LIFE INSURANCE COMPANY FINANCIAL STATEMENTS

Keys to successful reporting

R. ARTHUR SAUNDERS, FSA, FCIA

Library of Congress Catalog Card Number
85-51882

International Standard Book Number:
0-931028-74-4

Teach 'em, Inc.
160 East Illinois Street
Chicago, Illinois 60611

Society of Actuaries
500 Park Boulevard
Itasca, IL 60143

Printed in the United States of America

About the Author

Born in New York, R. Arthur Saunders received a Bachelor of Commerce degree from McGill University in 1933. Awarded a fellowship in the Actuarial Society of America in 1937, he is now a Fellow of the Society Actuaries (FSA) and a Fellow of the Canadian Institute of Actuaries (FCIA). He was first employed by the Federal Department of Insurance, Ottawa. He then joined the Equitable Life Insurance Company of Canada, of which he later became vice president and comptroller with responsibility for electronic data processing (EDP), annual statements, and income tax until retirement in 1978. Since then, he has acted as an EDP and actuarial consultant. He was active in the Insurance Accounting and Statistical Association, of which he was research director and president of the Ontario chapter for one term. For many years he was a member of the marketing research committee of the Life Insurance Agency Management Association and the Life Office Management Association automation committee. He also was a member of the annual statement and company income tax committees of the Canadian Life Insurance Association and chairman of the income tax section in 1978.

Contents

Acknowledgments

The writing of this book was facilitated by the provision of office space, access to the library, and the use of a wordprocessor by the Equitable Life Insurance Company of Canada. I would like to thank T. R. Suttie FIA, FCIA, chairman of the board, and D. L. MacLeod, president, for offering these facilities.

I was assisted in the preparation of the text by a review committee of the Society of Actuaries, chaired by Forrest A. Richen FSA, consisting of Donald A. McIsaac FSA, FCIA, nominated by the Canadian Institute of Actuaries; Edward S. Silins FSA, Robert W. Stein FSA, Thomas J. Leary FSA, and Paul R. Fleischacker FSA, nominated by the American Academy of Actuaries; William H. Aitken FSA, FCIA, Cecil D. Bykerk FSA, Linden N. Cole FSA, Michael D. Demner FSA, Sam Gutterman FSA, Martin S. Huey FSA, Burton D. Jay FSA, J. Alan Lauer FSA, Cande Olsen FSA, and Virgil D. Wagner FSA.

In addition, other authorities in the field read the sections dealing with their areas of expertise. For their many helpful criticisms and suggestions, I wish to thank Warren R. Adams FSA, James P. Addiego ASA, William H. Aitken FSA, FCIA, Faye Albert FSA, Janet F. Bleakney FSA, Samuel B. Coe FSA, Linden N. Cole FSA, Alan F. Exley ASA, Paul R. Fleischacker FSA, William J. Fox FSA, FCIA, Roland K. Heeb ASA, Rex D. Hemme FSA, Michael Krosky FSA, J. Alan Lauer FSA, Thomas J. Leary FSA, James H. Lehman FSA, Donald A. McIsaac FSA, FCIA, David R. McKusick FSA, George J. Melnick FSA, FCIA, James J. Murphy FSA, Cande Olsen FSA, Jane D. Pacelli FSA, Donald J. Perrie FSA, Frank G. Reynolds FSA, FCIA, Forrest A. Richen FSA, James K. Sample FSA, FCIA, Dennis J. Schettler FSA, FCIA, Thomas C. Scott FSA, Edward S. Silins FSA, James B. Smith, Jr. FSA, Steven B. Sommer FSA, Thomas R. Suttie FIA, FCIA, Ram Vaidyanath, Kurt von Schilling FSA, FCIA, and Virgil D. Wagner FSA. Finally, I am conscious of the many improvements in the text for which these reviewers are responsible. At the same time, I must take sole responsibility for any errors which remain.

Introduction

This book was written primarily for fellowship students of the Society of Actuaries, and most of the material was first prepared in the form of study notes. Since all students are required to have a general knowledge of life insurance statements, while a more detailed understanding is needed only by those specializing in one of those fields, the text has been divided into two parts. Chapters 1, 2 and 6 contain the general material; the other chapters provide more detailed treatment. Some material has been repeated to make the two sections more self-contained.

In the past 15 years there have been considerable changes in life insurance financial statements, because of a realization that the solvency requirements of statutory statements tended to distort the income statement. In describing the background for these changes I have relied on discussions of these issues in Canada, because the points of view of the accounting and actuarial professions, the regulatory authorities (in the person of the Superintendent of Insurance for Canada), and the insurance industry were clearly expressed in comprehensive reports.

Since this book concerns statements of life insurance companies, there has been no attempt to cover statements of other kinds of insurers (e.g., general insurance companies or health maintenance organizations).

Although life insurance practice in the United States and Canada, like the English spoken in the two countries, is basically quite similar, differences in practice and terminology can cause confusion. Since the text is intended for students in both countries, I have attempted to indicate differences in practices on the first occasion in which a practice is discussed. Where terminology differs, I have tried to use both on the first reference (e.g., shares of stock), and the appropriate term in the chapters dealing specifically with the statement of each country. A glossary has been included to assist students who have had little exposure to life insurance technical terms and also to indicate some of the terms which differ between the two countries.

In addition to providing helpful criticism of the text, one of the reviewers, Samuel B. Coe, FSA, pointed out that, in annual statement forms, there is little consistency in the directions to add or subtract items in calculating totals. For many statements, such as the balance sheet, this does not matter because all the items are added. In other statements, such as the **statement of surplus** and the **statement of changes of financial position,** some entries are added and others subtracted. A simple, consistent method of indicating the operation would facilitate their completion.

Coe has suggested placing an operation sign ("+", "−", or "=") before the description of each item, indicating the type of entry to which the sign applies in the description, where necessary (e.g., "net gain" or "increase"), and indicating a numerical entry requiring the opposite sign by parentheses. Additions or subtractions of subtotals can be indicated by instructions following the description of the result. Although his suggestion was made when it was too late to restructure all the statements, the National Association of Insurance Commissioners **statement of changes in financial position (Table 3.5,** page 76) is included as an example of this approach.

Chapter 1: Accounting and Financial Reporting

1.1 Introduction

All organizations dealing with money or goods must keep records of transactions to know their financial position and to have some assurance that assets are conserved and not stolen or wasted. Among the earliest writings found are records of temple or royal inventories and tax receipts. Simple records of receipts and disbursements may serve the second purpose adequately, but, as transactions become more complex, a better record of the sources and dispositions of possessions is required.

1.2 Accounts

The double entry system of accounting, developed in Renaissance Italy, provides such a record by recognizing the essential dual nature of a transaction, which requires a giver and a receiver, or, more generally, a source and a disposition. Thus, instead of merely recording that, say, $500 had been received from sales and $350 paid in wages, under the double entry system a company maintains records (accounts) for sales, wages and cash. The first transaction would be recorded by adding $500 to the cash account and $500 to the sales account; the second is recorded by subtracting $350 from the cash account and adding $350 to the wages account.

To distinguish between sources and dispositions, sources are credited and the dispositions debited. (Debits are regarded as positive and credits as negative so that the sum of all entries should be zero.)

In the above example, the entries should be:

SALES	CASH	SALES	WAGES
Debit cash	$500D		
Credit sales		$500C	
Credit cash	350C		
Debit wages			$350D
	$150D	$500C	$350D

(If the transactions are reversed, so are the entries. For instance, if an article sold for $50 is returned for cash, the entries would be debit sales $50, credit cash $50. This would reduce both sales and cash by $50.)

Accounts may be classified as assets, liabilities, income and disbursements. Asset accounts represent property owned by the organization, including amounts owed to it. Liability accounts include not only amounts owing to others, either directly or held for their benefit, but also reserves (amounts set aside to provide for some future contingency, such as reserves for bad debts), contributed capital and surplus (the excess of assets over the sum of liabilities, reserves and capital). These accounts may be considered as "status accounts," which show the current state of the amount owned, the amount owing, the reserve, capital or surplus.

Income and disbursement accounts, on the other hand, which represent operating transactions, are "historical accounts," which show the net amount received or disbursed during a given period. For instance, in order to have the sales account show the amount of sales for a calendar year, it is necessary to set it at zero at the beginning of the year. (See "Closing entries," 1.4.)

Increases in assets are debits and increases in liabilities, credits. Income increases assets and disbursements decrease them; therefore, in order to balance, increases in income must be credits and increases in disbursements debits, as illustrated above.

The concept of source and disposition also explains some apparent anomalies. For instance, contributed capital increases assets (usually cash); therefore the capital account must be a credit account. Surplus is the excess of assets over liabilities and capital; therefore it must also be a credit in order to balance. (If the organization is regarded as an entity separate from its proprietors, capital and surplus can be regarded as amounts owed to the proprietors.)

In summary:

DEBITS	CREDITS
Increases in assets	Increases in liabilities, capital, surplus and reserves
Disbursements	Income

Since every transaction results in equal debit and credit entries, the net sum of all accounts should be zero. This is one method of checking the accuracy of accounting procedures. As a result, a listing of all accounts is known as a "trial balance." If the net sum is not zero, it is necessary to correct one or more errors.

Accounts may be maintained on a cash basis or on a revenue (incurred or accrual) basis. When accounts are on a cash basis, only cash transactions are recorded; on the revenue basis, entries are made as income is earned or liabilities incurred. Statements prepared using the second method are more realistic and are required by good accounting practice. For instance, if goods are sold toward the end of a year but are not paid for until the following year, the transaction is correctly shown by including the sale in total sales for the former year and listing the amount owing as an asset, rather than by including the amount in the sales of the following year.

In the same way, consider a bond with semi-annual coupons due May 1 and November 1; on the cash basis, only the coupons actually collected would be credited to interest; on the revenue basis, in addition, at the end of the year one-third of the coupon due May 1 of the following year (accrued interest) would be added to the cash total, and the accrued interest taken into account at the end of the previous year deducted. The same principle applies to costs or charges incurred during the year of account and not paid until the following year.

1.3 Financial reporting

Periodically an enterprise must report on its financial position as of a given date and on the results of operations since the previous report. The report may be classed as (1) internal (i.e., to the management of the enterprise) or (2) external, (i.e., to the general public, which includes current and potential investors, customers or clients and creditors, who, in the words of the Financial Accounting Standards Board (FASB) of the American Institute of Certified Public Accountants (AICPA) "lack the authority to prescribe the financial information they want from an enterprise and therefore must use the information that management communicates for them."

For this reason, the form and content of published financial reports of business enterprises are prescribed by government agencies (e.g., securities commissions and insurance departments) and by the accounting profession, which sets reporting standards which an enterprise must follow to receive an audit certificate from a member of the profession.

For example, in the United States, the FASB has issued a **concepts statement** which describes the objectives of general purpose financial reporting. In the words of the statement, general purpose financial reporting "includes not only financial statements, but also other means of communicating information that relates, directly or indirectly, to the information provided by the accounting system—that is, information about an enterprise's resources, obligations, earnings, etc."

The FASB **concepts statement** summarizes the objectives of general purpose financial reporting as follows:

"Financial reporting should provide information that is useful to present and potential investors and creditors and other users in making rational investment, credit, and other similar decisions. The information should be comprehensible to those who have an understanding of business and economic activities and are willing to study the information with reasonable diligence.

"Financial reporting should provide information to help present and potential investors and creditors and other users in assessing the amounts, timing and uncertainty of prospective cash receipts from dividends, interest and the proceeds from the sale, redemption, or maturity of securities or loans.

"Financial reporting should provide information about the economic resources of an enterprise, the claims to those resources (obligations to transfer resources to other entities and owners' equity), and the effects of transactions, events, and circumstances that change resources and claims to those resources.

"Financial reporting should provide information about an enterprise's financial performance during a period. Investors and creditors often use information about the past to help in assessing the prospects of an enterprise. Thus, although investment and credit decisions reflect investors' and creditors' expectations about future enterprise performance, those expectations are commonly based, at least partly, on evaluations of past enterprise performance.

"The primary focus of financial reporting is information about an enterprise's performance provided by measures of earnings and its components.

"Financial reporting should provide information about how an enterprise obtains and spends cash, about its borrowing and repayment of borrowing, about its capital transactions, including cash dividends and other distributions of enterprise resources to owners, and about other factors that may affect an enterprise's liquidity or solvency.

"Financial reporting should provide information about how management of an enterprise has discharged its stewardship responsibility to owners (stockholders) for the use of enterprise resources entrusted to it.

"Financial reporting should provide information that is useful to managers and directors in making decisions in the interests of owners."

Because potential "information" about an enterprise is almost infinite (including the names and wages of all persons employed and details of all transactions, for example), some selection must be made. The objectives cited above are designed to meet the need for information on which to base investment, credit and similar decisions and on which to evaluate the management of an enterprise. Information provided should be relevant to those purposes, reliable and subject to verification. The information must also be material, and the cost of providing it should not be greater than its value.

Materiality is a very important but very subjective criterion. Essentially, the question of whether information would be relevant to a person making a financial decision about the enterprise is a matter of judgment. For example, if a company had a net income for a year of about $1,000,000, the loss of $50 due to the bankruptcy of a customer would obviously not be material, while a loss of $500,000 would, equally obviously, be material. Between those limits lies an area in which the determination of materiality can vary according to who is making the decision. In some cases, factors other than the amount involved might affect materiality. For example, the bankruptcy of an important customer might result in only a small current loss but could have a substantial effect on future sales. One guide to materiality is whether the amount exceeds five percent of the net income for the year.

The relevance of the above quotations, especially to life insurance companies, may be seen from some of the requirements of regulatory authorities. For instance, the number and amount of investments of most life insurance companies are too great for a detail listing in the general purpose statement to be either practical or useful (although such a listing is required in the statement to regulatory authorities). However, by providing for special treatment of securities in default and by recognition of market values in one way or another (in the United States, for example, by valuing common stocks at market values and in Canada by an investment reserve based on deficiencies from market values), information as to the uncertainty of future receipts from investments is provided.

Information about an insurance company's financial performance during the period is provided in the published statement, and more information is provided in the statutory statement by the requirement that the income statement be reported by line of business, so that one can determine whether net income is made up of profits in some lines and losses in others (a situation which, if not corrected, might create difficulties in future years, given the long-term nature of life insurance contracts). In Canada, the requirement for an analysis of income by fund enables both policyholders and shareholders to determine whether one group is benefiting at the expense of another.

1.4 General accounting

The principal statements included in financial reports of any organization are the balance sheet, the income statement and the statement of retained earnings (previously called the statement of surplus). In reading the general descriptions that follow it should be kept in mind that the terms and emphasis may vary somewhat from those used in life insurance accounting.

Balance sheet

The balance sheet for any organization is a statement of assets, liabilities, reserves, capital and surplus at a particular time. (In accounting practice reserves are amounts set aside to provide for possible future losses, such as bad debts, unfavorable judgments in pending court cases, etc.) The assets are shown first, grouped in categories and totalled. The liabilities are then listed, again in meaningful groupings, followed by reserves, capital and surplus. Since, as mentioned above, the surplus is the difference between the assets and the sum of liabilities, reserves and capital, the total of this second group must balance with the total assets. This, of course, is the reason for the name of the statement.

The balance sheet is important in determining the solvency of the organization, and is usually structured to highlight the important factors. For instance, most manufacturing and trading organizations have short term liabilities (such as accounts payable, short term bank loans, etc.) which will fall due in the near future, as well as long term liabilities, such as mortgages on property, outstanding bonds, etc. The assets are therefore usually displayed in order of liquidity, that is, the ease with which they may be converted into cash and used to pay amounts owed. Thus, current assets, cash, accounts receivable, prepaid accounts, merchandise inventories, etc. are shown first, usually with a total, and fixed assets, such as real estate, furniture and equipment, machinery, are listed below.

The relationship between current assets and short term liabilities is important in judging the solvency of an organization, because current assets are the resources out of which short-term liabilities can be paid. Purchasers of long term liabilities, on the other hand, although interested in the ratio of fixed assets to long-term liabilities, usually rely on the earning power of the company to provide the interest and repayments of principal on their loans, not on the liquidation of fixed assets.

Statement of income

The statement of income shows the income received from normal operations during the period (proceeds of sales, interest, rents, fees, etc.) less the cost of doing business (materials, expenses, taxes, etc.). This "normal operating income" may be compared with that of other periods and other, similar companies.

Until about 20 years ago, only the normal operating income was shown in the statement of income, while extraordinary income (nonrecurring income such as sales of assets of a capital nature) was included in a statement of surplus, in which the unallocated surplus at the end of the previous year was reconciled with that at the end of the current year by adding the normal operating income and extraordinary income to the former and subtracting dividends to shareholders and allocations to reserves.

In current accounting practice, the statement of income includes both normal operating income and extraordinary income. However, items of extraordinary income should be shown after the total of normal operating income, as special items, with explanatory notes, if necessary. The statement of retained earnings has replaced the statement of surplus.

[Note that income is used in two senses in accounting. It can mean amounts received from normal operations as contrasted with amounts paid (disbursements), and also "net income," the difference between income (in the first sense) and disbursements.]

Statement of retained earnings

The statement of retained earnings reconciles the statement of income with the unallocated surplus (retained earnings) shown in the balance sheets at the beginning and end of the period. It includes the net income from the statement of income, as well as such items as dividends to shareholders, adjustments relating to prior periods and allocations to reserves. It must balance with the change in unallocated surplus.

Closing entries

In addition to the ledger accounts, other data may also be used in financial statements. For instance, the change in the values of raw materials and goods held for sale over the accounting period is an important element in the gross profit on sales. If records of the amounts in stock are not maintained on a continuous basis in the ledger, the values at the end of each period must be ascertained by actual count or estimation (an inventory). The amounts in the ledger in such cases normally are the values at the end of the previous period. These amounts are credited to the inventory accounts and debited to income. The current amounts are debited to the inventory accounts and credited to income. Other amounts, such as estimates of uncollectable accounts receivable, depreciation of fixed assets, prepaid taxes and expenses, etc., may also be estimated or calculated and entered in the ledger in similar fashion.

After the final trial balance is listed and balanced for use in the preparation of the annual statement, the ledger is adjusted for the start of the new accounting period. The income and disbursement accounts are set to zero by debiting accounts with credit balances and crediting accounts with debit balances and making offsetting entries to the surplus account. For instance, if the sales account had a credit balance of $150,000 and salaries a debit balance of $80,000, the entries would be:

Debit Sales	$150,000
Credit Surplus	150,000
Debit Surplus	80,000
Credit Salaries	80,000

Similarly, allocations of surplus to reserves, say, would be made by debiting surplus and crediting the appropriate reserves. The income and disbursement accounts will then all be zero, and the asset, liability, reserves, capital and surplus accounts will be in accordance with the balance sheet. (In the above example the effect of the entries would be to increase surplus by $70,000.)

1.5 Life insurance accounting

Life insurance accounts in North America have been maintained on a cash basis, and annual reports have been prepared on a revenue basis with the aid of nonledger accounts (see 1.9). Only recently have some companies changed to the revenue basis. Although one reason was the fact that due and unpaid life insurance premiums are not enforceable debts (because a company cannot sue a policyholder for payment of premiums, literal adherence to accounting principles would require that they be excluded*), the principal reason was the volume of transactions and the

---

(*In practice, if policy reserves are computed on the assumption that all due premiums have been collected, it is legitimate to include any net due premiums which have not been collected in the assets as an offset to that liability.)

additional clerical work required to keep records on a revenue basis. For example, if we examine premium collections, admittedly a complicated case, but one involving many thousands of transactions for most companies, we can see some of the difficulties involved in revenue accounting.

On the cash basis, when a premium is actually paid, the amount is debited to cash and credited to premiums; if it is paid by automatic premium loan, it is debited to loan and credited to premiums. If the premium is not paid and the policy terminates or is changed to reduced paid-up or extended term insurance, no premium entry need be made. At the end of each accounting period the premiums due and unpaid, or paid in advance of the due date, are determined by inventory methods.

On the revenue basis, entries are made for all premiums due, and the treatment depends on the date of payment. Premiums paid before the due date must be credited to prepaid premiums when paid and additional entries must be made to credit premiums and debit prepaid premiums on the due date. For premiums unpaid on the due date, the amount of the premium is credited to premiums and debited to premiums due on that date, and credited to premiums due and debited to cash if and when the premium is paid. If the premium is advanced by loan, the entry will be to debit loan and credit premiums due. If the premium is not collected at all, premiums must be debited and premiums due credited. The number of entries is more than doubled, and the procedure is more complicated and liable to error.

As an example, let us assume a premium of $100 is due on a particular policy:

CASH		REVENUE	
a) Premium collected on or before due date:			
Dr. Cash	$100	Dr. Cash	$100
Cr. Premiums	100	Cr. Prepaid premiums	100
On due date (if premium previously collected):			
No entry		Dr. Prepaid premiums	$100
		Cr. Premiums	100
b) Premium outstanding on due date:			
On due date:		Dr. Premiums due	$100
No entry		Cr. Premiums	100
Premium collected after due date:			
Dr. Cash	$100	Dr. Cash	$100
Cr. Premiums	100	Cr. Premiums due	100
Premiums advanced by nonforfeiture loan:			
Dr. Loan	$100	Dr. Loan	$100
Cr. Premiums	100	Cr. Premiums due	100
Policy lapsed or changed to reduced paid-up etc.:			
No entry		Dr. Premiums	$100
		Cr. Premiums due	100

Because a high proportion of premiums are either paid on dates other than the due date or not paid at all, the revenue basis requires more than twice as many entries as the cash basis. On the other hand, on the revenue basis, prepaid premiums and premiums due and uncollected are available at any time from the ledger, while the cash basis requires an inventory of prepaid and unpaid premiums whenever that information is required.

With the large number of transactions involved in life insurance operations it was more economical to use the cash basis, and only the advent of computerized accounting has made revenue accounting practical for most life insurance transactions.

In addition, important liabilities, such as actuarial reserves and amounts on deposit, had to be calculated after the end of the accounting period, and other assets and liabilities which were obtained by inventory needed to be incorporated into the statement. These items are known as "non-ledger" accounts, since they do not appear in the ledger (see 1.9).

Ledger accounts

Life insurance companies must set up a number of ledger accounts in which to record financial transactions. However, the level of detail required of life insurance companies is so fine that it is most convenient to subdivide ledger accounts so that the required information will be available from the ledger rather than from collateral records or periodical analyses of transactions. With computerized accounting, it is relatively easy to combine many subaccounts into group totals as required.

For example, although the income statement (summary of operations) shows premiums and annuity considerations received as a single item, the exhibits in statutory statements require them to be subdivided by line of business (individual, group, life, annuity, etc.), by type (first year, single, renewal), by direct written, reinsurance acquired and reinsurance ceded, and by residence of policyholder. A company writing business in more than one country must also subdivide these items by country of origin and by currency. If the appropriate classification is made in the ledger as each transaction is recorded, no further analysis will be required. Similar subdivisions are required for commissions and payments to policyholders.

Accounts for invested assets include asset accounts and income accounts for regular income (such as interest, dividends and rents) and for capital gains and losses. These are usually subdivided by type of investment (bonds, common and preferred shares of stock, mortgages, etc.). In the United States, the National Association of Insurance Commissioners (NAIC) statement requires bonds to be subdivided into U.S. Government, tax-exempt, other bonds (unaffiliated) and bonds of affiliates. In addition, subdivisions by country and currency are required. Other classifications may be used to provide information to management, e.g., yield by type of bond, share or mortgage.

The subdivisions of expense accounts are determined by the requirements of the annual statement and of management information for expense control and other purposes. The classifications in the expense exhibits of statutory statements indicate the minimum number of accounts required, although additional accounts will usually be required for expense analysis and control. (For example, although statutory expense exhibits combine expenses for postage, overnight delivery, telephone and telegraph, most companies use separate accounts for these expenses.)

Because expenses must be allocated to investment operations and to the various lines of business, another level of subdivision may be used to facilitate the allocation. On the other hand, this requirement may coincide with management requirements, such as subdivision by department or cost center. (A cost center is a unit of the company determined to facilitate control of expenses and their allocation to departments and functions.)

1.6 Allocation of income and expenses

As life insurance companies increased the variety of their products, adding group insurance and group annuities to individual products and issuing accident and health insurance, it became necessary to prepare separate income statements for the different lines of business to determine the profitability of each line. In addition, regulatory authorities, concerned for the security of individual life insurance policyholders, required companies to provide this information to insure that new lines weren't being subsidized by older ones. As a result, statutory statements require income statements to be split by line of business. (In Canada, separate income accounts and funds must be shown for participating and non-participating policies, and the assets for accident and sickness business must be kept separate from the assets of the life business.)

Although such items as premiums, commissions and payments to policyholders may be allocated to lines of business in the ledger as each transaction occurs, as described above, investment income, except for such relatively small items as interest on policy loans and premiums, and most expenses cannot be so allocated, and methods must be devised to assign a reasonable proportion to each line of business. Investment income, after allocating interest on policy loans and premiums, may be allocated by using one or a combination of several different methods, including:

1. **In proportion to mean policy liabilities.** This method is simple, but may not be accurate, since it does not necessarily reflect the contributions of the various lines of business to the investment income of the company. Furthermore, changes in reserves due to changes in valuation bases will result in changes in the distribution of investment income.

2. **In proportion to mean funds.** This method requires that fund totals be established and maintained for each line of business. It is reasonably accurate when interest rates fluctuate within a relatively narrow range. However, when, for example, interest rates increase substantially over a period, lines of business whose funds are increasing slowly or decreasing will receive more than their proper share, and those whose funds are rapidly increasing will receive less.

3. **By use of the investment year method.** Allocation by the investment year method, which takes into account the yield on new investments for each year and the contribution of each line of business to the new investments of that year. This is a more accurate method but is obviously more complicated than either of the above methods.

4. By use of segmented assets. This method has recently been instituted by some of the major insurance companies. The cash flow for each line of business is invested separately in investments that are consistent with the expected future cash flow from that line. Because all the assets of the company must still support all the liabilities, a system of borrowing between lines must be developed, to be used whenever the cash flow and purchase of assets cannot be matched. (See Attwood and Ohman, T.S.A. XXXV.)

If the various lines of business in the annual statement are subdivided for management information purposes, other methods may be used for the allocations among such subdivisions, and combinations of the above methods may be used if it is felt that they will lead to reasonable results.

The allocation of expenses usually requires segregation of expenses by department or cost center and the allocation of such expense totals according to usage or activity. Overhead and executive salaries must be allocated by some reasonable formula. The methods used for internal cost control and profit analysis may also be used. As an example of the principles to be employed, the instructions for completing the NAIC statement may be quoted. (Section E, Item 6)

"In the distribution of a specific category of cost to lines of business, an appropriate index of the activity or activities giving rise to such cost shall be used. Such index should fluctuate with the specific category of cost and be capable of measurement. For example, as illustrations of principles only and not of required procedures:

"(1) Clerical salaries of operating departments may be distributed to lines of business on the basis of time or salary ratios, the former used where approximately the same rate of compensation is paid to clerks whose salaries are being distributed.

"(2) The cost of service departments may be distributed to other departments in proportion to the value of services rendered each department, e.g., the cost of a personnel department may be distributed to other departments on some general basis as number of clerks; a photostat section on a unit cost basis; or, in the case of a central tabulating unit, on an hourly rate reflecting the cost of each type of machine used.

"(3) Supervisory costs may be distributed to lines of business in the same proportions as the distribution of the salaries of the persons involved.

"(4) The cost of executive departments responsible for general administration of the company, including the salaries of executive officers, may be distributed to lines of business in the same proportions as the salaries of all other officers and employees.

"(5) Social security taxes may be distributed to lines of business in the same proportion to the corresponding distribution of taxable salaries.

"(6) Departmental rent charges may be made in proportion to the amount of floor space occupied, and distributed to lines of business on some appropriate basis, such as salaries.

"(7) Costs, such as meals for employees, telephone, telegraph, postage, stationery and supplies may be distributed first to departments on the basis of usage or on an appropriate general basis, and then distributed to lines of business on some appropriate basis, such as salaries.

"(8) In using number of transactions as a basis for distributing costs to lines of business, each type of transaction within an organisational unit may be weighted to reflect its relative cost. The average clerical cost per transaction may be used as a weight or, in special situations, such as the approval of death or disability claims, the relative weights may be determined by case studies.

"Estimates of time spent on activities may be used in the distribution of costs to lines of business only where such activities by their nature are not susceptible of objective measurement or where the cost of making time studies is disproportionate to the expense being distributed or where estimates of time are clearly appropriate."

1.7 Reinsurance

Because the essential characteristic of life insurance is the pooling of risks so that mortality losses will approximate the average mortality rate, insuring individual lives for amounts much greater than the average creates the risk of abnormal fluctuations in mortality losses. In order to protect against such fluctuations, companies establish maximum amounts of insurance which they will retain at their own risk and reinsure the excess with other companies.

As pointed out earlier, premiums, commissions and expenses, and claims payments on reinsurance ceded and acquired from other companies are posted to accounts separate from those used for transactions on the policies written directly by the company.

Reinsurance may be either facultative or automatic. On the facultative basis, the original (ceding) company applies for reinsurance in each case, submitting copies of the application and underwriting information to the reinsurer, which may accept, rate or reject each case. On the automatic basis, the reinsurer agrees to accept all amounts in excess of the original company's retention, up to an agreed limit, on the same terms as the original company's acceptance.

Reinsurance may be effected using one of the following methods:

1. Coinsurance. The company cedes a share of the original policy, paying the reinsurer a proportionate share of the gross premium (less an allowance for commissions and expenses). The reinsurer agrees to reimburse the original company for its share of death claims, dividends (if any) and cash values or maturity benefits paid. The original company holds the reserve on the whole policy but will normally be allowed a deduction for the reserve on the reinsured portion. (The deduction may not be allowed if the reinsurer is not licensed by the home jurisdiction of the original company.)

2. Risk premium (or YRT) reinsurance. The original company reinsures a portion of the amount at risk (the sum insured minus the terminal reserve) on a yearly renewable term basis. The original company pays a one-year term premium for the amount reinsured each year at the attained age of the insured, and the reinsurer agrees to reimburse the original company for the amount reinsured at the time a death claim occurs. The original company must hold the reserve on the original plan; only the reserve on the one-year term reinsurance is deducted.

In many cases there is provision for retroactive reductions in premium (experience refunds) determined in accordance with a specific formula, if experience is sufficiently favorable.

3. Modified coinsurance. Under certain circumstances (for example, when the deduction for reserves on reinsured policies is not permitted by the home jurisdiction of the ceding company), reinsurance may be effected through coinsurance with a provision that the reinsurer deposit the reserve on the reinsured portion (on which interest is payable at an agreed rate) with the original company. In such cases, each year the reinsurer pays the original company an amount equal to the net increase in reserves less interest on the amount held by the original company. This amount is normally reported as a special item of income, since it should not be deducted from reinsurance premiums paid but treated as an offset to the reserves set up on the policies reinsured.

1.8 Foreign exchange

Most corporations conduct operations in foreign countries by setting up subsidiaries which operate as independent companies. However, many life insurance companies set up branch operations to pool all the risks and allow the assets of the whole company to guarantee the solvency of each branch. In such cases, the company will hold assets in local currencies to guard against unfavorable fluctuations in exchange rates and to comply with legal requirements. (Most jurisdictions require foreign insurance companies to hold assets in the local currency at least equal to liabilities within that jurisdiction for the protection of domestic policyholders.)

In such cases the accounts of the company will include assets, liabilities and transactions in foreign currencies. In order to have all ledger balances in a single currency, foreign currencies are normally converted to the domestic currency at constant rates (book rates)—reasonable approximations of current exchange rates. When financial statements are prepared, the current exchange rates will usually differ from book rates. Assets and liabilities may be converted to current rates by multiplying the values in domestic currency by the ratio of current to book rates at the date of the statement. If this conversion reduces the excess of assets over liabilities, the difference should be held as a liability or appropriation of surplus; if it increases the excess, the difference may be held as an asset (as in the United States) or used to reduce a required investment reserve (as in Canada).

For example, if assets in sterling are £15,700,000 and liabilities £14,900,000 at book rates of 1£=$1.92, the book values would be $30,144,000 and $28,608,000 respectively, with an excess of assets over liabilities of $1,536,000. If the current value was $1.802 at the statement date, the excess would be reduced by the ratio 1.802/1.92 to $1,441,600, and a liability or allocation of surplus for the difference, $94,400, would be set up. (Alternatively, if liabilities are greater than assets, a decrease in current rates below book rates would result in an increase in surplus.)

Whenever it appears that current rates have changed enough that book rates are no longer reasonably close to current rates, the book rates may be changed to a value more closely approximating current rates. All assets and liabilities in that currency must then be revalued, and the resulting increase or decrease in surplus entered in the financial statement as an unusual item of income or an adjustment to surplus.

1.9 Nonledger accounts

Nonledger accounts are still used by many life insurance companies; they may include such assets as due and uncollected premiums, deferred premiums, due and accrued investment income, and such liabilities as actuarial reserves, reserves for supplementary contracts and amounts on deposit, prepaid premiums and incurred but unpaid claims, expenses and taxes, as well as investment and other contingency reserves and unallocated surplus. The analysis and treatment of nonledger accounts may be illustrated by following the progress of a new company.

A company starting business would have no nonledger accounts at its inception, and its ledger would be in balance throughout the year. At the end of the year, income and disbursement accounts would be closed off to a balance account, which would contain a substantial credit, since policy reserves, normally the dominant item among nonledger accounts, would not have been entered in the ledger. The balance account would, therefore, be numerically equal to the net sum of ledger assets and ledger liabilities at the end of the year.

When nonledger assets and liabilities are brought into the balance sheet and nonadmitted assets (i.e., assets which must be excluded from the balance sheet due to government regulation) are deducted, the difference between all assets and liabilities is the surplus, so that the balance account, which is the difference between ledger assets and liabilities, is equal to the net sum of the nonledger accounts, nonadmitted assets and surplus. In the second year, the balance account will remain equal to the net sum of the nonledger accounts, nonadmitted assets and surplus at the end of the previous year. This equality will continue as long as nonledger accounts are used.

If A_L, A_{NL}, and A_{NA} are ledger assets, nonledger assets, and nonadmitted assets, respectively, and L_L and L_{NL} ledger and nonledger liabilities, then the balance account

$$B = A_L - L_L, \text{ and the surplus,}$$
$$S = A_L + A_{NL} - A_{NA} - L_L - L_{NL}$$

so that,

$$B = A_L - L_L = S + L_{NL} - A_{NL} + A_{NA}.$$

A simple example may clarify this concept. Suppose capital paid in is $1 million, contributed surplus is $500,000 (received in cash) and organization expenses are $50,000. Before operations commence, the ledger would show:

Cash	$1,450,000D
Capital paid in	1,000,000C
Contributed surplus	500,000C
Expenses	50,000D
	0

(C indicates a credit balance and D a debit balance.)

During the first year, suppose premiums of $2,500,000 and interest of $115,000 are received, while expenditures include commissions of $400,000, additional expenses of $200,000, and claims of $175,000, with $3,100,000 invested in bonds.

The ledger entries, in summary, and the effect on the cash account, are:

	ASSET ACCOUNTS	INCOME ACCOUNTS	CASH ACCOUNT
Debit cash, credit premiums		$2,500,000C	$2,500,000D
Debit cash, credit interest		115,000C	115,000D
Debit commissions, credit cash		400,000D	400,000C
Debit general expenses, credit cash		200,000D	200,000C
Debit claims, credit cash		175,000D	175,000C
Debit bonds, credit cash	$3,100,000D		3,100,000C
Totals	$3,100,000D	$1,840,000C	$1,260,000C
Cash balance at beginning			$1,450,000D
Cash balance at end			$ 190,000D

The trial balance at the end of the year will be:

	DR.	CR.	BALANCE
Assets and liabilities			
Cash	$ 190,000		
Bonds	3,100,000		
Capital		$1,000,000	
Contributed surplus		500,000	
Assets—liabilities	$3,290,000	$1,500,000	$1,790,000D
Income accounts:			
Premiums		$2,500,000	
Interest		115,000	
Claims	$ 175,000		
General expenses	250,000		
Commissions	400,000		
Totals of income accounts	$ 825,000	$2,615,000	$1,790,000C
Totals	$4,115,000	$4,115,000	

When the income accounts are cleared, the balance account is debited with $825,000 and credited with $2,615,000, resulting in a net balance of $1,790,000C.

Suppose that, at the end of the year, the nonledger assets (A) and liabilities (L) are

Net due and deferred premiums	$75,000A
Unpaid claims	50,000L
Unpaid expenses and taxes	17,000L
Due and accrued interest	22,000A
Actuarial reserves	1,600,000L

and that $37,000 of bond values are nonadmitted.

The preparation of the balance sheet will be:

ASSETS	TRIAL BALANCE	NONLEDGER NONADMITTED	BALANCE SHEET
Cash	$ 190,000		$ 190,000
Bonds	3,100,000		
less nonadmitted		−37,000	3,063,000
Net due and deferred premiums		75,000	75,000
Due and accrued interest		22,000	22,000
	$3,290,000	$ 60,000	$3,350,000
LIABILITIES			
Actuarial reserves		$1,600,000	$1,600,000
Unpaid claims		50,000	50,000
Unpaid expenses		17,000	17,000
Capital	$1,000,000		1,000,000
Contributed surplus	500,000		500,000
Unallocated surplus			183,000
	$1,500,000	$1,667,000	$3,350,000
Balance account	$1,790,000C	$1,607,000D	$ 183,000C

As the last line indicates, the unallocated surplus is the difference between the balance account and the net sum of nonledger accounts and nonadmitted assets.

The trial balance is in balance because the balance account equals the excess of ledger assets over ledger liabilities, capital and contributed surplus. In the preparation of the balance sheet, each nonledger asset increases the difference between assets and liabilities and each nonledger liability and nonadmitted asset decreases that difference.

Thus the unallocated surplus in the balance sheet (the difference between the total admitted assets and liabilities, capital and contributed surplus) is equal to the balance account minus the sum of nonledger accounts and nonadmitted assets.

When nonledger accounts are brought into the statement, the same double entry system must be used as would be used if ledger entries were made. The amount of the nonledger account must be included in the assets or liabilities, and the change in the nonledger account for the period must be added to the appropriate income account. This may be done by subtracting the amount at the end of the previous period and adding the amount at the end of the current period.

For example, the actuarial reserve at the end of the current period is entered into the liabilities and added to the increase in actuarial reserves; the actuarial reserve at the end of the previous period is then subtracted from the increase in actuarial reserves. Current due and uncollected premiums are included in assets and added to premiums while the amount at the end of the previous period would be subtracted from premiums. In the same way, the total nonadmitted assets are deducted from the assets, and the change in nonadmitted assets is entered in the statement of surplus.

If the amounts entered for nonledger accounts and nonadmitted assets as of the end of the previous period are the same as those in the current statement, the increase in unallocated surplus determined from the income statement and the statement of surplus should equal the difference between the unallocated surplus in the current and previous balance sheets.

1.10 Problems of life insurance financial reporting

There are important differences between corporations which engage in short term contracts, such as manufacturing and trading companies, and life insurance companies, whose contracts are long term. At one extreme is, say, a trading company which purchases goods from manufacturers and sells them to dealers or the public, with the time between purchase and sale being measured in weeks or months. Once goods are sold and payment received, the transaction is complete and the profit or loss determined. For such companies the results for a single year will be an accurate report of the financial performance over the period, with uncertainty restricted to the areas of goods unsold (inventory) and the collection of amounts due (accounts receivable), which will normally be relatively small and subject to fairly accurate estimation. For example, the annual report for a large merchandising company showed sales of approximately $480 million, and accounts receivable and inventories totalling less than $60 million, or less than 12 percent of sales.

On the other hand, the "sale" of a life insurance contract initiates a long-term contract whose profitability will depend on future persistency, mortality, interest and expense rates, so that the income calculated for the current year depends on estimates of the future values of these rates.

Furthermore, the nature of life insurance requires assurance that the company will be able to meet its future obligations, since, in the event of insolvency, a policyholder may lose not only the money paid in, but also the much larger amount for which the company is liable in the event of a claim. Thus a certain degree of conservatism is required in making assumptions about future conditions. The more conservative the assumptions, the lower the income reported for a period when the company is growing. In a stock life insurance company there is therefore a conflict between the conservatism required to protect policyholders and the effect of this conservatism on the income statement and on shareholders' equity.

A further problem is that, due to the nature of level premium life insurance, even "those who have an understanding of business and economic activities and are willing to study the information with reasonable diligence" will probably not appreciate the effect of different assumptions about future conditions on the income statement—for example, the effect on income of a change of one percent in the assumptions about future investment earnings.

For many years, the emphasis in life insurance reports, especially in the United States and Canada, was on solvency, with the result that regulatory authorities prescribed conservative assumptions for future interest and mortality rates. These assumptions eventually became over-conservative because any changes tended to lag behind improvements in life expectancy and increases in interest rates. The consequent understatement of income was tolerated as a necessary evil. However, as explained in Chapter 2, this approach has been questioned in the past few decades, with the result that the use of excessively conservative assumptions is no longer considered satisfactory. It is very likely that companies will use more reasonable estimates of future conditions, recognizing the hazards of estimating economic conditions far into the future and the danger of unfavorable fluctuations.

In the United States, at present, stock companies under the supervision of the Securities and Exchange Commission must prepare two financial reports: a statutory report for the regulatory authorities, using the format and assumptions mandated by insurance departments, and a general purpose report for publication, using generally accepted accounting principles (GAAP) for stock life insurance companies, with actuarial reserves based on assumptions which are "realistically conservative" and which, it is hoped, will provide a more realistic income statement. For mutual companies and stock companies owned by mutual companies, the requirements of regulatory authorities are considered to be generally accepted accounting practices.

In Canada, the Federal Department of Insurance, which is responsible for the supervision of the vast majority of life insurance companies doing business in Canada, has changed the requirements for the statutory statement, permitting actuaries greater freedom in making assumptions about future conditions and in adhering to generally accepted accounting practices in the preparation of the income statement. Solvency is safeguarded by setting up certain required reserves as appropriations of surplus.

Assumptions about future interest rates, mortality, termination, expense, etc., are the responsibility of the actuary who certifies the adequacy of the valuation of the liabilities of a life insurance company. For statutory statements in the United States, these are controlled by statutory requirements, which, though conservative, have been liberalized in recent years. In Canada, statutory requirements have been eliminated, but the actuary must certify that the assumptions used are "appropriate to the circumstances of the company and the policies in force," and the assumptions must be acceptable to the Superintendent of Insurance.

At present, the accounting profession in Canada has not set up generally accepted accounting principles for life insurance companies, but a committee representing the accounting and actuarial professions and the Department of Insurance is engaged in developing such principles. It is hoped that, when these principles are established, statutory reports and reports prepared according to GAAP will be consistent, and it will not be necessary for companies to prepare two different reports.

In the United States, statutory statements are not subject to an audit certificate by an external auditor, but the assumptions used in preparing the actuarial liability for the GAAP statement must be "realistically conservative," and it appears that the actuary must be able to satisfy the auditor that this is the case. In Canada, although statutory statements require an audit certificate, the auditor is expressly permitted to "accept any reserve included in the annual statement in respect of which the valuation actuary has given the opinion required [by the Insurance Act]."

Review questions

1. What is the logic underlying double entry accounting? (**Answer:** See section 1.1.)

2. A $100,000 bond with interest of 11 percent per annum payable semiannually on April 30 and October 31 is purchased on May 1, 1980. The first interest payment is received November 5, 1980. Using the revenue basis, list the entries required to record the receipt of interest and the accrued interest on December 31, 1980.

Answer:

October 31, 1980	Dr. Bond interest due	$5,500.00
	Cr. Bond interest	$5,500.00
November 5, 1980	Dr. Bank	$5,500.00
	Cr. Bond interest due	$5,500.00
December 31, 1980	Dr. Accrued interest—bonds	$1,833.33
	Cr. Bond interest	$1,833.33

3. To whom are general purpose financial reports considered to be addressed?
(**Answer:** See section 1.3.)

4. What is the purpose of closing entries?
(**Answer:** See section 1.4.)

5. What are some of the reasons for the prevalence of cash basis accounting in the life insurance industry in North America?
(**Answer:** See section 1.5.)

6. Why are ledger accounts of life insurance companies broken into many subdivisions?
(**Answer:** See section 1.5.)

7. What methods are currently used by life insurance companies in the United States and Canada to allocate investment income among lines of business?
(**Answer:** See section 1.6.)

8. For a company using the cash basis for its ledger accounts, how can the amount in the balance account during 1980 be checked against the statutory statement for December 31, 1979?
(**Answer:** See section 1.9.)

Chapter 2: Principles of Life Insurance Financial Statements

2.1 Regulation and supervision of life insurance companies

In contrast to most commercial transactions, in which goods or services are provided to a customer who in turn pays for them, the "sale" of an insurance contract requires payments to be made by the customer, in return for which he/she receives a promise of payment by the insurer when a specified contingency occurs. In life insurance, especially, the insurer's payment may be deferred for many years.

As a result, the solvency of the insurer is important to its policyholders, and governments have enacted legislation regulating the conduct of the insurance business and requiring detailed financial statements from insurers, so supervisory authorities can satisfy themselves that the insurer has complied with the law and is able to meet future obligations.

> "The paramount interest of policyholders far transcends all other interests (in the insurance industry). In the ordinary enterprise a stockholder's or creditor's risk of loss is limited to the funds he has advanced or the credit he has extended, and this he can control. The risk of loss by the holder of an insurance policy is not limited to the amount of premiums he has paid; in the event that the insurance company becomes insolvent he has at risk the full amount of any loss he incurs which he thought was covered by insurance. Recognizing this, all state regulatory laws today contain provisions seeking to protect the policyholder." (Samuel J. Broad, "The Applicability of Generally Accepted Accounting Principles", **Journal of Accountancy,** September, 1957).

In the United States and Canada almost all aspects of the insurance business are regulated by government. The incorporation of life insurance companies is regulated to insure that new companies have adequate surplus funds to protect them against unfavorable fluctuations in mortality and other contingencies, and every jurisdiction has an official (called a superintendent, commissioner or director) responsible for the licensing and supervision of insurance companies. Companies must be licensed by each state or province in which they wish to transact business and must deposit securities with government authorities to guarantee the payment of claims. The classes of investments which may be made are prescribed to ensure that assets are conserved, and minimum standards for the valuation of liabilities are established to ensure solvency. To provide policyholders with additional protection in their dealings with life insurance companies, agents must be licensed, and certain provisions, such as incontestable clauses and non-forfeiture benefits, must be included in policies.

Financial statements in prescribed form must be submitted annually to all jurisdictions in which an insurer is licensed, and the accounts of the company are audited periodically by officials of the supervisory authority. In the event that the financial statements show that the surplus of the company has been reduced below the minimum required by statute, the license to transact business may be restricted or revoked.

United States

In the United States the regulation and supervision of insurance has been the responsibility of the states. Until a 1944 U.S. Supreme Court decision, insurance was not considered commerce and therefore interstate insurance was not subject to federal regulation. After that decision, since the states had assumed jurisdiction and the federal government was not prepared to take over the responsibility, the McCarran Act was passed, providing that the states could legislate insurance matters and that no act of Congress would supersede any state law unless the federal statute expressly mentioned insurance.

The regulation of insurance by over 50 different supervisory authorities creates problems for companies which transact business in more than one state. Some degree of uniformity has been attained by the National Association of Insurance Commissioners, which has developed a standard annual statement (the NAIC statement) and uniform rules for the valuation of securities and liabilities. Most states accept a certificate of solvency from the state in which a company is domiciled (the home state) and, with a few exceptions, deposits of securities need be made only in the home state. To avoid the confusion and expense of audits by every state in which a company is licensed, states are grouped into zones, and audit examinations are conducted under the supervision of officials of the home state with a representative from each zone in which the company is licensed. For companies incorporated outside the United States, a state must be designated the home state.

Nevertheless, a lack of uniformity among the states still exists. Although required policy provisions are broadly similar, there are sufficient differences so that obtaining approval of policy forms from all states in which a company is licensed may present problems. In particular, all companies operating in New York must comply with much stricter rules than those which apply to companies which only operate in other states. Some states prohibit mutual companies from writing non-participating insurance. Some restrict the amount of profits from participating business written by stock companies which may be credited to shareholders, while other states have no such restrictions. In addition, there are wide variations in the size, competence and authority of state insurance departments. In the majority of states, the responsibility for supervision of insurance companies is placed in a separate department under a superintendent or commissioner; in others the responsible official has other duties or is subordinate to some other department. The minimum capital and surplus a life insurance company must have before it can commence operations varies from $150,000 in Arizona to $3,000,000 in New York.

Canada

In Canada, jurisdiction over insurance companies is shared by the federal and provincial governments. Domestic companies may be incorporated by either the federal or provincial governments, but British and foreign companies may only be registered by the federal Department of Insurance. The provincial governments, however, have jurisdiction over the dealings between the policyholders and the companies, and regulate matters such as policy provisions, licensing of agents and the solvency of provincially incorporated companies. The federal government is responsible for the solvency of federally registered companies (which represent about 94 percent of the business in force in Canada).

All companies must be licensed by each province in which they transact business, but the provinces accept federal financial statements and the reports of examinations made by the federal Department of Insurance of federally registered companies. The provisions of provincial insurance acts regarding incorporation, investments and actuarial reserves and the financial statements required of provincially incorporated companies tend to be patterned on federal provisions.

The regulatory policies of the provincial superintendents of insurance are coordinated through the Association of Superintendents of Insurance of the Provinces of Canada. There is considerable uniformity among the insurance acts of the provinces (except for certain policy provisions in Quebec, whose civil law differs from that of the other provinces).

The federal Department of Insurance supervises some 400 life and casualty insurance companies and fraternal societies, in addition to trust, loan and finance companies, and is large and well staffed. Since its establishment in 1875, there have been only seven superintendents of Insurance, of whom six have been actuaries. The staff includes more than ten fellows of the Canadian Institute of Actuaries.

2.2 Statutory financial statements

The statutory financial statements required of life insurance companies by supervisory authorities in the United States and Canada are similar in format to those of other corporations. They include:

1. a statement of assets,
2. a statement of liabilities, capital (for stock companies) and surplus,
3. an income statement (called a summary of operations in the NAIC statement), and
4. a surplus account.

In addition to these principal statements, there are supplementary statements, such as the analysis of income by line of business, and a large number of exhibits and schedules, which provide details of items summarized in the various statements. For example, the total value of bonds owned by a company is shown as a single asset item, but information on every bond owned must be provided in a separate schedule. Again, although the total net investment income is shown in the income statement, the gross investment income from each class of investment must be shown in an exhibit and the total then converted to net investment income by deducting investment expenses and taxes and depreciation of invested assets such as real estate. There are also exhibits and schedules which reveal data not included in the financial statements, such as exhibits of insurance and annuities written, terminated and in force, and schedules of dividends per $1,000 of insurance on participating policies for specified plans and ages.

The statutory statements required of life insurance companies are therefore much more comprehensive and provide far more information concerning the operations of the company than the financial statements typically prepared by other corporations.

The most important statutory statements are the NAIC life and accident and health statement in the United States and the life and accident and sickness statement in Canada (Form INS-54). In the United States, additional statements must be submitted for separate account contracts: the separate account statement for contracts without life insurance benefits, and the variable life insurance separate account statement for those including such benefits. In Canada a separate statement is required for all such contracts (the segregated fund statement).

In the preliminary discussion of statutory statements, reference will be made to the current NAIC statement and to the pre-1978 Canadian life insurance statement, because both are based on what might be called traditional statutory accounting principles. In 1978 the Canadian statement was modified to be more consistent with generally accepted accounting practices in Canada. Additional revisions were made in 1981, when the life insurance statement and the accident and sickness insurance statement were combined.

Financial statements for a period include a balance sheet as of the end of the period, a statement of net income for the period, and a statement showing the disposition of that net income (a surplus account). The balance sheet consists of a statement of assets, the property owned by the company and amounts owed to the company, and a statement of liabilities, capital and surplus. The liabilities are obligations to others, while the difference between the assets and the liabilities constitutes the interest of the proprietors, which is divided into capital contributed by shareholders and contributed and earned surplus.

1. Statement of assets

The statement of assets lists all assets owned by the company, except those excluded by government regulation. It includes:

a) Invested assets, e.g., bonds, mortgages, shares of stock, investment real estate and home office property, policy loans, cash and bank deposits. In the United States, bonds (except for securites in default) are included at amortized values, mortgages at the principal balance outstanding and preferred shares at cost. Common shares are included at market values and real estate at cost less depreciation.

In Canada, before 1978, there were no requirements for valuing assets to be used in the statement, but an investment reserve was required for the excess of book values of bonds and shares over approved values (or the average of the excesses for the current and preceding two years, if less). Approved values were amortized values for bonds of the Canadian, U.S., and provincial governments and mortgages not in default, and market values for all other bonds and for shares.

b) Assets acquired in the course of business, e.g., investment income due but not yet received, or accrued at the end of the year but not yet due; premiums due but unpaid as at the end of the year; amounts due from reinsurers on ceded reinsurance, such as expense allowances or reimbursements on claims or refunds paid, and other receivable amounts, such as advances made to agents in anticipation of commissions.

c) Depreciated values of electronic data processing equipment. Other furniture and equipment is excluded by government regulation as "nonadmitted assets" (see 2.3).

d) Assets in special funds, e.g., assets of segregated fund contracts.

2. Statement of liabilities, capital and surplus

a) Liabilities for unmatured obligations on insurance and annuity contracts, e.g., policy reserves.

b) Provision for dividends to be allocated in the next calendar year on participating contracts.

c) Liabilities for amounts deposited by policyholders, such as prepaid premiums, premium deposit funds (amounts deposited to pay future premiums, but not yet credited to the premium account), dividend accumulations and supplementary contracts under settlement options.

d) Amounts owing to policyholders and others, e.g., unpaid claims, dividends due but unpaid, prepaid premiums, prepaid interest, and expenses, commissions and taxes due but unpaid.

e) Liabilities of special funds, e.g., segregated fund contracts and staff pension and insurance funds.

f) Investment and contingency reserves required by regulatory authorities or set up voluntarily to provide for possible future losses.

g) Capital stock, if any.

h) Unappropriated surplus, i.e., the difference between the total assets and the sum of the preceding items.

3. Income statement (summary of operations)

The income statement shows the earnings of the company in the year of account. Receipts are shown first, with a subtotal, followed by disbursements and other charges to income. All amounts are included on a revenue (accrual) basis.

a) Receipts include premiums, considerations for supplementary contracts and net investment income, i.e., gross investment income less investment expenses and taxes, and depreciation of real estate. Capital gains and losses on investments are not included in this item but are reported in the surplus account. (In Canada, this procedure was modified in 1978.)

Income from supplementary contracts is shown separately from premiums received because it results not from money received by the company but rather from proceeds of claims and surrender values which are retained by the company either on deposit at interest or to be paid to the beneficiaries as annuities. In order to show the correct amount of claims incurred, the amounts retained are included in claims and also shown as income in this item. Disbursements on these contracts are shown separately to avoid inflating claims since the proceeds from which the disbursements arise have already been included.

The NAIC statement includes amounts left on deposit with other supplementary contracts without life contingencies. Amounts left on deposit are included with considerations, interest paid thereon and amounts withdrawn with disbursements and the increase in reserve included with the increase in reserve for supplementary contracts. In Canada, considerations and payments on all supplementary contracts other than amounts on deposit are combined and the increase in reserve included with the increase in reserves for other policies. Amounts left on deposit or withdrawn are not shown separately, but the excess of the increase in reserve plus amounts withdrawn over the amounts left on deposit is shown as a single item, "interest credited to amounts on deposit." This has the effect of treating amounts on deposit in the same manner as borrowed money, and is consistent with the way banks account for deposits.

An example will illustrate the difference in treatment of amounts on deposit in the two statements. Suppose the amount of proceeds on deposit at the end of a year is $100,000 and interest is credited at 6 percent, with all transactions taking place at mid-year. The account may be presented as follows:

	Amount	Accrued Interest	Liability (Amount on Deposit Plus Accrued Interest)
On deposit January 1	$100,000	$3,000	$103,000
Interest capitalized	6,000		
Deposits	50,000		
Withdrawals (including interest)	−20,000		
On deposit December 31	$136,000	$4,080	$140,080

Interest credited is $6,000 capitalized plus the increase in accrued interest, $1,080, for a total of $7,080. (The interest can also be calculated as 6 percent of the average amount on deposit, $118,000.)

The NAIC statement would show the following entries:

Income (included in income from supplementary contracts without life contingencies)	$50,000
Disbursements (included similarly)	−20,000
Increase in reserve	−37,080
Income minus disbursements	−$7,080

In the Canadian statement the only item would be interest credited on amounts on deposit calculated as follows:

Reserve at December 31	$140,080	
Plus withdrawals	20,000	$160,080
Less:		
Reserve at January 1	$103,000	
Deposits	50,000	153,000
Interest credited		$ 7,080

(This appears to be the method used for premium deposit funds in the NAIC Statement and is the method required in GAAP statements in the United States for the increase in reserves for supplementary contracts life and supplementary contracts certain and dividend accumulations.)

b) Amounts paid to policyholders, e.g., death and disability claims, matured endowments, surrender values, dividends, etc.

c) Normal increases in the liabilities for unmatured obligations to policyholders, such as policy reserves. The normal increase is the increase in reserves calculated using the same assumptions for interest and mortality and the same valuation method. Changes in policy reserves due to changes in assumptions or methods are shown in the surplus account. The Canadian statement shows the increase in the provision for dividends to participating policyholders in the next calendar year separately, while in the NAIC Statement this amount is included with dividends paid.

d) Commissions, expenses and taxes.

The net amount, the net income after provision for policyholder dividends and income tax, is transferred to the surplus account.

4. Surplus account

The surplus account shows the reconciliation between the amount of surplus at the end of the previous year and the amount at the end of the current year. In addition to net income, the surplus account includes items which do not occur regularly, such as capital gains and losses, and items which can be regarded as allocations of surplus, such as dividends to shareholders and additions to contingency reserves. The surplus account includes:

a) Unappropriated surplus at the end of the previous year.

b) Net income transferred from the income statement.

c) Net capital gains or losses on investments, including changes in book values of investments.

d) Changes in actuarial reserves due to changes in valuation bases.

e) Changes in investment and contingency reserves.

f) Amounts transferred to other funds, e.g., separate accounts and, in Canada, the accident and health branch.

g) Changes in capital and contributed surplus in stock companies.

h) Dividends to shareholders.

i) Unappropriated surplus at the end of the current year (the net sum of the above items).

The balance sheet and income statement are interrelated, because items of income and expenditure affect assets and liabilities, and the treatment of assets and liabilities affects net income. For example, charging higher depreciation on property will increase expenses as well as decrease assets, and increasing liabilities by using more conservative valuation assumptions will increase actuarial reserves and thus reduce income.

The NAIC statement contains a reconciliation of ledger assets which accounts for the increase in ledger assets from the end of the previous year to the end of the current year. This exhibit has been retained from the pre-1951 NAIC statement in which income and disbursements were reported on a cash basis. Although such an exhibit is not strictly necessary now that the summary of operations is on a revenue or accrual basis, it fulfills an audit function for supervisory authorities and provides an audit trail from the balances in the ledger to the amounts which appear in many exhibits. This exhibit would be more appropriately entitled reconciliation of total ledger assets, because it does not trace the increases and decreases in each ledger asset during the year, but summarizes the net cash transactions and changes in book values of assets for the year and verifies that they account for the net increase in total ledger assets.

The reconciliation of ledger assets lists income collected and disbursements actually made, along with all other transactions affecting ledger assets such as loans made and repaid; capital and surplus paid in, and amounts transferred to and from separate accounts. The net difference added to the ledger assets at the beginning of the year must equal the ledger assets at the end of the year.

In Canada, there is a reconciliation of funds, because of provisions in the Canadian Insurance Act which require 1) that separate accounts must be maintained for participating policies, nonparticipating policies and the shareholders' interest, if any, and 2) that a minimum percentage of the profits earned on participating policies (ranging from 90 to 97½ percent, depending on the size of the participating fund) be retained for the benefit of participating policyholders. The totals in the individual funds must therefore be updated each year, and the income statement must be split to show the net income in the different funds, including segregated funds if equity-linked policies are issued.

Because fund totals represent the assets contributed by the members of each fund, e.g., participating policyholders, non-participating policyholders or shareholders, the fund totals at the end of each year are increased by the net income for the year, and adjustments are made for charges to income which do not affect assets, such as the increase in reserves. Transfers between funds and to or from other funds, and any other credits or charges such as dividends to shareholders must also be included. The balances are the fund totals at the end of the year. The sum of the individual funds plus amounts owing must equal the total assets.

The fact that the sum of funds and amounts owing equals total assets reflects the reality that assets arise from the net contributions of policyholders and shareholders and from amounts which have actually been borrowed or which are due but unpaid. In the calculation of total funds, increases in policy reserves and the reserve for dividends payable in the following year which do not result in asset changes must be excluded from net income. Such items are subsequently added to net income in the reconciliation of funds.

The logic behind this procedure can be seen from a few examples. Claims incurred and paid will decrease income and assets; claims incurred but unpaid will decrease income and increase amounts owing, so that the reduction in the fund will be balanced by the increase in amounts owing. An increase in policy reserves will not affect assets, while the payment of a claim unpaid at the end of the previous year will decrease both assets and amounts owing. To illustrate the two reconciliations, let us assume that the only ledger asset is cash and that income and disbursements consist of premiums, claims and increases in policy reserves. The balance sheet at the end of Year 1 is as follows:

Cash	$100,000	Policy reserves	$50,000
Premiums due and unpaid	5,000	Unpaid claims	20,000
		Surplus	35,000
	$105,000		$105,000

Suppose that, for Year 2, premiums collected are $50,000, claims paid are $30,000 and the increase in reserves is $9,000. Premiums due and unpaid at the end of the year are $7,000 and unpaid claims $26,000. The income statement for Year 2 will show:

Premiums collected	$50,000	
Due at end of year	7,000	
	$57,000	
Due at end of previous year	(5,000)	
Revenue premiums		$52,000
Less: Claims paid	$30,000	
Unpaid at end of year	26,000	
	$56,000	
Unpaid at end of previous year	20,000	
Incurred claims		($36,000)
Increase in policy reserves		(9,000)
Net income		$ 7,000

The balance sheet at the end of Year 2 will be:

Cash	$120,000	Policy reserves	$ 59,000
Premiums due and unpaid	7,000	Unpaid claims	26,000
		Surplus	42,000
	$127,000		$127,000

The Reconciliation of Ledger Assets will be:

Premiums collected	$ 50,000
Claims paid	(30,000)
Difference	$ 20,000
Ledger assets at end of previous year	100,000
Ledger assets at end of current year	$120,000

The reconciliation of funds will be:

Fund balance at end of previous year	$ 85,000
(Total assets of $105,000 minus amounts owing of $20,000)	
Net income	7,000
Plus increase in reserve	9,000
Fund balance at end of current year	$101,000
Amounts owing	26,000
Total assets	$127,000

The U.S. and Canadian statements both split the income statement (summary of operations) by line of business. In the NAIC statement the lines of business are:
1. Industrial
2. Ordinary:
    life insurance
    individual annuities
    supplementary contracts
3. Credit life insurance
4. Group:
    life insurance
    annuities

5. Accident and health:
    group
    credit
    other

In Canada there are ten lines of business: eight combinations of participating and non-participating, individual and group, insurance and annuities for life insurance; and individual and group accident and sickness insurance.

The NAIC statement also has an exhibit showing increases in reserves which presents the reserves at the end of the previous year, with increases due to net premiums, considerations for supplementary contracts, tabular interest, etc., and decreases due to deaths and other terminations, cost of insurance, annuity and supplementary contract payments, with a total of the reserves at the end of the current year. Before 1951, this exhibit was structured to show gains and losses from sources such as loadings, interest, mortality and terminations. It was changed to its present form when it became clear that gains and losses depended on the valuation bases used and that results would be misleading whenever such bases differed from those on which premiums were calculated or when multiple valuation bases were used.

2.3 Special features of life insurance statements

For corporations that do not sell insurance, the important statement is the income statement. Present and prospective shareholders are interested in the profitability of the enterprise, and creditors want to know how much is available from profits to service debt. Accountants, therefore, are interested in insuring that the income statement is correct and informative; this has generally determined how the assets and liabilities are presented. For instance, the Canadian Institute of Chartered Accountants, in its recommendations on inventory valuation, states "The method selected for determining (the value of inventory items) should be one which results in the fairest matching of costs against revenues regardless of whether or not the method corresponds to the physical flow of goods."

Life insurance policyholders, and supervisory authorities, on the other hand, are interested primarily in the ability of the company to meet its long-term obligations (i.e., its solvency), and therefore in the balance sheet. This has affected the statutory income statement. For example, assets such as furniture and equipment and advances to agents, which other corporations would include as assets in their balance sheets, have been excluded from the statutory balance sheets of life insurance companies. The reason was explained by the federal Superintendent of Insurance of Canada in his report for 1972:

> "The principle here is to reflect in the assets only those items that seem to represent a realizable amount. This is considered important since the resulting surplus figure is the only figure that can be used in testing solvency. If an effort were made to reinsure the obligations

of a life insurance company, the only assets taken into account by a reinsurer would be those that are considered as admitted assets for statement purposes. Even though furniture and fixtures, for example, might be expected to serve the needs of the company over many years and there might be a strong argument for spreading the costs over those years, the fact is that on liquidation or reinsurance there is very little value to used furniture and equipment. Thus, from a solvency aspect, it would be misleading to accept this as a valid asset for balance sheet purposes. Also, one of the most serious criticisms of the deferred acquisition expense idea is that it would result in showing on the asset page a relatively large figure representing unamortized acquisition expenses and these are not, in fact, realizable assets.

"It is recognized that in pursuing this principle, the consequence is one of forcing companies to write off as an expense in the year of purchase, items that can be expected to have many years of use. This is the main point in the criticism of the income statement as shown in the government statement. It must be admitted that some of these requirements do have the effect of depressing earnings in years when heavy expense is incurred. This, traditionally, has been accepted as a lesser evil than inflating the surplus figure by reason of assets that may not be realizable."

This conservative approach, which applies to many other items, such as initial policy expenses and the valuation of assets and liabilities, affects the income statement and the surplus of a life insurance company to a considerable extent.

Initial policy expenses

Because mortality costs tend to increase with age, on a policy with equal annual premiums it is necessary to set aside a portion of each premium received (the gross premium) to provide for current and future benefits. This portion is the valuation premium. Only the balance of the gross premium (the expense allowance) is available to defray expenses. Under the net level premium reserve system, the valuation premiums in all policy years are equal and, therefore, so are the expense allowances.

In the United States and Canada, expenses incurred in the first policy year normally exceed the net level expense allowance in the premium by a substantial margin, while those incurred in subsequent policy years are less than the expense allowances. If net level premium reserves are set up, a substantial deficit is incurred on business written in the current year and surpluses are generated from premiums paid on previously written business. As long as adequate premiums are charged, and premiums, expenses and the amount of business written in each year remain constant, a steady state will be reached in which the deficit on new business is balanced by surpluses from business written previously. However, if the amount of new business increases from year to year, the deficits on new business will reduce reported earnings, even though the "going concern concept" (i.e., the assumption that the company will continue in business indefinitely and will not be liquidated or reinsured in the near future) calls for surpluses expected from future premiums on the new business to be shown as an asset.

These deficits may be reduced by using "modified reserve systems" under which the valuation premium in the first year may be lower than the net level valuation premium (but not less than some statutory minimum), offset by higher valuation premiums in subsequent years. This procedure increases the first year expense allowance and decreases subsequent expense allowances. Nevertheless, the deficit on new business is still significant in most cases. There has been a reluctance to go farther, not only because of the solvency principles stated above, but also to prevent unrestricted competition for new business. An increase, say, in first year commissions, spread over all the gross premiums to be paid, will increase each premium by a relatively small amount. The competitive disadvantage of a slightly higher gross premium may well be outweighed by the additional incentive to sales created by higher commissions.

Nonadmitted assets

All jurisdictions place restrictions on the investments which may be made by insurance companies. For example, corporate bonds must meet certain criteria; only first mortgages are acceptable as assets in the balance sheet—and these are limited to some percentage of the value of the property mortgaged; investment in comon and preferred shares is prohibited in some states (if permitted, shares are subject to earnings criteria and limited to a specified percentage of assets), and investments in real estate, apart from property used by the company in its operations, are generally restricted. Investments which do not meet these criteria (except for small percentages in some jurisdictions, e.g., 7 percent in Canada and specified percentages of certain types of investment in New York) may not be included in the balance sheet.

As noted earlier, furniture and equipment (except electronic data processing equipment) and advances to agents in anticipation of commissions must also be excluded. In Canada, before 1978, expenditures on these items were charged as expenses in the year incurred. In the United States ledger assets may be set up, and only depreciation of furniture and equipment and expected losses due to nonrepayment of amounts advanced may be charged as expenses, but any such ledger assets must be treated as nonadmitted assets and excluded from the balance sheet.

Policy reserves

Life insurance companies must set up a liability for the excess of the value of benefits payable in future years over the value of the premiums to be collected under the contracts. Both countries have established minimum standards for these reserves. In the United States, the reserves are based on specific mortality tables and interest rates tied to the issue date of the policy, although other mortality tables and interest rates may be used if they result in equal or larger reserves. In Canada, before 1978, companies could either use one of a number of specified tables, with certain maximum interest rates, or apply to the Superintendent of Insurance for approval of other tables and interest rates higher than the maximum rates for particular classes of policies. In both countries a minimum reserve method is specified, permitting a first-year valuation premium that is less than the net level premium, with compensating additions to renewal valuation premiums.

In both countries, these policy reserves must be certified by a qualified actuary. In the United States, the certificate includes a statement that "the reserves are based on actuarial assumptions which are in accordance with or stronger than those called for in policy provisions." In Canada, the actuary must certify that "the reserves are not less than those required by the Insurance Act." In addition, in both countries the actuary must verify that "the reserves make good and sufficient provision for all the unmatured obligations of the company guaranteed under the terms of its policies."

Investment reserves

Investment reserves are prescribed by statute in order to protect the company against future investment losses. In the United States, the mandatory securities valuation reserve (MSVR) also serves to reduce the impact on surplus of realized and unrealized capital gains and losses on securities. The specified maximum is based on varying percentages of the admitted values of the different classes of securities held, with specified mandatory and optional annual increases, based on smaller percentages of admitted values of securities and on net realized and unrealized capital gains. A portion of net capital losses is charged against the reserve.

In Canada, before 1978, the investment reserve was based on the excess of book values of bonds (other than bonds of the Canadian, United Kingdom, or United States governments or bonds of Canadian provinces) and shares over market values.

Gains and losses on investments

Realized gains and losses from investments arise when investments are sold or otherwise disposed of at values greater than or lower than the values at which they are carried in the ledger. Unrealized gains and losses occur when the statement values of investments at the end of a year are greater or less than the statement values at the end of the previous year, except for the normal change in amortized values of bonds and mortgages.

In the United States, bonds are shown in the statement at amortized values and preferred shares at cost. (Market values are used for securities in default.) Common shares are also shown at market value. Therefore realized gains and losses will arise from sales at values different from statement values; unrealized gains and losses from changes in market values of common shares, and changes in market values of any bonds or preferred shares valued at market. The total net realized and unrealized capital gains, less any income tax payable on the gains, is credited to the surplus account as a separate item. However, the effect on unappropriated surplus is reduced by the charge against the MSVR of realized and unrealized losses and the inclusion of some of the gains in this reserve.

In Canada, before 1978, realized gains and losses were included in the surplus account and therefore affected unappropriated surplus. The required investment reserve was based on the net difference between market values and book values, but no additional reserve was necessary if the voluntary investment reserve held by the company exceeded the required reserve. As a result, unrealized gains and losses affected unappropriated surplus only when the difference between market values and book values exceeded the investment reserve normally held.

2.4 Criticisms of statutory financial statements

Statutory financial statements, which emphasize solvency, generally show lower current earnings than do statements prepared according to the principles on which financial statements of other corporations are based. Because published statements of most life insurance companies use data from the statutory statements, accountants and investment analysts have criticized the statements because of the difficulty of estimating the earnings or net worth of life insurance companies on a "going concern" basis.

The principal features of statutory accounting that have been criticized are:

1. Initial expenses. Critics have argued that, instead of writing off all expenses when incurred, with an insufficient allowance for initial expenses in policy reserves, normal accounting practice requires that expenses directly due to acquisition of new business should be amortized to the extent that they are considered recoverable, and an asset account established for unamortized deferred expenses. This would prevent the depression of earnings by the sale of increasing amounts of new business, if the new business can be expected to be profitable.

2. Nonadmitted assets. Excluding nonadmitted assets from the balance sheet on the basis of statutory provisions unduly depresses assets and earnings. It has been maintained that nonadmitted investments should be included in the assets at realistic values, that furniture and fixtures be included (less reasonable depreciation) and that receivables be included (less a reserve for amounts considered uncollectable).

3. Policy reserves. Since statutory provisions prescribe only minimum reserves, and actuaries could certify liabilities on more conservative bases, some method should be devised to prevent undue conservatism and make statements of different companies more comparable.

4. Capital gains and losses on investments. Many accountants have held that income should include capital gains and losses on investments, since these are normal results of investment operations.

5. Investment and contingency reserves. Although conceding that the long-term nature of life insurance obligations make investment and contingency reserves necessary, many critics have contended that these reserves should be included in surplus, except to the extent that they provide for specific contingencies, such as expected losses on securities in default.

Replies to these criticisms have pointed out that "traditional accounting systems reflect the fact that most businesses have a relatively fast turnover of goods and services and that the emergence of profits can conveniently be measured annually. Life insurance obligations, however, can span many years and therefore profits are not so readily identifiable." (Report of the Canadian Life Insurance Association committee on Life Insurance Accounting.)

Furthermore, the amount of detailed information on assets, liabilities and operations required in statutory statements and published by insurance departments provides information which can be used to assess the operations of an individual company. However, this assessment requires more and more technical knowledge of insurance as operations become more complex. In practice, it is only made by officials of insurance departments who are in a position to warn companies that their business practices are considered unsound and require improvements. As a last resort, if the company becomes technically insolvent, the conservative values used for assets and liabilities will very often enable a regulator to take over the administration of the company while there is still a good chance to rescue the interests of the policyholders.

For many years, this supervision was satisfactory; most life insurance companies were well managed and, since most stock companies were closely held, there was little trading in life insurance company shares. As long as only a few new companies were formed, their operations could be monitored by insurance departments. In view of these circumstances, in the United States the financial statements of life insurance companies were exempt from certification by external auditors in reports or regulatory statements filed under the Securities Exchange Act of 1934. In Canada auditors certified life insurance statements as "prepared using principles prescribed or permitted by regulatory authorities."

After 1945, however, new insurance companies proliferated in the United States. At the end of 1945, there were 473 life insurance companies in the United States; by 1950, there were 611, and in the following 25 years 2,552 new life insurance companies were formed. The majority of the new companies were formed in states where insurance supervision was relatively weak. The fact that over 1,400 companies discontinued business in the same period demonstrates that many were poorly managed and that, in many cases, supervision was ineffective, at least from the investors' point of view.

The use of statutory accounting principles in published statements made it difficult for investors to determine whether a new company was properly managed. Under these principles, new companies generally show deficits, because the surplus on previously written business isn't enough to compensate for the deficits on new business. As a result, investors cannot distinguish well-managed companies with deficits caused merely by the effect of new business from those whose deficits also reflect poor management.

This was equally true in Canada, although the number of new companies was much smaller and most were supervised by the federal Department of Insurance and the stronger provincial departments. However, the deficits shown even by well-managed new companies made it difficult to raise capital.

As a result, investment analysts and accountants demanded the development of principles for the preparation of published statements of life insurance companies which would permit better estimates of earnings. In 1971, the Securities and Exchange Commission (SEC) in the United States proposed an amendment to delete the exemption from certification. This made the adoption of generally accepted accounting principles for life insurance companies urgent, since certification required an unqualified opinion of an external auditor. Under the principles of the American Institute of Certified Public Accountants (AICPA), a life insurance company statement presented in conformity with regulatory practices would normally receive a qualified or adverse opinion.

2.5 Developments in the United States

In 1966, the Committee on Insurance Accounting of the AICPA published an audit guide for property and casualty insurers and undertook the development of a similar guide for life insurance companies. In 1967, the American Life Convention and the Life Insurance Association of America established the Joint Committee on Financial Reporting Principles to work with the AICPA Committee in the development of the audit guide. In 1970, a Joint Actuarial Committee was formed by the American Academy of Actuaries, the Society of Actuaries, the Canadian Institute of Actuaries, and the Conference of Actuaries in Public Practice with an observer from the Casualty Actuarial Society. A year later, the AICPA Committee published an exposure draft of an audit guide. In 1972, the AICPA Committee issued an audit guide for stock life insurance companies. Mutual companies were not included, apparently because the committee did not agree on accounting principles for mutual companies. Moreover, the SEC rules applied only to companies issuing publicly traded shares.

In the introduction to the listing of generally accepted accounting principles for general purpose statements of life insurance companies, the AICPA Audit Guide points out that:

"The interests of policyholders and of the public in the financial integrity of the life insurance industry make it important and proper that the solvency of life insurance companies be demonstrated to regulatory authorities. Consideration of these interests, together with the uncertainties inherent in the future, has resulted in the conservative accounting practices prescribed or permitted by insurance regulatory authorities (regulatory accounting practices). Solvency must be continuously demonstrated for a life insurance company to be permitted to offer its services to the public. Federal income taxation of life insurance companies is also based primarily on these insurance regulatory accounting practices. The use of generally accepted accounting principles, as discussed herein, should not be construed as an indication that such accounting principles should also be used in reporting to insurance regulatory or taxing authorities.

"Statement on auditing procedure number 33 states that the basic postulates and broad principles of accounting comprehended in the term "generally accepted accounting principles" which pertain to business enterprises in general apply also to regulated companies, including insurance companies. Regulatory accounting practices differ in some respects from generally accepted accounting principles. The purpose of this chapter is to discuss the difference between these two bases, and to set forth appropriate guidelines for accounting and financial reporting in conformity with generally accepted accounting principles for general purpose financial statements. The object of such statements is to provide reliable financial information about economic resources and obligations of a business enterprise and changes in net resources resulting from its business activities, measured as a going concern."

The Audit Guide also notes that "conservatism in valuing assets and liabilities and in accounting for revenue and costs is necessary because of the uncertainties inherent in the use of actuarial assumptions for contracts guaranteeing performance over long periods of time and the risk of adverse deviations. However, as contemplated by generally accepted accounting principles, such conservatism must be reasonable and realistic."

The Audit Guide further points out that the choice of actuarial assumptions and the regulation of that choice are primarily responsibilities of the actuarial profession. The related responsibility of the auditor is to form a judgment as to whether the actuary has been guided in his work by considerations which are consistent with generally accepted accounting principles:

"However, the actuary's choice of assumptions to be used in connection with general purpose financial statements is disciplined by the principles of his profession. His responsibility to use assumptions which are 'adequate and appropriate' is consistent with the concept, under generally accepted accounting principles, that actuarial assumptions be characterized by conservatism which is 'reasonable and realistic'. The auditor should expect the actuary to be able to demonstrate that assumptions used in determining actuarial items in a general purpose financial statement meet such standards."

The Audit Guide lists a number of areas in which statutory accounting principles differ from generally accepted accounting principles and sets forth principles which must be followed for published statements. The principles which govern the most important areas are discussed in detail in Chapter 4, section 4.2, pages 141-157.

2.6 Developments in Canada

In Canada, although life insurance companies traditionally have been audited by external auditors, the Canadian Institute of Chartered Accountants (CICA) specifically excludes life insurance from generally accepted accounting principles. Accountants certify financial statements on the basis of "principles prescribed or permitted by regulatory authorities."

Although a number of new life insurance companies were formed in Canada after 1945, the majority were federally registered or incorporated in provinces where capital and surplus requirements for new companies paralleled those of the federal government, so that relatively few caused the problems which concerned the SEC in the United States. Nevertheless, the discussion of generally accepted accounting principles for life insurance companies in America increased interest in the subject in Canada and the CICA formed a research committee to study accounting and auditing practices of life insurance companies and recommend improvements. The committee included an actuary and was assisted by the Assistant Superintendent of Insurance for Canada who participated in the discussions but had no part in the preparation of the report or responsibility for the views expressed in it.

The CICA research report issued in 1972 broadly concluded that life insurance company published statements should be based on the same accounting principles applied to the preparation of statements of other corporations. (A number of reservations were made by the actuary on the committee in a minority report.)

The publication of the report stimulated further study by the Federal Department of Insurance, and by committees of the Canadian Life Insurance Association and the Canadian Institute of Actuaries. Reports made by all three which agreed with some of the criticisms of the CICA research study but held that the special nature of life insurance required modification of generally accepted accounting principles. The principal modifications related to the treatment of capital gains and losses on investments, the exclusion of "nonadmitted assets," deferred acquisition expenses, actuarial reserves, and income taxes.

To illustrate the arguments on both sides, the recommendations and reasons set out in the CICA research study are listed below, followed, in each case, by excerpts from the 1972 report of the Superintendent of Insurance, and from the reports of the committees on life insurance accounting of the Canadian Institute of Actuaries (CIA) and of the Canadian Life Insurance Association (CLIA).

I. Capital gains and losses

Recommendations of CICA research report

1. The "completed transaction" method (reporting a capital gain or loss in the year in which the asset is sold) is appropriate for accounting and statement presentation of all capital gains or capital losses. If gains or losses have been significant in relation to other sources of net income for

the year, an explanatory comment may be warranted in a note or annual report textual material. (Whether an amount is "significant" or "material" is a question of judgment. If net income is $1,000,000, $2,000 would normally not be considered significant or material, but $200,000 would be.)

2. Capital gains and capital losses on income-yielding assets should enter into the determination of net income. The net gain or net loss should be disclosed separately in the income statement.

Reasons

"The study group concludes that net realized capital gains and losses on income-yielding assets are part of the normal investment activity of a life insurance company, and should be shown separately in the income statement as an ordinary item. It is inappropriate to show such gains as an extraordinary item or as a retained earnings adjustment. All gains taken into income in a year should flow through and be included in net income without any offsets." (CICA, Chapter 7)

Superintendent's comments

"The study suggests that realized capital gains should be shown as part of income (although as a separate item) rather than as an adjustment to surplus which is the existing requirement in the government statement.

"The present practice was adopted at a time when equity investments represented a much smaller proportion of assets of life insurance companies than is the present case. Exclusion from the income statement thus did not distort investment earnings but, instead, left net earnings as a more reliable indicator of the normal experience and trends. With growth in equity type investments, many of which are made on grounds of expected capital appreciation rather than regular income, it becomes more difficult to justify any treatment that does not reflect capital gain as part of investment return. However, to complete the picture unrealized capital gains must be given consideration. Inequity can well occur between generations of policyholders if today's assets are invested in low-yielding shares or real estate with the idea of capital gain. The investment income can be depressed by such action if the capital gains are not recognized until disposal of the asset—this could be many years away. It seems desirable, therefore, to devise some way of recognizing at least some part of the unrealized capital gain for income purposes. For shareholders the point is not important since the unrealized gain is probably reflected in share prices, but for participating policyholders, the deferment of income can represent a permanent loss." (P. 45A.)

CIA comments

"The disposal before maturity of bonds held at amortized cost will usually produce capital gains or losses. These gains or losses are more apparent than real as the proceeds on sale must be reinvested at current rates. If a company immediately takes these amounts into its income statement, a distortion, which can be substantial, will result. Such gains or losses should be amortized over the lifetime of the original bond to be consistent with the holding of policy reserves on the basis assumed in the original pricing of the product." (P. 69)

(*Note:* Bond prices generally reflect current interest rates. Therefore, as long as the proceeds of a bond sale are reinvested at current rates, the gain or loss incurred when a bond is sold at a price reflecting current yields may be considered only a nominal gain or loss. For example, if a $10,000 7 percent bond with semi-annual coupons, purchased at par, is sold 10 years before maturity when current yields are 10 percent, the proceeds will be $8,130.67, a book loss of $1,869.33.

However, if the proceeds are reinvested in a 10 percent 10-year bond at par, the transaction will be the exchange of an income stream of $700 per annum for 10 years plus $10,000 at the end of the period for $813.07 for 10 years plus $8,130.67 at the end of the period. If the additional $113.07 per annum can be invested at 10 percent as it is received, it will amount to $1,869.33 at the end of the period, and the two income streams will be identical. It can therefore be argued that spreading the loss over the 10 years during which the additional income is to be received is more appropriate than showing a substantial loss in the year of sale and higher income in subsequent years. This argument does not apply, of course, if the proceeds are not reinvested.)

Additional CIA comments

"Funds received in respect of participating policyholders are a major source of the cash available for investment and some of this money will be used to acquire assets where appreciation in value is expected. Unrealized capital gains should be recognized in some form when determining the dividend scale if equity is to be maintained among generations of policyholders. Equity will not be achieved if only realized gains are recognized as distributable because they may arise in an irregular fashion and may not emerge until after the termination of many policies entitled to the gains.

"Under the present system, the distribution through dividends of any part of the unrealized capital gains on common stocks would lead to the undesirable situation of having paid out earnings before they are taken into the financial statements. Although this may not have been a major problem up to now, it will become an increasing one as companies invest relatively more in assets where a capital appreciation is a significant part of the expected investment return. Similarly, losses should be recognized as they occur rather than only on realization.

"Something less than unrealized capital gains or losses on the basis of full current market values would seem to be desirable; that is, some system which draws the present level of book values towards the market values. Any such system would give only partial recognition to current market conditions but, whatever its shortcomings, it would be preferable to ignoring capital gains or losses completely or recognizing the entire market swing in the annual earnings." (Pp. 71-2.)

CLIA comments

"It is important that accounting principles adopted should not inhibit investment officers from pursuing investment policies which take advantage of temporary market situations or which maximize investment results. The use of amortized values for bonds provides stability while the bonds are held, but sales may have a distorting effect on income and surplus since amortized values can differ appreciably from market values." (P. 13.)

The last comment refers to the possibility that, when interest rates are high, there may be a reluctance to trade short-term low interest bonds for longer term bonds with higher interest rates due to the effect on surplus if the full capital loss incurred on the sale of the bonds held is recognized in the year of sale.

II. Nonadmitted assets

Recommendations of CICA research report

1. All so-called "nonadmitted" assets should be recorded at original cost in the accounts of a life insurance company. Arbitrary values of something less than cost (e.g., including furniture and equipment at zero) are not considered appropriate accounting.

2. The balance of these assets which has not yet been expensed should be reflected in the balance sheet.

CIA comments

"The exclusion of 'nonadmitted' assets from the balance sheet has been motivated by the need for a demonstration of the solvency of a life insurance company. However, this tends to distort the income statement to the extent that it portrays a 'going concern.' For example, while the inclusion of furniture as an asset might be inappropriate in a solvency test, the expensing of the entire cost in the year of purchase is misleading, when it is recognized that the furniture will serve a productive purpose for many years.

" 'Nonadmitted assets' should be included in the financial statements for life insurance companies, as they are for other business enterprises. Recognizing that these assets are not distributable and are of questionable value in a solvency test, an offsetting amount of retained earnings should be appropriated." (Pp. 74-5.)

III. Deferred acquisition expenses

Recommendations of CICA research report

1. Deferrable acquisition expenses are those expenses which vary with or arise from the sales of new life insurance policies or annuity contracts. These expenses relate to production of new business and normally arise in the year of sale. Renewal commissions telescoped into early policy years may also be considered as deferrable acquisition expenses.

2. Deferred acquisition expenses should be amortized block by block

according to the regularly updated persistency experience of the individual company.

3. Deferred acquisition expenses should be reflected as an asset on the balance sheet.

Reasons

"Superintendents of Insurance, through their regulatory practices, require that commissions in connection with acquiring new business be charged against income as incurred in the statutory statements filed with them. Usually, there is no provision for deferral. One exception to this rule is the Canadian modified method of determining actuarial liabilities. At the end of the first policy year, the liability is established on a preliminary term basis to leave a greater portion of the premium to offset high first year expenses. Except for this partial allowance, acquisition expenses are not treated in a manner which produces matching of income and expense. In many cases the current statutory actuarial liability methods produce a negative result, in that acquisition expenses and the actuarial provision for the first year are deducted from policy premiums of the first year. A company actively expanding and writing an increasing volume of business can thus produce a loss on operations. Conversely, a company which is not writing new business may reflect large emerging profits. The concern that policyholders, shareholders and the public at large do not understand the emergence of profits of insurance companies is well founded. The identification of acquisition expenses is necessary if generally accepted accounting principles are to be applied to a life insurance industry." (CICA, Chapter 10)

Superintendent's comments

"Generally, it appears to me that a modified reserve method such as presently available continues to be the best way to ease the impact of a high first year expense. It might be appropriate to adopt a new version of modified reserves whereby some prescribed proportion of the first year premium would be released to meet the first year expenses and the actuarial reserve would be built up using a correspondingly higher net premium for subsequent years. The present maximum first year allowance linked to full preliminary term reserves on the whole life plan could perhaps be replaced by some more appropriate limit.

"Such an approach would have the advantage of uniformity amongst companies, it would act as a check on extravagance (additional expenses would have to be financed from surplus) and the need to determine amortization periods for blocks of business would disappear. Also, controversy over what expenses should be deferred would not arise.

"Of course, the adoption of even a new system of modified reserves as acceptable for government statement purposes would not be synonymous with requiring modified reserves to be used by all companies. Presumably, the approach would be for those companies that continued to use net level premium reserves to reveal in the audited shareholders' or policyholders' statement the adjustment to earnings that would result from using modified reserves and so 'deferring' part of the acquisition expense." (Pp. 40A, 41A.)

CIA comments

"The committee concluded that the acquisition cost element is best treated as an intrinsic part of the reserving system, by the use of a 'modified' reserving system. However, the committee recommends that the amount to be deferred or amortized in the reserving system, instead of being determined by arbitrary formulae applicable to all companies, be determined by the actuary as part of a process of selecting reserve assumptions adequate and appropriate to the characteristics of the particular company.

"The committee further recommends that such a modification be a mandatory element of the policy reserves, rather than an optional one as is presently the case, and that the unamortized acquisition cost element be separately disclosed as a deduction from the reserve for future policy obligations." (Pp. 42-3.)

IV. Actuarial reserves

Recommendations of CICA research report

1. The mortality assumptions and actuarial liabilities for new policies should be based on tables which reflect realistic estimates of expected mortality at the time premiums are established or policies are issued.

2. An appropriate interest rate as determined by the company actuary should be utilized in the actuarial liability valuation in published financial statements.

3. The valuation of actuarial liabilities for cash value policies is only appropriate if it produces an actuarial liability at least equal to the aggregate guaranteed cash surrender value.

4. The net level premium method is appropriate for actuarial liability valuation in published financial statements.

5. When the valuation basis of actuarial liabilities in general purpose financial statements differs materially from statutory actuarial liabilities in statements filed with regulatory authorities, the latter amount and the differences should be disclosed by note to the financial statements.

6. The basis of valuation of actuarial liabilities should be disclosed by note to the financial statements to reflect mortality tables, interest assumptions, and valuation method utilized.

Superintendent's comments

"The study expresses considerable concern that the reserves computed and certified by the actuary may be excessive. They seek the determination of what they refer to as 'appropriate' actuarial reserves, feeling that this would avoid concealed surplus and depression of earnings because of excessive allocation to actuarial reserves.

"It appears to me that the concern expressed in the study is excessive in this regard. I think it is extremely important to avoid computation and publication of two different sets of actuarial reserves. This is probably the aspect of life insurance statements that is least understood and is most dependent on subjective judgment. If two different sets of reserves are produced, confusion would undoubtedly result. The computation of actuarial reserves is not an exact science since we are dealing not with absolute liabilities but with an estimate of the resources that will be needed to meet future obligations. It is not possible to arrive at an exact amount that will be 'appropriate.' Also, I believe that it would be dangerous to launch any program that would have the effect of cutting actuarial reserves to the bone. I think, therefore, that it is important to rely on one set of actuarial reserves—those certified by the actuary as making good and sufficient provision.

"With respect to interest rates, the underlying requirement that actuarial reserves must cover the cash surrender values again leaves the actuary of a company very little room to maneuver as respects older business on the books. If premiums have been determined at rates of interest that are much lower than current rates and cash values have been computed assuming that lower rate of interest, the actuary cannot now adopt higher rates of interest without producing reserves that are inadequate to cover the cash surrender values.

"The research report is critical of 'contingency reserves' that sometimes appear in the actuarial reserves. The report suggests that all such items should be removed from actuarial reserves and reflected in the free surplus figure. It is difficult to be categorical over this matter. It must be admitted that if amounts are included among actuarial reserves that are, in fact, free surplus, then there may be some lack of full disclosure. However, sometimes amounts labelled as contingency reserves in the statement of actuarial liabilities are really the beginning of the accumulation of sums necessary to strengthen actuarial reserves, and sometimes may be amounts that the actuary feels are necessary in order to justify his certificate of adequacy. In such cases, they are in fact, a part of the actuarial reserves and perhaps they should be more appropriately labelled than 'contingency reserves.' It would seem that any amounts necessary to justify the certificate of the actuary cannot be considered free surplus and are properly held with the other actuarial reserves." (P. 42A.)

CIA comments

"One reserving system should be used to meet the requirements of the users of financial statements.

"The reserving system should consider explicitly or implicitly all elements of risk and policy cost, provide for appropriate deferral and amortization by sound actuarial methods of acquisition costs, and incorporate necessary solvency safeguards.

"The choice of assumptions, including the amount of acquisition costs to be deferred, is the responsibility of the actuary. Such assumptions should be appropriately conservative with due regard for the current and future interests of policyholders and shareholders, the particular circumstances of the company, and the bases of asset valuation.

"The balance sheet should show as a liability the policy reserves (i.e., the reserve for future policy obligations less unamortized acquisition costs), with the two components separately disclosed, and, as an appropriation of surplus, any amounts held in addition in order to satisfy solvency requirements.

"Income both before and after appropriation for solvency safeguards and other purposes should be disclosed.

"Reserves for specific contingencies deemed actuarially necessary by the actuary should be treated as part of the reserve for future policy obligations. General contingency reserves should be treated as appropriations of retained earnings.

"A general statement of the method of valuation should be disclosed (along with any material changes in basis) in the published financial statements." (Pp. 49-50.)

V. Income taxes

Recommendations of CICA research report

1. When timing differences occur between accounting income and taxable income, life insurance companies should account for income taxes on the tax allocation basis, which relates the provision for income taxes to the accounting income for the period.

CLIA comments

"The tax legislation for life companies is highly complex and relatively new in Canada. Because the tax calculation is temporarily surrounded by uncertainties, it seems unrealistic at this time to attempt refinements such as deferred tax accounting. Complications also arise because of the taxes imposed by the various foreign jurisdictions in which companies do business." (P. 5.)

Although these recommendations of the research study were not adopted by the CICA nor implemented by the Department of Insurance, the criticisms were taken into account by the Department in proposing the 1977 amendments to the Insurance Act and in the 1978 and 1981 revisions of the Canadian Statement.

2.7 1978 revisions of the Canadian annual statement

Despite differences in opinion about the treatment of specific items, there was substantial agreement on at least two important points: 1) that it is desirable to have a single statement that can be used for both supervisory authorities and for the public (including policyholders and present and prospective shareholders) and 2) that solvency requirements should not distort the income statement.

The Superintendent of Insurance asked the three associations (CICA, CIA, and CLIA) to suggest members for an advisory committee which would work with Department officials who were preparing recommendations for amendments to the Insurance Acts regarding annual statements and solvency requirements. The advisory committee also included representatives of the Association of the Provincial Superintendents of Insurance.

After considerable discussion, the Superintendent recommended amendments to the Insurance Acts to the Minister of Finance. These amendments were enacted in 1977 and made effective for 1978 statements.

The memorandum of instructions for Canadian life insurance companies referred to the changes in the statement in the following words:

"Efforts have been made to accommodate, where possible, the views of various parties such as the Canadian Life Insurance Association and the Canadian Institute of Chartered Accountants.

"Many of the changes were made to bring the Annual Statement form more in line with financial statements prepared using generally accepted accounting principles. It continues to be our objective to have the statement filed with the Department report a balance sheet and income statement identical to those contained in the report to the company's members."

The principal changes were:

1. Appropriated surplus. Before 1978, the surplus shown in the statement was the excess of assets over liabilities and capital, while liabilities included contingency reserves either required by the Insurance Act or considered necessary by management. Beginning in 1978, such contingency reserves were treated as appropriated surplus, and the excess of assets over liabilities, capital and appropriated surplus is called unappropriated surplus. Increases or decreases in appropriated surplus will not be included in the income statement but will be treated as appropriations of surplus.

This procedure permits assets previously treated as "nonadmitted" to be included in the statement in accordance with generally accepted accounting principles, although a reserve for the amount of such assets must be included in appropriated surplus.

For example, the amount expended on furniture and equipment will increase the amount of the assets, and the only charge in the income statement will be normal depreciation. However, the difference between the amount expended in the year and the depreciation will be treated as an increase or a decrease in appropriated surplus. Thus the income statement is prepared on a "going concern" basis, while the unappropriated surplus takes into account the fact that the asset is not considered realizable for solvency purposes.

2. Invested assets. Taking into account the fact that life insurance company liabilities are long-term and that proceeds of the sale of investments are usually reinvested, the regulations provide that bonds and mortgages be valued at amortized cost and gains and losses on their sale be included in investment income in equal amounts over the remaining term of the securities sold, but not more than 20 years. A valuation reserve, equal to 10 percent of the excess of book values over market, must be established. (Market values of mortgages are calculated on the basis of current interest rates, but reasonable approximations may be used.)

Suppose, in 1978, the first year in which this method was prescribed, a company sold bonds maturing in 1988, incurring a book loss of $220,000. The loss would be spread over 11 years (the current year and the remaining 10 years to maturity). One-eleventh of the loss ($20,000) would be charged to investment income in 1978 and the unamortized balance of $200,000 taken as an asset to increase the book values of the bonds. In each future year the same amount would be charged to investment income, and the unamortized balance reduced until it reached zero. As other bonds are sold, the gains and losses would be treated in the same manner.

Book values of shares are shown at cost. In order to recognize at least part of the appreciation or depreciation in the values of shares and to avoid fluctuations in income when gains and losses are realized, according to the regulations implemented in 1978, seven percent of the net excess of market values over adjusted book values would be included in investment income and added to the book values in total. As gains and losses are realized, the net gain is deducted from the adjusted book values. (In 1984, the 7 percent was increased to 15 percent.)

Let us assume further that, at the end of year 1, the adjustment account (the amount added to book values of shares in total) is $250,000, and in year 2 profits on the sale of shares amount to $150,000 and losses to $24,000 (calculated on the basis of the actual book values of the shares sold). If, at the end of the year, book values of shares were $3,175,000 and market values $3,650,000, the following adjustments would be made:

Adjustment account, end of year 1	$ 250,000
Plus losses on sale	24,000
Less profits on sale	−150,000
Preliminary adjustment account, year 2	$ 124,000
Book values, end of year 2	3,175,000
Preliminary adjusted book values	$3,299,000
Market values, end of year 2	3,650,000
Excess of market values over adjusted book	$ 351,000
15% of excess	$ 52,650*
Preliminary adjustment account, year 2	124,000
Final adjustment account, year 2	$ 176,650
Book values of shares	$3,175,000
Adjusted book values, end of year 2	$3,351,650

*Amount included in investment income

The adjustment account is added to the book values whether it is positive or negative. For instance, if the adjustment account at the end of the previous year happened to be zero, the preliminary adjustment account at the end of the year would be −$126,000, the excess of market values over adjusted book values $601,000, and the amount included in investment income $90,150. The final adjustment account would be −$126,000 + $90,150 = −$35,850, and the adjusted book value $3,139,150.

The adjustment account at the end of any year is the difference between the net realized and unrealized capital gains included in income since December 31, 1977 and the net realized capital gains incurred since that date.

A life insurance company is also required to maintain a valuation reserve for shares equal to the deficiency of market values from adjusted book values (less any market excess of bonds, mortgages and real estate) or the average net deficiency for the current and preceding two years (if less).

Because life insurance obligations are long-term, the full market deficiency of secure bonds and mortgages is an excessive reserve, since a company may hold most such securities until the market value appreciates or the debt matures. To take this into account, the valuation reserve on debt securities is 10 percent of the market deficiency (less any market excess on shares and real estate) with a minimum of 1.5 percent of the total book value. The total investment reserve must not be less than 1.5 percent of the total book value of debt securities and is to be treated as an appropriation of surplus instead of a liability.

Since many accident and sickness contracts cover relatively short terms (e.g., group business and cancellable individual policies), the treatment of invested assets related to these contracts is different. Realized capital gains and losses on securities are included in full in the income statement and, for the investment valuation reserve, debt securities are considered either short-term (maturing in 5 years or less) or long-term. The market deficiency on short-term bonds and short-term mortgages may be ignored, unless the book value of mortgages is over 40 percent of the total book value of assets (increased to 80 percent in 1984).

The full market deficiency on long-term debt securities and real estate (less any excess on shares), as well as the average market deficiency on shares for the current and previous years, must be included in the investment valuation reserve. However, to recognize the fact that some obligations are long-term and the corresponding assets entitled to treatment similar to that in life insurance, the reserve may be reduced by applying the factor $1.10 (1 - .5T)$, where T is the ratio of the reserve on long-term obligations to total liabilities. (See Chapter 5, 5.13 and Example 5.4.)

As has always been the case, investments in subsidiaries must be shown separately, but shares in subsidiaries must be valued using the equity method. Under the equity method, the value of each share of stock is considered to be the sum of the capital paid in plus (minus) the surplus (deficit) divided by the number of shares outstanding.

3. Actuarial liabilities. The minimum method for calculation of actuarial reserves has been changed to permit higher deferred acquisition costs (up to 150 percent of the net level valuation premium for the plan but only to the extent the costs are recoverable from future premiums). In addition, withdrawal rates may be used in the calculation of reserves. Negative reserves and reserves less than cash values may be included, but, if this is done, an appropriation of surplus must be made for the amount of negative reserves and cash value deficiencies.

No mortality tables or maximum interest rates are specified in the current act, but the board of directors of each company must appoint a valuation actuary (who must be a fellow of the Canadian Institute of Actuaries) and notify the Superintendent of Insurance of the appointment. The statutory statement must include a report from the valuation actuary stating that, in his or her opinion, the reserves 1) make sufficient provision for the liabilities of the company; 2) are calculated by a method that produces reserves at least equal to the minimum reserves specified in the Insurance Act, and 3) "that the rate or rates of interest and the rate or rates of mortality, accident, sickness or other contingencies used in calculating the reserves are appropriate to the circumstances of the company and the policies in force." Moreover, the assumptions used must be "acceptable to the Superintendent."

The Insurance Act also provides that the auditor of a company may accept any reserve included in the annual statement as a fair presentation of the company's obligations connected to the policies for which the reserve is calculated if the valuation actuary has given an opinion that the reserves meet the requirements of the act.

In the annual statement, in addition to the reserve certified by the valuation actuary (the "statement reserve"), the net level premium reserve calculated using the same assumptions must be shown, with the difference between the two listed as "deferred acquisition costs." The reserve calculated on the same assumptions but using the minimum method specified in the Insurance Act must also be shown in a footnote.

In the income statement the normal increase in actuarial reserves must be split into the "mandatory provision," the increase in the minimum reserves and the "additional provision," the balance of the normal increase in statement reserves.

4. Income statement. The income statement is divided into four parts:

1. Normal income from insurance operations. This is the income from normal insurance transactions which is comparable with that of other periods and of similar companies.

2. Unusual income from insurance operations. Unusual items are defined by the CICA as "gains, losses, and provision for losses resulting from normal business operations which are both abnormal in size and caused by rare or unusual circumstances." Examples would be changes in actuarial reserves due to changes in valuation bases; net capital gains or losses from invested assets other than bonds, mortgages or shares, and net gains or losses due to changes in book rates of exchange. (Companies with business in other currencies usually convert all assets, liabilities and transactions to Canadian currency on the basis of a standard rate of exchange, the "book rate." If management considers the book rate of exchange unrealistic, in view of the trend of current rates, the book rate may be changed to one closer to the current rate. Any change in surplus due to revaluation of assets and liabilities at the new rate must be treated as an unusual item, even if it is not "abnormal in size.")

3. *Extraordinary income from insurance operations.* "Gains, losses and provision for losses which, by their nature, are not typical of the normal business activities of the enterprise, are not expected to occur regularly over a period of years and are not considered as recurring factors in any evaluation of the operations of the enterprise." An example would be the gain or loss from the sale of a subsidiary.

4. *Income from subsidiaries and ancillary operations.* In Canada, life insurance corporations may carry on any business that is reasonably ancillary to life insurance. For instance, management services may be provided to a subsidiary insurance corporation. Income from such operations must be shown in an exhibit and included in this section of the income statement.

The net income is the sum of items 1, 2, 3 and 4. The net income is then transferred to a reconciliation of surplus, which includes changes in reserves such as investment reserves; reserves for assets not considered realizable; reserves for cash value deficiencies (which are treated as appropriations of surplus); dividends to shareholders; transfers of surplus to and from the company's Accident and Sickness branch or segregated funds, and any surplus contributed by shareholders during the year.

2.8 1981 revisions of the Canadian annual statement

In 1981 the annual statements were revised to include life insurance and accident and sickness insurance in a single statement so that the balance sheet and income statement could be prepared on a consolidated basis. (Because the Canadian and British Insurance Companies Act provides that assets held in the life and accident and sickness branches of a company be kept separate, there are separate statements and schedules for assets and liabilities in each branch as well as the consolidated statements.)

The income statement for accident and sickness business was made consistent with that for the life branch, and capital gains on securities held by the accident and sickness branch are now included in investment income. For each branch, a statement of changes in financial position (a cash flow statement) is required.

The inclusion of accident and sickness business requires two additional funds for policyholders and shareholders in the accident and sickness branch—and two more lines of business—individual and group accident and sickness insurance.

Provision is also made for showing income tax in conformity with generally accepted accounting principles (GAAP) by permitting companies to include deferred income taxes in the statement, although the liability is listed separately, between "total liabilities" and "capital, surplus and reserves."

In addition, except for the exhibit of dividends per $1,000 paid to policyholders on selected plans and the schedules of invested assets, entries in statements, exhibits and schedules are rounded to the nearest $1,000.

Effect of changes in the Canadian statement

The new form of statement enables companies to prepare statements which conform more closely to generally accepted accounting practices in many respects, since the amounts required to be set aside for solvency purposes, such as reserves for furniture and equipment and other assets not considered realizable, as well as increases in reserves for cash value deficiencies and in investment and contingency reserves, are treated as appropriations of surplus and not charged against net income for the year.

The category of "nonadmitted assets" (which many accountants criticized because the exclusion of any asset, no matter how "unrealizable" it may be considered to be, is not in keeping with the principle of full disclosure), has been replaced with a provision allowing the inclusion of such assets with reserves of 100 percent of the statement value.

The 1981 revisions extended conformity with generally accepted accounting practices by presenting the balance sheet and income statement on a consolidated basis; including the Statement of Changes in Financial Position, and permitting companies to include income tax on the tax allocation basis.

The treatment of invested assets, while not following the recommendations of the CICA Study Group, is consistent among companies and in accordance with the nature of the liabilities and the investment operations of life insurance companies.

The provisions regarding actuarial reserves permit a recognition of deferred acquisition expenses to a much greater extent than previously, and provide for separate presentation of the amount, although it is shown as a deduction from a liability rather than as an asset. They also preserve the independence of the actuary by allowing greater freedom to choose valuation assumptions and by permitting the auditor to accept the actuarial reserves certified by the actuary, while making it a legal responsibility of the latter to use appropriate rather than merely safe assumptions in the reserve calculations.

Both the net level premium and the statement reserves are shown in the liabilities (with the minimum reserve shown in a footnote). Also, the normal increase in reserves is split into mandatory and additional provisions. Therefore, if the statement reserve is greater than the minimum reserve, it is possible for a reader of the statement to calculate what the deferred acquisition costs, income and surplus would be if minimum reserves were held.

2.9 Differences between NAIC and Canadian statements

Although the balance sheets and income statements required in the United States and Canada are basically similar, there are a number of differences in the treatment of accounts and in the data required.

In the United States, classes of accident and health insurance are treated as separate lines of business in a consolidated statement. In Canada, on the other hand, life and accident and sickness business must be carried on by separate branches, and, although the balance sheet and income statement are consolidated, assets, liabilities, capital and surplus must be shown separately for each branch.

In the United States, the income statement is split by line of business only. In the Canadian statement it is also split by fund and there is a reconciliation of funds. As a result, the amounts of credits such as investment income and capital gains, and charges such as expenses, taxes and capital losses, allocated to participating policyholders, non-participating policyholders, the accident and sickness branch and shareholders, and the surplus or deficit in each fund are shown in the statement and published in the Annual Report of the Superintendent of Insurance.

In Canada, in addition to showing income tax actually payable, companies may also show it according to generally accepted accounting principles.

1. Invested assets. In the statement adopted by the National Association of Insurance Commissioners, book values are left to the discretion of the company but the amount carried in the statement must be the approved (Association) value. In practice, for bonds not in default, Association values are amortized values; preferred shares are valued at cost. However, for common shares, Association values are market values, so that changes in market values of shares result in unrealized capital gains and losses. Realized and unrealized capital gains and losses are reflected in the surplus account, but in many cases are balanced by adjustments in the mandatory securities valuation reserve.

For the Canadian statement, book values are prescribed by regulation and are therefore approved values. Amortized values are used for bonds and mortgages not in default, and cost values for common and preferred shares. However, in the life branch, realized capital gains and losses on bonds and mortgages, and both realized and unrealized capital gains and losses on shares, are amortized and brought into income, and the unamortized amounts are used to adjust book values in total (see 2.7, 2). In the accident and sickness branch realized gains and losses on securities are included in income in full in the year realized.

2. Investment reserves. In the United States, a maximum mandatory securities valuation reserve must be held. This is based on percentages of the NAIC values of all bonds and shares, according to category. For example, the percentages are zero for United States and Canadian government bonds, 2 percent for the highest rated corporate bonds, 5 percent for preferred shares in good standing and 33.33 percent for common shares.

As long as the reserve is less than the maximum, it must be increased annually (subject to certain qualifications). The increase is the sum of the percentages of the Association values of securities (.1 percent for highest rated corporate bonds, .25 percent for preferred shares in good standing, 1 percent for common shares) plus the net realized and unrealized capital gains, minus income tax on realized gains. Net realized and unrealized capital losses less income tax are charged to the reserve. Limited voluntary additions to the reserve may also be made until it reaches the maximum value.

Including capital gains in the increases and charging capital losses to the reserve means that net capital gains on securities (except U.S. government bonds in certain cases) will not affect unappropriated surplus unless the reserve is too small to absorb all the losses or too large for all the gains to be used in the increase. The reserve is included in the liabilities, but the increase is treated as an appropriation of surplus.

In Canada the investment valuation reserve is based on net deficiencies of market values from book values for real estate and securities. For life insurance, the reserve for bonds and mortgages is only 10 percent of the market deficiency (with a minimum of 1.5 percent of the book value of bonds and mortgages). In the accident and sickness branch the investment valuation reserve is calculated differently, with exemptions for market deficiencies on short-term bonds and mortgages, in order to take into account the different nature of accident and sickness obligations.

3. Other accounts. In the NAIC statement premiums due and uncollected at the end of the year and deferred premiums (fractional premiums due in the following calendar year prior to the policy anniversary) less loadings are included in assets. The increases in these items are included in premiums, with an adjustment in the summary of operations for the increase in loadings. In the Canadian statement due premiums less commissions and estimated losses in collection are included in assets, but deferred premiums less loadings are deducted from the actuarial liability. Therefore, only the increases in due premiums and commissions on them are included in premiums and commissions in the income statement.

In the Canadian statement deposits and withdrawals of claims, dividends, premium deposits and other amounts left to accumulate at interest are not treated as income or disbursements. Only the interest credited appears in the income statement. In the NAIC statement transactions arising from such deposits (except premium deposit funds) are included with supplementary contracts without life contingencies (see 2.2, 3), although the liabilities are shown separately. Premiums waived by disability are excluded from both premium income and claims and are shown only in an exhibit in the Canadian statement, but are included in premiums and claims in the NAIC statement.

In the NAIC statement assets such as furniture and equipment and amounts advanced to agents are treated as nonadmitted assets. Any increases in such assets are charged to surplus. In Canada, they may be treated as nonadmitted assets with the annual increases charged to expenses, or they may be held as assets subject to the inclusion of a 100 percent reserve in appropriated surplus, with only annual depreciation of furniture and equipment and actual and anticipated losses in collection of the amounts advanced charged to expenses. Although all three methods will have the same effect on unappropriated surplus, the third procedure is more in accordance with generally accepted accounting principles.

2.10 Responsibilities of the actuary

The requirements of the *Audit Guide for Stock Life Insurance Companies* in the United States and the 1977 legislation in Canada place new formal responsibilities on actuaries in connection with the preparation of financial statements. The American Academy of Actuaries and the Canadian Institute responded by issuing opinions on professional conduct in connection with the preparation of insurance company financial statements (Opinions A-6 and CIA-6 respectively). The respective committees on financial reporting principles issued formal recommendations for, and interpretations of, a number of aspects of financial statements.

The guides to professional conduct of the American Academy and the Rules for Professional Conduct of the Canadian Institute are very similar. In general, the opinions differ only in matters peculiar to each country, such as the *Audit Guide for Stock Life Insurance Companies* in the United States and the responsibilities of the valuation actuary in Canada.

Because paragraph 1(b) of both guides to professional conduct states that "the member will bear in mind that the actuary acts as an expert when he gives actuarial advice, and he will give such advice only when he is qualified to do so," Opinion A-6 states that an actuary should undertake to prepare or verify reserves or other actuarial elements of financial statements only if he or she is familiar with the purposes and uses of such statements, and, in the case of financial statements prepared in accordance with generally accepted accounting principles, with the application of generally accepted accounting principles to life insurance accounting.

Opinion CIA-6 similarly states that "the member should not accept appointment as valuation actuary if he does not have the necessary practical experience, except where arrangements are made for him to have recourse on a professional and formal basis to a member who has such experience."

Furthermore, since paragraph 4(b) of both guides states that "the member will exercise his best judgment to ensure that any calculations or recommendations made by him or under his direction are based on sufficient and reliable data, that any assumptions made are adequate and appropriate, and that the methods employed are consistent with sound principles established by precedents or common usage within the profession", paragraph 7 of Opinion A-6 points out that this "requires that the actuary, in selecting actuarial assumptions and methods for use in any financial statement prepared in accordance with generally accepted accounting principles, take into consideration the published formal recommendations of the Committee on Financial Reporting Principles of the American Academy of Actuaries. An actuary who makes use in any such financial statement of any assumption or method which conflicts with such recommendations must be prepared to support his use of such assumption or method."

Opinion CIA-6 makes similar reference to the recommendations for insurance company financial reporting of the Canadian Institute of Actuaries.

To date, the Committee on Financial Reporting Principles of the American Academy of Actuaries has issued nine recommendations and interpretations:

Recommendation 1 concerns actuarial methods and assumptions for use in financial statements of stock life insurance companies prepared in accordance with generally accepted accounting principles. It describes actuarial methods and assumptions satisfactory to both the accounting and actuarial professions.

Recommendation 2 gives advice concerning the actuary's relations with the auditor in connection with the review of financial statements of stock life insurance companies.

Recommendation 3 defines the content of actuarial reports and of statements of actuarial opinion.

Recommendation 4 deals with reinsurance ceded.

Recommendation 5 deals with recognition of premium income.

Recommendation 6 deals with participating policies issued by stock life insurance companies.

Recommendation 7 concerns the statement of actuarial opinion for life insurance company statutory statements.

Recommendation 8 concerns the statement of actuarial opinion for fire and casualty company statutory annual statements.

Recommendation 9 gives advice regarding "materiality."

The recommendations for insurance company financial reporting of the Canadian Institute of Actuaries include:

1. verification of data;
2. assumptions for valuation of policy benefit liabilities;
3. methods for valuation of policy benefit liabilities;
4. the actuary's report in published financial statements, and
5. the report by the valuation actuary in the government statement.

Both committees have emphasized that a number of important issues are not yet dealt with in the recommendations and that further recommendations will be made to deal with these issues.

It is apparent, therefore, that in both countries, an actuary may not undertake the responsibility of preparing statutory or published financial statements unless he or she has the necessary experience and understanding and is familiar with the recommendations of the relevant committee on insurance company financial reporting.

Review Questions

1.   Why is the solvency of life insurance companies considered a government responsibility?
(**Answer:** See section 2.1.)

2.   What are the principal statements required of life insurance companies in their statutory statements?
(**Answer:** See section 2.2.)

3.   Why is income from supplementary contracts shown separately from premiums in the income statement of a life insurance company?
(**Answer:** See section 2.2)

4.   Why does the conservative valuation of assets and liabilities reduce the net income of a life insurance company?
(**Answer:** See sections 2.2, 2.3.)

5.   Explain why the sum of the funds of a life insurance company plus amounts owing equals the total assets.
(**Answer:** See section 2.2.)

6.   What is the reason for the use of "modified" reserve methods specified in the United States and Canada?
(**Answer:** See section 2.3.)

7.   List five criticisms made of life insurance statutory accounting in North America.
(**Answer:** See section 2.4.)

8.   Are the requirements of the AICPA Audit Guide for actuarial reserves inconsistent with the actuary's professional responsibility? Explain your answer.
(**Answer:** See section 2.5.)

9.   Why do some authorities contend that the total realized capital gains and losses on bonds of life insurance companies should not be included in income in the year the gains or losses are realized?
(**Answer:** See section 2.6.)

10.   What effect can including capital gains and losses on shares only on realization have on participating policyholders?
(**Answer:** See section 2.6.)

11.   Were the recommendations of the CICA research report on life insurance accounting in Canada adopted by the CICA?
(**Answer:** See section 2.6.)

12.   A Canadian life insurance company whose shares are all in Canadian dollars has an adjustment account for the value of shares of $1,570,000 at the end of 1983. In 1984 the realized gains on shares are $480,000 and losses $75,000. At the end of 1984 the total book value of shares is $18,450,000 and the total market value $19,950,000.

What are the realized and unrealized gains to be included in income in 1982? What is the adjusted value of shares at the end of the year?

Answer:

Adjustment account December 31, 1983	$ 1,570,000
Plus realized losses	75,000
	$ 1,645,000
Less realized gains	480,000
Preliminary adjustment account	$ 1,165,000
Book values at December 31, 1984	18,450,000
Preliminary adjusted book value	$19,615,000
Market values December 31, 1984	19,950,000
Excess of market values over book	$ 335,000
Realized and unrealized gains 15%	50,250
Preliminary adjustment account	1,165,000
Final adjustment account	$ 1,215,250
Total book values	18,450,000
Adjusted book values December 31, 1984	$19,665,250

The amount included in income is $50,250.

13.   Recalculate the figures in Question 12 on the assumption that total market values of shares at December 31, 1984 are $17,500,000.

Answer:

Adjustment account December 31, 1983	$ 1,570,000
Plus realized losses	75,000
	$ 1,645,000
Less realized gains	480,000
Preliminary adjustment account	$ 1,165,000
Book values at December 31, 1984	18,450,000
Preliminary adjusted book value	$19,615,000
Market values December 31, 1984	17,500,000
Excess of market values over book	−$ 2,115,000
Realized and unrealized gains 15%	− 317,250
Preliminary adjustment account	1,165,000
Final adjustment account	$ 847,750
Total book values	18,450,000
Adjusted book values December 31, 1984	$19,297,750

The amount included in income is −$317,250.

Chapter 3: The NAIC Life and Accident and Health Statement

3.1 Annual statements for life insurance companies

Life insurance companies transacting business in the United States must file annual statements in standard form in all states in which they are licensed. A statement must be filed for each calendar year by March 1 of the following year. The statement must contain an affidavit completed by the president, secretary and treasurer of the company certifying the accuracy of the statement and a statement by a qualified actuary setting forth his or her opinion relating to policy reserves and other actuarial items. Although the balance sheet must include assets and liabilities of separate account business, companies writing such business must file additional statements: the Separate Accounts Statement for contracts not providing life insurance, and the Variable Life Insurance Separate Accounts Statement for those providing life insurance benefits (see Chapter 6, section 6.5).

The annual statement contains financial statements consisting of a balance sheet (statements of assets and liabilities, surplus and other funds); a summary of operations (a statement of normal income and disbursements), and a surplus account, followed by exhibits and schedules which provide detailed information on items summarized in the financial statements as well as other information, such as summaries of insurance, annuity and health contracts written and terminated during the year and in force at the end of the year.

The statements, exhibits and schedules are prescribed by the National Association of Insurance Commissioners, as are the values at which assets must be included in the statement. For instance, amply secured bonds must be included at amortized values, preferred stocks at cost and common stocks at market value. Minimum policy reserves are prescribed by the standard valuation law adopted by individual states, and a mandatory securities valuation reserve prescribed by the NAIC must be held to provide for possible future losses on securities and to reduce the impact on surplus of realized and unrealized capital gains and losses.

To assist the student in understanding the statement, prepared financial statements have been created, using sample data. (See Example 3.) Because the NAIC statement implicitly assumes that ledger accounts will be on a "cash" basis and requires that the calculation of incurred amounts for premiums, claims and investment income be shown in the exhibits, the sample data have been prepared on this basis and nonledger accounts have been appended. (In the listing of ledger items, D represents debits and C credits; for nonledger items, A represents assets and L liabilities.)

The balance account (see Chapter 1, section 1.9) at the end of the year 19B ($101,327,020C) can be checked as numerically equal to the assets minus liabilities at the end of the year 19A, and also as the net sum of the nonledger liabilities minus nonledger and nonadmitted assets, plus unassigned surplus at the end of the year 19A. (In this calculation, nonledger assets arising from the excess of statement values over ledger values must be included.)

	YEAR 19A
Nonledger accounts attributed to line of business (Ex. 3.6)	
Par insurance	$ 49,710,949L
Non par insurance	21,982,012L
Par annuities	5,688,997L
Non par annuities	17,254,300L
Accident and health	481,429L
Miscellaneous (Ex. 3.8)	1,057,121A
Stock values (Ex. 3.9, 302)	344,575A
Less nonadmitted assets (Ex. 3.21)	− 1,387,859A
Agents' credit balances (Ex. 3.5, 64)	145,075L
Unassigned funds (Ex. 3.24, 29B)	6,078,095L
	$101,327,020L

The first step in preparing the statement is to calculate incurred income and disbursements, using ledger and nonledger data shown in Examples 3.10 to 3.14. The totals of nonledger assets and liabilities must agree with the totals in Examples 3.6, 3.7 and 3.8. It is best to include all income and disbursement accounts, so that the totals may be checked against the ledger balances and the column totals cross-checked. (These checks are shown at the end of Examples 3.11, 3.12, 3.13 and 3.14.)

The nonledger data for the year 19B can be used to prepare the nonledger items in the balance sheet, while the incurred figures are used to prepare the Summary of Operations by line of business and in total.

3.2 Assets

Because life insurance obligations are long-term, the solvency of a life insurance company is important to policyholders. For that reason supervisory authorities prescribe values at which assets must be carried in the annual statement. For example, assets such as furniture and equipment have value to a company on a going-concern basis (i.e., assuming that it continues to operate). However, if the solvency of the company is in question, such assets are of little value; therefore, the values of furniture and equipment (except for EDP equipment) must be excluded from the statement. For all assets, values are prescribed by state law or by the NAIC (Association values). Any excess of ledger values over prescribed values must be deducted as a "nonadmitted" asset in preparing the statement. If the Association value exceeds the ledger value, the excess must be added as a nonledger asset. These adjustments must be displayed in Exhibit 13, described below. (See also Example 3.21 and Example 3.22.)

Note: In the description of asset and liability items, paragraph numbers refer to the line numbers of the items in the current NAIC statement, pages 2 and 3.

1. Bonds. Because life insurance obligations are long-term, life insurance companies can generally anticipate holding bonds until they mature without being forced to liquidate any on a depressed market. The association values of amply secured bonds not in default are therefore amortized values, calculated by writing bonds purchased at a premium or discount down or up annually so that the value at maturity will be equal to the maturity value. U.S. and Canadian government bonds are considered amply secured. Other bonds must pass certain tests of assets and income of the issuer. Bonds which fail the tests or are in default must be carried at values published by the NAIC, usually market values.

2.1 Preferred stocks. Preferred stocks on which dividends have been paid for the past three years issued by corporations whose earnings meet certain requirements (preferred stocks "in good standing") must be carried at cost; others must be carried at market value.

2.2 Common stocks. Common stocks must be carried at market values. Because it is not usually convenient to adjust the ledger values of stocks for market fluctuations, ledger values are normally at cost, and the net difference from market values is treated as a nonadmitted or nonledger asset.

3. Mortgage loans. Mortgage loans must be first liens and must not exceed some percentage of the value of the property, which tends to vary between 66.67 and 75 percent. Loans not in default which meet the requirements are carried at the principal outstanding. For loans which do not meet these requirements, all or part of the principal outstanding must be treated as a nonadmitted asset. Loans in default must be carried at a value which takes the probability of loss into consideration.

4. Real estate. Real estate must be shown in three categories: properties occupied by the company, properties acquired in satisfaction of debt and investment real estate. Real estate is usually carried at cost less depreciation and net of any mortgages. If state laws limit the amount of investment real estate, any excess must be treated as a nonadmitted asset. For properties occupied by the company, an appropriate rent must be charged and treated as investment income (less interest paid on any mortgage on the property), while real estate expenses, taxes and depreciation of the property are added to investment expenses.

5. Policy loans. The excess of any policy loan over the reserve on the policy must be treated as a nonadmitted asset.

6. Premium notes. The excess of any unsecured premium note over the reserve on the policy must be treated as a nonadmitted asset.

7. Collateral loans. Collateral loans must not exceed some percentage (e.g., 75 percent in New York) of the market value of the collateral. Any excess is a nonadmitted asset.

8. Cash on hand and on deposit. Full details must be shown in an exhibit.

9. Other invested assets. This will include assets such as property on lease-back contracts.

10. Total of cash and invested assets. This is used to calculate the average rate of interest earned. Although investments not permitted by state legislation must generally be treated as nonadmitted assets, some states allow companies to include such investments as admitted assets up to some small percentage of admitted assets, the percentage varying from state to state.

11. Reinsurance ceded. Amounts due from reinsurance companies for reinsurance ceded, such as amounts due on reinsured claims paid, commissions and expense allowances due and experience rating refunds due.

14. Federal income tax recoverable.

17. Life insurance premiums and annuity considerations deferred and uncollected. Although life insurance companies do not have the right to enforce payment of premiums, actuarial reserves are usually calculated on the assumption that premiums are payable annually and were collected on the anniversary, so that deferred premiums (installments falling due in the current policy year after the date of the statement) and uncollected premiums due on or before the date of the statement, less loadings, are included in the assets as an offset to the overstatement of reserves.

19. Investment income due and accrued.

20. Net adjustments to assets and liabilities due to exchange rates. Companies transacting business in foreign currencies normally use a constant rate of exchange, the book rate, to convert transactions in such currencies to U.S. dollars. If the actual rate of exchange at the date of the statement differs from the book rate, the U.S. dollar values of assets and liabilities are recalculated using the actual rate. If the net change in surplus is positive, it is shown in this item; if negative, it is shown in item 21 of the liabilities.

26. Total assets at statement values excluding separate account assets which are included in items 27A and 27B). The asset values are taken from Exhibit 13, Assets, in which ledger assets, nonledger assets, and assets not admitted are listed in three columns, and statement values are calculated by adding nonledger assets and subtracting nonadmitted assets. (Example 3.21, Example 3.22.) These adjustments affect surplus, through either the Summary of Operations or the Surplus Account.

The change in gross deferred and uncollected premiums affects incurred premiums, while the change in loadings is entered in the Summary of Operations as a separate item. The change in investment income due and accrued affects net investment income while the change in the excess of statement values over ledger values is included in unrealized capital gains and losses on investments.

Among nonadmitted assets, the changes in nonadmitted due and accrued investment income affect net investment income, while changes in the deficiency of statement values of invested assets from ledger values affect unrealized gains and losses from investment.

The changes in the remaining nonadmitted assets are summarized in Exhibit 14, and the total entered in the Surplus Account. One point to be noted is that the asset not admitted for agents' balances in Exhibit 13 is the net of agents' debit balances and agents' credit balances. In order to charge surplus with the increase in debit balances, the increase in credit balances is included in Exhibit 14.

Table 3.1: Nonledger assets

	YEAR 19B	YEAR 19A	DIFFERENCE
Gain from change in admitted values (302)	$ 519,827	$ 344,575	$175,252
Incurred premiums (201-204)			
Insurance Due	30,000	20,000	
	14,500	11,250	
	680,000	600,000	
	352,000	295,000	
Deferred	215,800	202,500	
	106,478	97,550	
	1,654,006	1,431,030	
	633,408	555,241	
Annuities Due	550	1,190	
	22,400	27,700	
Deferred	38,415	42,518	
	189,715	180,950	
	$3,937,272	$3,464,929	472,343
Accident and health	8,496	7,969	
	80,931	75,046	
	$ 89,427	$ 83,015	6,412
Loading insurance (207-210)	$ −754,025	$ −657,734	
Annuities	−39,825	−43,200	
	$ −793,850	$ −700,934	−92,916
Due and accrued investment income (550)			
	1,220,534	1,090,121	130,413
Totals	$4,973,210	$4,281,706	$691,504

(Numbers in parentheses in this and following tables refer to reference numbers in examples. See Example 3.1)

Table 3.2: Nonadmitted assets

	YEAR 19B	YEAR 19A	DIFFERENCE
Net loss from changes in association values			
Bonds (Ex. 3.9, 303)	$ 814,522	$ 753,230	$−61,292
Mortgages (304)	83,915	107,827	23,912
Not admitted due investment income (305)	10,840	8,752	−2,088
Exhibit 14 (Ex. 3.23)	758,459	663,125	−95,334
	$1,667,736	$1,532,934	
Less agents' credit balances (64)	164,515	145,075	
Exhibit 13 (Ex. 3.21, Ex. 3.22)	$1,503,221	$1,387,859	

The change in surplus for agents' balances is the sum of $37,594 and $19,440 (Ex. 3.23), or $57,034, which is equal to the increase in debit balances from $425,625 to $482,659.

3.3 Liabilities, surplus and other funds

The liabilities of a life insurance company may be divided into five classes:

1. Liabilities to provide for payments to policyholders and beneficiaries falling due in future years, such as policy reserves, claims reserves on accident and health policies, provision for dividends falling due in years subsequent to the date of the statement.

2. Benefits to policyholders and beneficiaries due but unpaid, such as claims in course of settlement and estimates of claims incurred but unreported at the date of the statement.

3. Amounts payable to creditors other than policyholders, amounts received in advance or held for others such as taxes deducted from payments, and amounts received but not yet allocated.

4. Adjustments to asset values.

5. Special reserves required by law or set up voluntarily by management. (Generally accepted accounting principles class these as appropriations of surplus.)

1. Treatment of liabilities to provide for payments falling due in future years

1. Aggregate reserves for life policies and contracts. These amounts are summarized in Exhibit 8. The increase in reserves calculated on the same valuation bases is shown in the Summary of Operations. Any increase or decrease due to changes in valuation bases is shown in the surplus account.

POLICY RESERVES	YEAR 19B	YEAR 19A
Insurance (518)	$ 72,323,014	$65,625,523
Supplementary contracts (518)	1,127,334	1,067,400
Annuities (518)	27,580,971	22,215,015
	$101,031,319	$88,907,938

2. Aggregate reserve for accident and health policies, summarized in Exhibit 9. The amounts in the balance sheet are taken directly from Ex. 3.13, 518.

3. Reserves for supplementary contracts without life contingencies, summarized in Exhibit 10. The amounts in the balance sheet are taken directly from Ex. 3.11.

5. Reserves for accumulations of policyholder dividends and coupons, summarized in Exhibit 10. The increase is charged to the Summary of Operations.

DIVIDENDS ON DEPOSIT (223)	YEAR 19B	YEAR 19A	INCREASE
Insurance	$2,511,250	$2,357,500	$153,750
Annuities	830,700	782,580	48,120
	$3,341,950	$3,140,080	$201,870

7. Provision for dividends payable in the following calendar year. The increase is included in dividends credited in the Summary of Operations. (Ex. 3.10, Ex. 3.12, 515)

10. Liability for premium deposit funds. This amount is taken directly from the nonledger liabilities. The excess of the increase in liability plus amounts withdrawn over new amounts deposited is entered in the Summary of Operations as "interest on policy or contract funds."

2. Treatment of benefits to policyholders due but unpaid

4. Policy and contract claims, summarized in Exhibit 11, which can be prepared from the nonledger data in Ex. 3.6 and 3.7.

	YEAR 19B	YEAR 19A
Insurance death claims (211, 215)	$350,000	$281,000
Insurance maturity values (212)	62,000	30,000
Annuity claims (211)	15,300	24,860
	$427,300	$335,860
Accident and health claims (213, 215)	$ 68,475	$ 54,248

6. Policyholder dividends due and unpaid. Nonledger liabilities from Ex. 3.6 and 3.7.

11. Policy and contract liabilities not included elsewhere. Miscellaneous liabilities such as unpaid surrender values on terminated policies, provision for experience rating refunds on group policies, etc.

3. Treatment of amounts payable to creditors other than policyholders, amounts in advance, etc.

9. Premiums and annuity considerations received in advance.

	YEAR 19B	YEAR 19A
Insurance first year par (205)	$ 1,100	$1,000
Nonpar	825	450
Renewal Par (206)	6,000	5,000
Nonpar	2,450	2,200
	$10,375	$8,650

13. Commissions to agents due or accrued.

13A. Commission and expense allowances on reinsurance assumed due or accrued.

14. General expenses due or accrued.

Insurance (220)	$179,500	$159,800
Accident and health (220)	2,942	2,598
Investment (258)	12,430	11,000
	$194,872	$173,398

15. Taxes, licenses and fees due or accrued.

Insurance (219)	$ 42,000	$ 39,000
Accident and health	1,052	876
	$ 43,052	$ 39,876

15A. Federal income tax due or accrued.

17. Unearned investment income, e.g., mortgage interest paid in advance.

(The above items are normally nonledger liabilities.)

18. Amounts withheld by company as agent or trustee.

19. Amounts held for agents' account.

20. Remittances and items not allocated. Amounts held as deposits on policies in course of issue, amounts received at the end of the year and not allocated at the date of the statement.

22. Liabilities for benefits to agents and employees not included above.

23. Borrowed money and interest thereon.

24. Dividends to stockholders due and unpaid.

(Most of the above items are ledger liabilities.)

4. Treatment of adjustments to asset values

16. Cost of collection on premiums and annuity considerations in excess of loadings.

21. Net adjustment to assets and liabilities due to foreign exchange rates. Corresponds to asset item 20.

5. Treatment of special reserves

25.1 **Mandatory securities valuation reserve.** The MSVR is a reserve required by law to provide for future losses on securities and to absorb fluctuations in the values of securities so as to smooth out their effect on unassigned surplus. In addition to regular increases based on statement values of securities held, most realized and unrealized capital gains, less income tax, and realized and unrealized capital losses must be used to increase or decrease the reserve, respectively. A company may also make voluntary additions to the reserve, in order to build it up more quickly or to rebuild it after depletion by realized or unrealized capital losses. The reserve has two basic components, each of which has a specified maximum as a percentage of the statement values of securities. No additions may be made to a component that will increase it above the maximum, and no component may be negative.

Bond and preferred stock reserve component

The first component is the bond and preferred stock component. All bonds and preferred stocks are classified into categories according to tests applied to the financial position of the issuer. Maximum reserves and factors for annual increases are established for each category. Apart from U.S. government bonds, for which no reserve need be held, bonds are divided into three categories and preferred stocks into two. Federally insured building and savings and loan shares carried as preferred stocks are in a separate category.

The factors for maximum reserves and required annual additions are:

Category	Maximum	Annual Addition
Highest category bonds	.02	.001
Second category bonds	.10	.005
Lowest category bonds	.20	.02
Preferred stocks "in good standing"	.05	.0025
Other preferred stocks	.20	.01
Federally insured building and savings and loan shares	.02	.001

1. Required additions to component

a) The rates in the second column above are applied to the statement values of the securities to obtain the required addition. For companies in business less than five years or whose reserve component at the end of the previous year was less than 50 percent of the maximum, this amount must be doubled.

b) Net realized and unrealized capital gains on bonds and preferred stocks (except on U.S. government bonds), less income tax, must also be added.

2. Voluntary additions to component

a) Up to twice the required addition described in 1 a) may be added.

b) If the common stock component is at its maximum, any realized or unrealized capital gains on common stocks, less tax, which cannot be used to increase that component may be added to the bond and preferred stock component.

3. Deductions from component

Net realized and unrealized capital losses on bonds (except U.S. government bonds) and preferred stocks must be charged to this component unless the company has been in business less than five years.

No additions may be made that will increase the component above the maximum.

Common stock reserve component

The second component is the common stock reserve component. The maximum for this component is 20 percent of the statement value of stocks of controlled or affiliated companies and of federally chartered banks, and 33⅓ percent of all other common stocks.

1. Required additions to component

a) The required annual addition is one percent of the statement values of all common stocks.

b) Net realized and unrealized capital gains on stocks, less income tax, also must be added.

2. Voluntary additions to component

a) Up to two percent of the statement values of common stocks may be added.

b) Net realized and unrealized capital gains on preferred stocks and bonds, less income tax, which cannot be added to the previous component because it is at its maximum, may be added to this component.

3. Deductions from component

Net realized and unrealized losses on common stocks must be deducted from this component unless the company has been in business less than five years.

No additions may be made which will increase the component above the maximum.

Temporary excess reserve component

In 1965 the requirements for the MSVR were changed, and the reserve at the end of 1964 was distributed to the two components described above. Any excess was allotted to this component. No additions could be made to it, and all net realized and unrealized capital losses were charged to it until it was exhausted. Therefore, very few companies have any amount in this component.

Calculation of the MSVR is shown in Example 3.15. The bond and preferred stock component has been set at $700,000 to illustrate the calculation of the ratio of the reserve to the maximum.

The total net capital loss on bonds has been reduced by the net loss on U.S. government bonds, since capital gains and losses on such bonds do not affect the reserve.

25.2 Reserves on policies reinsured in unauthorized companies (Ex. 3.7, 226). The amounts on line 1 are net of reinsurance ceded (other than modified coinsurance). If any amounts deducted from aggregate reserves on line 1 are for reinsurance in unauthorized companies, such amounts must be added back on line 25.2.

Liabilities of separate accounts and variable life insurance separate accounts, if any, are entered in total from the appropriate statements on lines 25A and 25B in order that this page will show the total liabilities of the company. The amount of total liabilities is entered on line 26.

The remaining items include capital stock, contributed surplus and special surplus funds; the amount required to balance with the total assets is the unassigned surplus.

3.4 Closing accounting entries

At the end of the year all income accounts are transferred to the balance account by debiting or crediting the balance of each one and making the opposite entry to the balance account so that the income accounts are all zero at the beginning of the year. At the same time liability accounts are adjusted, as necessary. For instance, the MSVR may be either a ledger or nonledger liability. If it is a ledger liability, as in the example, it must be increased or decreased to show the new balance. In this case it must be increased from $1,250,000 to $1,639,003, or credited with $389,003. The change in the MSVR reduces the difference between ledger assets and ledger liabilities to $114,481,186.

The entries to the balance account are:

Par insurance accounts (Ex. 3.3)	$ 479,960C
Nonpar insurance accounts	643,930C
Par annuity accounts	62,159D
Nonpar annuity accounts	3,681,026C
Accident and health accounts	21,369D
Investment and miscellaneous accounts (Ex. 3.4)	8,821,781C
Increase in MSVR (Ex. 3.15)	389,003D
	$ 13,154,166C
Balance account before entries (Ex. 3.5)	101,327,020C
New balance	$114,481,186C

This balances with the new figure for assets minus liabilities and equals the nonledger liabilities minus nonledger assets plus nonadmitted assets plus unassigned surplus.

YEAR 19B

Nonledger assets and liabilities		
Par insurance (Ex. 3.7)		$ 54,459,534L
Nonpar insurance (Ex. 3.7)		24,365,424L
Par annuities (Ex. 3.7)		6,093,016L
Nonpar annuities (Ex. 3.7)		22,256,700L
Accident and Health (Ex. 3.7)		544,372L
Miscellaneous (Ex. 3.8)		1,183,362A
Excess of market values of common stocks over ledger values (302)		519,827A
Nonadmitted assets (Ex. 3.22)	1,503,221	
Agent credit balances (Ex. 3.23)	164,515	1,667,736L
Unassigned funds (Ex. 3.24)		6,797,593L
		$114,481,186L

3.5 Reconciliation of ledger accounts, Exhibit 12

This is merely a check that all accounts in the ledger have been included in the Summary of Operations and the Surplus Account, since the balance is implicit in double-entry accounting.

At the beginning of the year, when all income accounts have been closed off,

$$\text{Assets} - \text{liabilities} = \text{balance account}$$

or, $A_0 - L_0 = B$.

At the end of the year,

$$\text{Assets} - \text{liabilities} - \text{income} + \text{disbursements} = \text{balance account}$$

or, $A_1 - L_1 - I + D = B = A_0 - L_0$

so that $A_1 - A_0 = I - D + (L_1 - L_0)$.

The increase in ledger assets is equal to income minus disbursements plus the increase in ledger liabilities.

Ledger assets − ledger liabilities 19A (Ex. 3.5)		$101,327,020
Plus liabilities: agent credit balances (64)		145,075
MSVR (70)		1,250,000
paid up capital (71)		1,500,000
Total ledger assets 19A		$104,222,095
Income − disbursements 19B:		
Par insurance (Ex. 3.3)	$ 479,960C	
Nonpar insurance (Ex. 3.3)	643,930C	
Par annuities (Ex. 3.3)	62,159D	
Nonpar annuities (Ex. 3.3)	3,681,026C	
Accident and health (Ex. 3.3)	21,369D	
Miscellaneous (Ex. 3.4)	8,821,781C	$ 13,543,169
Increase in agents' credit balances (64)		19,440
Total ledger assets 19B		$117,784,704
Ledger assets − ledger liabilities 19B (Ex. 3.5)		*$114,870,189
Plus liabilities: agents' credit balances (64)		164,515
MSVR (70)		1,250,000*
paid-up capital (71)		1,500,000
		$117,784,704

Since ledger assets for the reconciliation are taken from Exhibit 13, in which agents' credit balances are netted against agents' debit balances, the increase in agents' credit balances is the only ledger liability whose increase need not be entered in the exhibit. The increases and decreases in other ledger liabilities must be included, such as, for instance, increases or decreases in borrowed money, in items 9 and 31, and increases or decreases in paid-up capital, in items 7 and 29.

---

*Before closing entries.

3.6 Summary of operations

The Summary of Operations (income statement) is shown in total on page 4 of the NAIC statement, along with corresponding figures for the previous year. The breakdown of the totals by line of business is shown on page 5. Although premiums and claims are shown on a net basis, i.e., direct written plus reinsurance assumed minus reinsurance ceded, commissions on reinsurance ceded are shown among the income items (line 5) while commissions on direct business and on reinsurance assumed are shown separately among the disbursements (lines 21 and 21A).

The lines of business into which transactions must be allocated are:

> Industrial life
> Ordinary: life insurance
> individual annuities
> supplementary contracts
> Credit life (group and individual)
> Group: life insurance
> annuities
> Accident and health: group
> credit (group and individual)
> other
> Other

The data come either directly from the trial balance or from the calculation of incurred figures (Examples 3.10 to 3.14).

However, investment income and interest on claims must be allocated among lines of business by some reasonable method. In the example, the allocation is by mean funds, although other methods may be used. (See Chapter 1, section 1.6.) The funds for each line of business are the shares of the assets of the company contributed by each line. The total funds of the company must equal the total assets minus amounts owing (see **Table 3.4**), since, for example, borrowed money will increase assets without increasing the fund totals.

The funds of the sample company at the end of the year 19A amount to $106,103,760, calculated as follows:

Total assets		$106,970,867
Less amounts owing (Ex. 3.24, Liabilities)		
Outstanding claims: life and annuity (4.1)	$335,860	
accident and health (4.2)	54,248	
Dividends due and unpaid (6)	35,000	
Premiums received in advance (9)	8,650	
Due and accrued expenses (14)	173,398	
taxes, licenses and fees (15)	39,876	
income tax (15A)	53,000	
interest on claims (25.6)	22,000	
Agents' credit balances (19)	145,075	867,107
Total funds		$106,103,760

The allocation of funds at the beginning of the year is usually taken from previous fund accumulations, illustrated in **Table 3.3.** In this example, the funds at the beginning of the year are given.

The mean fund for each line of business is the average of the fund at the beginning of the year and the end of the year, or the fund at the beginning of the year plus half the net increase. In this case, since the mean funds are to be used to allocate certain income items, the increase in the funds will be the "direct income," which excludes items to be allocated. We therefore obtain the direct income by including all income items except (a) net investment income and interest on policyholders' funds (which are the items to be allocated) and (b) increases in reserves (which do not affect fund totals). Adding half the direct income to the funds at the beginning of the year gives the mean funds, and the ratio of the mean fund for each line of business to the total is then calculated (Example 3.17).

Interest on policy loans is deducted from net investment income and allocated among lines of business according to mean policy loans outstanding. The balance of the net investment income is then split according to the calculated ratios.

In the example, the same split is used for interest on claims. The rationale for allocating this item in this fashion, instead of according to amounts of claims, as seems plausible, is that net investment income includes earnings from the investment of funds arising from unpaid claims.

(In the example, for simplicity, it was assumed that income tax had been allocated before investment income. In many instances, income tax may be allocated according to net gain or in proportion to the amount of tax calculated for each line of business as though it were a separate enterprise. In such cases the direct income before income tax would be used in the calculation of mean funds, and the allocation of income tax made after the allocation of investment income.)

The amounts allocated are then entered in the analysis of operations and the net gains calculated.

3.7 Capital and surplus account

The capital and surplus account is the reconciliation of capital and unassigned surplus at the end of the current year with that at the end of the previous year. As can be seen in Example 3.19 the reconciliation process starts with the capital and unassigned surplus at the end of the previous year. To this is added the net gain from the Summary of Operations, net capital gains or (losses) from Exhibit 4 (Ex. 3.18) and net increases in nonadmitted assets and related items from Exhibit 14 (Ex. 3.23). Increases in reserves due to changes in valuation bases, in the MSVR, and in the reserve for reinsurance ceded to unauthorized insurers are deducted, as well as dividends to stockholders.

Other items which affect capital or surplus, but are not normal constituents of net gain, such as changes in the surplus of separate accounts, capital paid in or surplus contributed by stockholders, must be included in this account so that the net total will agree with the sum of capital and unassigned funds in the balance sheet.

As a starting point for the following year's allocation of investment income, and as a check on the accuracy of the statement, the year-end funds for each line of business may be calculated at this point. Since increases in reserves do not affect fund totals, the items which have to be included and allocated among individual lines of business are net capital gains or losses; increases in nonadmitted assets and dividends to stockholders.

It is reasonable to allocate the first two according to mean funds, the ratios for which were calculated for the allocation of investment income (Ex. 3.17). The allocation of dividends to stockholders will depend on many factors, including state laws and the company charter, either or both of which may restrict the portion of the surplus arising from participating business which may be credited to stockholders. In this case we shall assume that there are no such restrictions, and dividends to stockholders will be allocated among lines of business according to the shares of the net gain before dividends to policyholders but after income tax (**Table 3.3**).

Table 3.3: Calculation of Fund Balances Year 19B

	TOTAL	INSURANCE	ANNUITIES	SUPP. CONTRACTS	ACCIDENT AND HEALTH
Net gain before dividends and income tax (Ex. 3.16)	$ 3,908,665	$ 2,907,317	$ 741,917	$ 143,988	$ 115,443
Less income tax (Ex. 3.16)	600,200	347,200	213,000		40,000
	$ 3,308,465	$ 2,560,117	$ 528,917	$ 143,988	$
Ratios %	100.00	77.38	15.99	4.35	2.28
Fund balances Year 19A (Ex. 3.17, 9)	$106,103,760	$75,142,684	$25,178,422	$3,766,683	$2,015,971
Net gain (Ex. 3.16, 31)	1,300,665	682,617	398,617	143,988	75,443
Increase in policy reserves (Ex. 3.16, 17)	12,177,989	6,697,491	5,365,956	59,934	54,608
Increase in reserves on supplementary contracts and dividends accumulations (Ex. 3.16, 18)	338,195	153,750	48,120	136,325	
Increase in reserve for dividends (225)	224,000	220,000	4,000		
Net capital gains (Ex. 3.18)	255,072*	178,066	63,411	8,902	4,693
Change in nonadmitted assets (Ex. 3.23)	−95,334*	−66,553	−23,700	−3,327	−1,754
Dividend to stockholders (Ex. 3.4)	−250,000	−193,450	−39,975	−10,875	−5,700
Fund balances 19B	$120,054,347	$82,814,605	$30,994,851	$4,101,630	$2,143,261

*Allocated according to ratio A, Example 3.17.

One test of the accuracy of the summary of operations and the surplus account is that the total funds obtained above should agree with the total assets minus amounts owing:

Table 3.4

Total assets year 19B (Ex. 3.24)		$121,090,178
Less amounts owing: (Ex. 3.24, Liabilities)		
Outstanding claims life, annuity (4.1)	$427,300	
accident and health (4.2)	68,475	
Dividends due and unpaid (6)	42,500	
Premiums received in advance (9)	10,375	
Due and accrued expenses (14)	194,872	
taxes, licenses, fees (15)	43,052	
income tax (15A)	60,000	
interest on claims (25.6)	24,742	
Agents' credit balances (19)	164,515	1,035,831
Total funds		$120,054,347

3.8 Analysis of increase in reserves during the year

This exhibit is a relic of the pre-1951 NAIC statement, which was actually a statement of income and expenses on a cash basis instead of a true income statement (summary of operations). Such a statement could not account for the increase in unassigned surplus shown in the balance sheet from that of the previous year. To rectify this deficiency, a gain and loss exhibit was developed which used incurred figures, along with additional data from the calculation of statutory reserves, to show the increase in surplus for the year as the sum of:

a) interest earned minus interest required to maintain reserves,

b) expected mortality minus actual mortality less reserves released,

c) loadings on premiums minus actual expenses and

d) reserves released by terminations other than death, minus surrender values, maturity payments on endowments, etc., minus dividends, plus miscellaneous items such as gains and losses on disability and accidental death benefits, capital gains and losses, etc.

The fact that all the comparisons in this exhibit were based on statutory valuation bases, which were much different from those used for calculating premiums or dividends, prompted C. O. Shepherd to comment, "It would be difficult to exaggerate the unsuitability of these statutory valuation factors as a standard for testing a company's experience." (RAIA, XXVI, p. 105) Reserve standards may quite properly differ from the bases on which premiums were calculated. If more than one valuation basis is used, even comparisons between years may be meaningless.

In 1925 an exhibit of changes in surplus was introduced into the NAIC statement by appending changes in nonledger assets and liabilities to the cash income and disbursement figures. The gain and loss exhibit was retained, however.

The analysis of increases in reserves is of considerable value to management, auditors and examiners, since it can be used by those in a position to compensate for these restraints to analyze experience trends by line of business. Furthermore, it has an audit value, since it breaks the large increase in reserves into smaller components, in which errors may be more easily detected by year to year comparisons. (See Chapter 6, 6.2). However, such an audit is more properly done by auditors or examiners, and details of this nature are not normally considered appropriate for published financial statements.

Formulas for this analysis are included in the NAIC Statement instructions. A derivation of the formulas is given in Chapter 6, section 6.13.

3.9 Statement of changes in financial position

This statement is essentially a cash flow statement. The net gain from operations is shown first, and adjusted for items not affecting cash (e.g., increases in policy reserves and in reserves for amounts on deposit), and for changes in nonledger assets and liabilities (e.g., due and deferred premiums, due and accrued investment income and outstanding and unreported claims). (Investment income must also be corrected to reflect amortization of premium and accrual of discount.) Expenses such as depreciation must be added back, and increases in nonadmitted assets such as agents' balances and furniture and equipment, which represent cash outlays not reported in the summary of operations, must be deducted.

The decreases in book values of investments due to sale, maturity or repayment are then added, and profits (losses) on sale added (subtracted) so that the net increase will be the net proceeds. Increases in borrowed money; sales of capital stock and other capital inflows, and any other acquisitions of cash, are added to give the total of net cash available.

The cost of investments acquired, the increase in policy loans, dividends to stockholders and other cash outlays are then deducted, leaving the net increase in cash and short-term investments. Adding this amount to the cash and short-term investments at the end of the previous year should result in the total at the end of the current year.

In using the data on sales, maturities and repayments of investments (as shown in Example 3.9), it is advisable to check that the investment transactions balance with the net change in book values for the year.

The statement of changes in financial position is shown in **Table 3.5.**

Table 3.5: Changes in Financial Position

FUNDS PROVIDED

+	1. Net gain from operations (Ex. 3.16, 31)	$ 1,300,665
+	2. Increases in policy and contract reserves (*L1,2)	12,177,989
+	3. Increase in policy and contract claims (L4)	105,667
+	4. Increase in other policy and contract liabilities (L 3,5,6,9,25.6)	350,162
+	6. Increase in liability for dividends (L7)	224,000
+	7. Increase in commissions, expenses, taxes due and accrued (L14,15)	24,650
+	8. Increase in federal income tax due and accrued (L15A)	7,000
−	9. Increase in premiums receivable (A17,18)	385,839
−10.	Increase in net investment income receivable (A19)	128,325
+11.	Depreciation of real estate (28,29)	144,000
+12.	Amortization of premium (06)	1,635
−13.	Accrual of discount (05)	16,303
−14.	Increase in agents' balances (64,65)	37,594
−15.	Increase in furniture and equipment (62)	38,300
+16.	Depreciation of EDP equipment (63)	350,000
=17.	Funds provided by operations	$14,079,407

INVESTMENTS SOLD, MATURED OR REPAID

+18.	Bonds (314,318)	597,830
+19.	Stocks (315,319,320)	538,297
+20.	Mortgage loans (321)	746,673
+23.	Net gains or (losses) on investments (314,315)	117,200
=25.	Total investments sold, matured or repaid	$ 2,000,000
30.	Total funds provided (line 17 + line 25)	$16,079,407

FUNDS APPLIED

INVESTMENTS ACQUIRED

+31.	Bonds (318)	7,307,212
+32.	Stocks (320)	1,495,134
+33.	Mortgage loans (321)	6,244,826
=38.	Total investments	$15,047,172

OTHER FUNDS APPLIED

+39.	Dividends to stockholders (20)	250,000
+40.	Net increase in policy loans (60)	830,800
=44.	Total other funds applied	$ 1,080,800
45.	Total funds applied (line 38 + line 44)	$16,127,972
46.	Increase in cash (line 30 − line 45)	(48,565)

CASH ON HAND AND ON DEPOSIT

47.	Beginning of year (A8)	249,024
48.	End of year (line 46 + line 47) (A8)	$ 200,459

*A and L references are to asset and liability items respectively.

3.10 Supporting exhibits

a) Exhibits of premiums, claims outstanding and claims incurred. These exhibits are prepared by line of business, and show direct written, reinsurance assumed, reinsurance ceded and net totals. Premiums are also split into first year, single and renewal. Ledger data is assumed to be on a cash basis, and the calculation of incurred figures is shown.

b) Exhibit of commissions. Commissions are split by line of business. Commissions incurred on first year, single and renewal premiums are shown separately for direct business, reinsurance assumed and reinsurance ceded. The net of ceded less assumed reinsurance is also shown.

c) Dividends. Dividends and coupons applied to pay premiums and to purchase additions or shorten the endowment or premium-paying period must be shown by line of business. The second group is also included with single premiums collected. In Exhibit 7 dividends and coupons paid during the year must be shown separately for life and for accident and health, according to the disposition of the dividends. The figures are converted to the incurred basis by adding unpaid dividends and the reserve for dividends payable in future years and subtracting the corresponding figures for the previous year.

d) Investment income. The exhibit of gross investment income shows the calculation of incurred income for each class of investment by adding income due and accrued to the amount collected; subtracting unearned and nonadmitted income at the end of the current year, and adjusting for the corresponding figures at the end of the previous year.

The total gross investment income is carried to the exhibit of net investment income, where investment expenses and taxes, depreciation of invested assets and interest on borrowed money are deducted. The balance, net investment income, is carried to the summary of operations and also used in the calculation of the average rate of investment income earned during the year, the ratio of net investment income to mean invested assets, using the formula

$$\frac{2I}{A + B - I}$$

where I is the net investment income and A and B are the invested assets at the end of the previous and current years respectively (item 10A of the assets page) plus due and accrued investment income (line 19) minus borrowed money (liabilities line 23). If investment expenses of separate account investments have been included in investment expenses, they must be added back to the net investment income before the ratio is calculated. The calculation in the example is:

A Ex. 3.24, 10A	$101,792,488		
19	1,081,369		
B	115,747,635		
	1,209,694		
A + B	$219,831,186		
I (551)	9,130,976	2I	$18,261,952
A + B − I	$210,700,210		
2I/(A + B − I) = .08667			

The exhibit of capital gains and losses on investments uses the same categories of investments as that of gross investment income. Increases and decreases in book values are shown separately, as are gains and losses from sale or maturity and the net gains and losses from the changes in difference between statement values and ledger values. The net sum of these amounts is the net capital gain or loss, which is carried to the capital and surplus account.

e) General expenses and taxes, licenses and fees. These exhibits list general expenses, taxes, licenses and fees in several categories, split by life, accident and health, and investment, on an incurred basis. Since cash expenditures are required for the reconciliation of ledger assets, the totals are adjusted by adding back the amounts due and unpaid at the end of the previous year and subtracting the corresponding figures at the end of the current year. The incurred totals for life and accident and health are entered in the summary of operations. The totals for investment are deducted from gross investment income in the exhibit of net investment income.

f) Aggregate reserve for life policies and contracts. The reserves for life insurance and annuity contracts are split by industrial, ordinary, credit (including group) and other group. The reserves are listed as gross figures by valuation basis, with the gross total, total reinsurance ceded and net reserve for:

• Life insurance,
• Annuities,
• Supplementary contracts with life contingencies,
• Accidental death benefits,
• Disability, active lives,
• Disability, disabled lives,
• Miscellaneous, including reserves for deficiencies of gross premiums from valuation net premiums, reserves for nondeduction of fractional premiums, and reserves for cash values in excess of reserves.

The net totals for each category are summed to obtain the total reserve, which is carried to the liabilities. All changes in reserves due to changes in valuation bases must be shown in Exhibit 8A.

g) Aggregate reserve for accident and health policies. This exhibit is split into the following lines of business:

• Group
• Credit (group and individual)
• Collectively renewable
• Other individual policies:
    Noncancellable
    Guaranteed renewable
    Nonrenewable for stated reasons only
    Other accident only
• All other.

For active life reserves, unearned premiums, additional reserves, reserves for future contingent benefits and reserves for rate credits are shown separately. Claims reserves are separated into 1) the present value of amounts not yet due on claims, including incurred but unreported claims, and 2) reserves for future contingent benefits. Gross totals are shown for each category, with reinsurance ceded deducted. The total net reserve is carried to the liabilities.

h) **Reserves on supplementary contracts without life contingencies.** The reserves for supplementary contracts without life contingencies, divided into the present value of amounts not yet due and amounts on deposit, and dividend and coupon accumulations, are listed according to valuation interest rate and contract rate.

i) **Exhibit of life insurance.** The number of policies and amounts of insurance in force at the end of the previous year, split by industrial, ordinary, credit and group, are reconciled to those in force at the end of the current year by adding new issues, reinsurance assumed, revivals, net increases and additional insurance purchased by dividends, and by subtracting terminations occurring during the year, listed by mode of termination. The amount of reinsurance ceded to other companies at the end of the year is deducted from the gross amount in force to give the net amount.

j) **Exhibits of annuities and supplementary contracts.** An exhibit similar to that for life insurance, but more condensed, must be prepared for individual and group annuities and supplementary contracts with life contingencies. A second exhibit classifies the annuities and supplementary contracts outstanding at the end of the year into income now payable, deferred, fully paid and deferred, not fully paid.

k) **Accident and health exhibit (Schedule H).** This exhibit displays financial data on accident and health policies, in total and broken down into more detailed categories than those in the analysis of operations. Types of policies covered include:

1. Group accident and health (excluding credit insurance).

2. Individual and group credit insurance.

3. Collectively renewable, i.e., individual policies issued to groups either by agreement with employers, associations, unions, etc., or issued under mass enrollment procedures under which renewal of an individual policy will not be refused unless it is refused to all other policies in the group.

4. Noncancellable, i.e., policies renewable for life or to a specified age at guaranteed premium rates.

5. Guaranteed renewable, i.e., policies renewable for life or to a specified age under which the insurer reserves the right to change the scale of premium rates.

6. Nonrenewable for stated reasons only, i.e., policies in which the insurer has reserved the right to cancel or refuse renewal for one or more stated reasons, but has agreed not to cancel or decline renewal solely because of deterioration of health after issue.

7. Other accident only, i.e., policies that provide health coverage only in the event of accident.

8. All other, i.e., individual policies not included in the above categories.

The financial data for the company are shown on a "net" basis, including reinsurance assumed minus reinsurance ceded. Written and earned premiums, incurred claims and commissions on reinsurance ceded and assumed are shown separately in Part 4.

Part 1. Analysis of underwriting operations. Premiums written (cash premiums plus the increase in due and uncollected premiums) are shown, followed by earned premiums (premiums written minus the increase in premium reserves shown in Part 2, Section A). Incurred claims, agreeing in total with the Exhibit of Policy and Contract Benefits (Exhibit 3, Part 1), are then shown, followed by the increase in policy reserves (Part 2, Section B) and, commissions, agreeing in total with the Exhibit of Commissions (Exhibit 2, Part 2). Expenses and taxes come last. The totals of commissions, expenses and taxes are then shown, followed by the net gain after dividends. In addition to dollar amounts, the percentage of earned premiums must be shown for all items following earned premiums.

Part 2, Section A: Premium reserves. Unearned premiums, advance premiums and the reserve for rate credits are shown, followed by the total, the total premium reserve for the previous year, and the increase for the year (which is deducted from written premiums to get earned premiums).

Part 2, Section B: Policy reserves. Additional reserves for deferred benefits, e.g., reserves on noncancellable contracts, are shown, followed by reserves for future contingent benefits, e.g., deferred maternity benefits, and the total is shown, with the prior year total and the increase for the year, indicated in Part 1.

Part 2, Section C: Claims reserves and liabilities. The current year total (which must agree in total with the liability at the end of the current year in the Exhibit of Policy and Contract Benefits (Exhibit 3, Part 2)) is shown, followed by the total for the prior year and the increase for the year, shown in Part 1.

Part 3: Test of previous year's claim reserves and liabilities. The sums of the claims paid during the year and the reserve for claims (including amounts outstanding at the end of the year) are split into claims incurred before and during the current year. The sum of the amounts paid on claims incurred before the current year and the related claims reserve at the end of the year is compared with the claims reserve at the end of the previous year to determine the accuracy of the latter reserve.

l) Accident and health policy experience exhibit. Further information on direct written accident and health business must be provided in the accident and health policy experience exhibit which may be filed separately.

Earned premiums; incurred losses; the ratio of losses to earned premiums; commissions incurred and the rates of commission paid, and incurred dividends must be shown for the different policy forms issued in five major categories:

1) group policies, conversions and individual policies with annual premiums of $7.50 or less per person,

2) credit (group and individual),

3) hospital, medical and surgical policies,
4) loss of time policies and
5) all other policies.

The last three categories must also be subdivided into collectively renewable, noncancellable, guaranteed renewable, nonrenewable for stated reasons only, other accident only, and all other. The totals for direct written business must be shown and adjusted for net reinsurance assumed less ceded to obtain the net totals, which must check with the corresponding data from the annual statement.

Example 3.1

Original Data	RFERENCE	Example Number
Additional data	301-322	3.9
Incurred income 19B: Insurance	501-535	3.10
Supplementary contracts	516-541	3.11
Annuities	501-535	3.12
Accident and health	502-535	3.13
Investment 19B	532-553	3.14
Nonledger accounts: line of business, 19A	201-226	3.6
19B	201-226	3.7
Miscellaneous, 19A, 19B	250-260	3.8
Trial balance: line of business, 19A	101-125	3.2
19B	101-125	3.3
Miscellaneous income, 19A, 19B	01-30	3.4
Assets and liabilities, 19A, 19B	50-90	3.5
Allocation of investment income and interest on claims	550-551	3.17

Statement or exhibit	Example Number
Analysis of nonadmitted assets Ex. 14	3.23
Analysis of operations 19B	3.16
Assets Ex. 13 19A	3.21
Assets Ex. 13 19B	3.22
Calculation of MSVR 19B	3.15
Capital and surplus account 19B	3.19
Capital gains and losses Ex. 4, 19B	3.18
Reconciliation of ledger assets 19B	3.20
Statement of assets 19A, 19B	3.24
Statement of liabilities, surplus and other funds 19A, 19B	3.24

Index to Reference Numbers

Number	19A Ex.	19B Ex.
01-30	3.4	3.4
50-90	3.5	3.5
101-125	3.2	3.3
201-226	3.6	3.7
258-260	3.8	3.8
30i-322	3.9	3.9
501-535 Insurance		3.10
516-535 Supplementary contracts		3.11
501-535 Annuities		3.12
502-535 Accident and health		3.13
532-553 Investment		3.14

Example 3.2
TRIAL BALANCE YEAR 19A

	INSURANCE		ANNUITIES		ACCIDENT AND HEALTH
	PAR	NONPAR	PAR	NONPAR	
101 Premiums: single	$ 30,000C	$ 52,000C	$ 30,300C	$4,462,000C	
102 First year	750,000C	400,000C	163,400C		$ 79,240C
103 Renewal	4,600,000C	2,350,000C	770,000C	4,950C	746,175C
Commissions					
104 Single	900D	1,560D	990D	130,300D	
105 First year	525,000D	280,000D	60,000D		33,075D
106 Renewal	184,000D	86,000D	38,500D	120D	42,038D
Payments to policyholders					
107 Death claims	600,000D	350,000D	18,500D	63,550D	
108 Maturity values	300,000D	160,000D			
109 Surrender values	1,250,000D	575,000D	592,700D	306,520D	
110 Disability payments	5,000D	2,400D			631,800D
111 Annuity payments			67,200D	812,350D	
112 Considerations for supp. contracts life	82,000C	37,000C			
113 Supp. contract payments life	70,000D	32,500D			
114 Dividends: cash	15,745D		3,475D		
115 applied	1,434,255D		101,500D		
116 used to purchase additions	1,020,000C				
117 left on deposit	300,000C		92,700C		
118 Dividend deposits withdrawn	250,000D		82,475D		
119 Proceeds: left	150,000C	72,000C			
120 withdrawn	140,000D	68,000D			
121 Income tax paid	140,000D	78,000D	8,000D	15,000D	15,000D
122 Other taxes, licenses and fees	130,500D	62,000D	1,350D	2,650D	17,824D
123 General expense	1,134,771D	577,717D	103,500D	147,100D	80,807D
124 Supp. contract expenses	979D	583D			
125	$ 750,850C	$637,240C	$ 21,790D	$2,989,360C	$ 4,871C

Example 3.3
Trial Balance Year 19B

		Insurance		Annuities		Accident and Health
		Par	Nonpar	Par	Nonpar	
101	Premiums: single	$ 40,000C	$ 47,000C	$ 43,000C	$5,650,000C	$ 82,247C
102	First year	800,000C	435,000C	137,000C	3,850C	783,508C
103	Renewal	4,800,000C	2,565,000C	742,000C		
	Commissions					
104	Single	1,200D	1,410D	1,530D	154,500D	
105	First year	560,000D	304,000D	48,200D		34,362D
106	Renewal	192,000D	93,500D	34,300D	115D	44,119D
	Payments to policyholders					
107	Death claims	625,000D	340,500D	19,150D	66,700D	
108	Maturity values	330,000D	180,000D			
109	Surrender values	1,375,000D	615,000D	546,527D	497,124D	
110	Disability payments	8,000D	2,700D			653,359D
111	Annuity payments			80,450D	919,000D	
112	Considerations for supp. contracts life	94,000C	41,500C			
113	Supp. contract payments life	81,000D	37,600D			
114	Dividends: cash	17,530D		4,580D		
115	applied	1,632,470D		121,720D		
116	used to purchase additions	1,100,000C				
117	left on deposit	350,000C		117,350C		
118	Dividend deposits withdrawn	315,000D		102,758D		
119	Proceeds: left	175,000C	78,000C			
120	withdrawn	160,000D	71,000D			
121	Income tax paid	175,000D	165,200D	48,000D	165,000D	40,000D
122	Other taxes, licenses and fees	141,500D	72,500D	1,400D	3,970D	19,242D
123	General expense	1,264,325D	638,510D	92,894D	166,415D	96,042D
124	Supp. contract expenses	1,015D	650D			
125		$ 479,960C	$ 643,930C	$ 62,159D	$3,681,026C	$ 21,369D

Example 3.4

TRIAL BALANCE—MISCELLANEOUS INCOME

		YEAR 19A	YEAR 19B
01 Interest on bonds: U.S. government		$ 110,114C	$ 127,110C
02	tax-exempt	203,758C	237,735C
03	other unaffiliated	3,921,098C	4,349,430C
04	affiliated	25,000C	25,000C
05 Accrual of discount		15,307C	16,303C
06 Amortization of premium		1,725D	1,635D
07 Dividends on stocks: preferred		55,118C	60,784C
08	common	117,882C*	148,216C*
09 Interest on mortgages		3,004,091C	3,405,180C
10 Interest on policy loans		348,000C	378,000C
11 Interest on bank deposits		18,640C	20,330C
12 Income from real estate: home office		300,000C	315,000C
13	investment	325,000C	350,000C
14 Net loss on sale of bonds		22,500D	125,800D
15 Net gain on sale of stocks		9,800C	243,000C
16 Interest paid on borrowed money		73,500D	82,400D
20 Dividends paid to stockholders		250,000D	250,000D
21 Interest paid on claims		47,000D	49 500D
25 Real estate expenses: home office		45,800D	49,250D
26 Other investment expenses		125,733D	141,942D
27 Investment taxes		8,250D	9,780D
28 Real estate depreciation: home office		75,000D	75,000D
29	investment	69,000D	69,000D
30		$7,735,300C	$8,821,781C
*Includes dividends on affiliates		250C	250C

Example 3.5

TRIAL BALANCE—ASSETS AND LIABILITIES

	YEAR 19A	YEAR 19B	YEAR 19B AFTER CLOSING ENTRIES
50 Bonds: U.S. government	$ 1,376,420D	$ 1,563,872D	$ 1,563,872D
51 tax-exempt	3,424,500D	3,945,115D	3,945,115D
52 other nonaffiliated	46,609,830D	52,625,813D	52,625,813D
53 affiliated	250,000D	250,000D	250,000D
54 Stocks: preferred	787,400D	1,053,200D	1,053,200D
55 common: unaffiliated	2,685,400D	3,376,437D	3,376,437D
56 affiliated	5,000D	5,000D	5,000D
57 Mortgages	35,460,970D	40,959,123D	40,959,123D
58 Real estate: home office	2,675,000D	2,600,000D	2,600,000D
59 investment	2,585,426D	2,516,426D	2,516,426D
60 Policy loans	6,200,000D	7,030,800D	7,030,800D
61 Cash	249,024D	200,459D	200,459D
62 Furniture and equipment	237,500D	275,800D	275,800D
63 EDP equipment	1,250,000D	900,000D	900,000D
64 Agent credit balances	145,075C	164,515C	164,515C
65 Agent debit balances	425,625D	482,659D	482,659D
70 MSVR	1,250,000C	1,250,000C	1,639,003C
71 Capital stock	1,500,000C	1,500,000C	1,500,000C
80	$101,327,020D	$114,870,189D	$114,481,186D
90 Balance account	$ 89,231,189C	$101,327,020C	$114,481,186C

Example 3.6

NONLEDGER ASSETS AND LIABILITIES YEAR 19A
(BY LINE OF BUSINESS)

	INSURANCE		ANNUITIES		ACCIDENT AND HEALTH
	PAR	NONPAR	PAR	NONPAR	
Premiums due and uncollected					
201 First year	$ 20,000A	$ 11,250A	$ 1,190A	$	$ 7,969A
202 Renewal	$ 600,000A	295,000A	27,700A		75,046A
Deferred					
203 First year	202,500A	97,550A	42,518A		
204 Renewal	1,431,030A	555,241A	180,950A		
Advance					
205 First year	1,000L	450L			
206 Renewal	5,000L	2,200L			
Loadings					
207 Due first year	16,600L	9,563L	702L		
208 renewal	90,000L	38,350L	2,216L		
209 Deferred first year	168,075L	82,918L	25,806L		
210 renewal	185,405L	66,823L	14,476L		
Payments to policyholders					
211 Due but unpaid death claims	150,000L	75,000L	5,560L	19,300L	
212 maturities	20,000L	10,000L			
213 disability payments					
214 Disability payments not yet due					46,498L
215 Unreported due but unpaid	35,000L	21,000L			163,864L
216 Unreported not yet due					7,750L
217 Due but unpaid dividends	35,000L				25,574L

(continued)

Example 3.6 (Continued)

NONLEDGER ASSETS AND LIABILITIES YEAR 19A
(BY LINE OF BUSINESS)

	INSURANCE		ANNUITIES		ACCIDENT AND HEALTH
	PAR	NONPAR	PAR	NONPAR	
Due and accrued expenses					
218 Income tax	33,000L	20,000L			876L
219 Other taxes	27,000L	12,000L			2,598L
220 General expenses	110,000L	49,800L			
Reserves					
221 Supp. contracts L	736,506L	330,894L			
222 Policy reserve	44,459,396L	21,166,127L	4,980,015L	17,235,000L	317,284L
223 Dividends on deposit	2,357,500L		782,580L		
224 Proceeds deposited	1,537,500L	840,500L			
225 Dividend reserve	1,700,000L		130,000L		
226 Reserve for reins. in unauthorized companies	297,497L	215,428L			
230	$49,710,949L	$21,982,012L	$5,688,997L	$17,254,300L	$481,429L

Example 3.7

Nonledger Assets and Liabilities Year 19B
(By Line of Business)

	INSURANCE		ANNUITIES		ACCIDENT AND HEALTH
	PAR	NONPAR	PAR	NONPAR	
Premiums due and uncollected					
201 First year	$ 30,000A	$ 14,500A	$ 550A	$	$ 8,496A
202 Renewal	$ 680,000A	352,000A	22,400A		80,931A
Deferred					
203 First year	215,800A	106,478A	38,415A		
204 Renewal	1,654,006A	633,408A	189,715A		
Advance					
205 First year	1,100L	825L			
206 Renewal	6,000L	2,450L			
Loadings					
207 Due first year	24,510L	12,687L	326L		
208 renewal	100,640L	45,408L	1,770L		
209 Deferred first year	176,309L	93,168L	22,742L		
210 renewal	227,062L	74,241L	14,987L		
Payments to policyholders					
211 Due but unpaid death claims	200,000L	85,000L	3,600L	11,700L	
212 maturities	50,000L	12,000L			
213 disability payments					
214 Disability payments not yet due					59,573L
215 Unreported due but unpaid	42,000L	23,000L			187,329L
216 Unreported not yet due					8,902L
217 Due but unpaid dividends	42,500L				30,496L

(continued)

Example 3.7 (Continued)

NONLEDGER ASSETS AND LIABILITIES YEAR 19B
(BY LINE OF BUSINESS)

| | INSURANCE | | ANNUITIES | | ACCIDENT AND HEALTH |
	PAR	NONPAR	PAR	NONPAR	
Due and accrued expenses					
218 Income tax	35,000L	25,000L			1,052L
219 Other taxes	30,000L	12,000L			2,942L
220 General expenses	120,000L	59,500L			
Reserves					
221 Supplementary contracts L	783,497L	343,837L	5,335,971L		343,505L
222 Policy reserve	48,788,247L	23,534,767L	830,700L	22,245,000L	
223 Dividends on deposit	2,511,250L	889,700L			
224 Proceeds deposited	1,624,625L				
225 Dividend reserves	1,920,000L		134,000L		
226 Reserve for reins. in unauthorized companies	356,600L	258,227L			
230	$54,459,534L	$24,365,424L	$6,093,016L	$22,256,700L	$544,372L

Example 3.8

NONLEDGER ASSETS AND LIABILITIES—MISCELLANEOUS

	YEAR 19A	YEAR 19B
Interest due		
250 Bonds	$ 5,000A	$ 5,700A
251 Mortgages	25,765A	27,465A
Interest accrued		
252 Bonds: U.S. government	19,941A	23,211A
253 tax-exempt	36,900A	42,792A
254 other non-affiliated	710,259A	782,897A
255 Mortgages	122,256A	150,034A
256 Policy loans	170,000A	188,435A
258 Due and accrued investment expenses	11,000L	12,430L
259 Accrued interest on claims	22,000L	24,742L
260	$1,057,121A	$1,183,362A

Example 3.9
ADDITIONAL DATA

	19A	19B	GAIN/(LOSS)
301 Market values of common stocks less book values (55)	$3,029,975 / 2,685,400	$3,896,264 / 3,376,437	
302 Nonledger asset	$ 344,575	$ 519,827	$ 175,252
Nonadmitted assets			
303 Bonds	$ 753,230	$ 814,522	($ 61,292)
304 Mortgages	107,827	83,915	23,912
305 Due and accrued interest on mortgages	8,752	10,840	(2,088)
310 Bonds in 20% maximum reserve class	$1,874,190	$1,482,916	
311 10% maximum reserve class	Nil	Nil	

Realized capital gains and losses

	GAINS	LOSSES	NET GAIN
312 Bonds: U.S. government		$ 32,016	
313 tax-exempt		15,974	
314 other (unaffiliated)	$ 23,415	101,225	$ -125,800
315 Common stocks	$ 275,000	$ 32,000	$ 243,000

Policy loans by line of business

	LIFE INSURANCE	ANNUITIES	TOTAL
316 19A	$5,757,143	$ 442,857	$6,200,000
317 19B	6,547,784	483,016	7,030,800

Investment transactions

	SALES, MATURITIES AND REPAYMENTS	COST OF NEW INVESTMENTS
318 Bonds	$ 472,030	$ 7,307,212
319 Preferred stocks	0	265,800
320 Common stocks	781,297	1,229,334
321 Mortgages	746,673	6,244,826
322 Totals	$2,000,000	$15,047,172

Example 3.10

CALCULATION OF INCURRED INCOME YEAR 19B INSURANCE

	LEDGER	NONLEDGER 19B	NONLEDGER 19A	INCURRED
Premiums				
Single par	$ 40,000C			
(101) nonpar	47,000C			
Dividends applied to aditions (116)	1,100,000C			
501	$ 1,187,000C			$ 1,187,000C
First year: par	800,000C			
(102) nonpar	435,000C			
Due: par		$ 30,000A	$ 20,000A	
(201) nonpar		14,500A	11,250A	
Deferred: par		215,800A	202,500A	
(203) nonpar		106,478A	97,550A	
Advance: par		1,100L	1,000L	
(205) nonpar		825L	450L	
502	$ 1,235,000C	$ 364,853A	$ 329,850A	$ 1,270,003C
Renewal: par	4,800,000C			
(103) nonpar	2,565,000C			
Due: par		680,000A	600,000A	
(202) nonpar		352,000A	295,000A	
Deferred: par		1,654,006A	1,431,030A	
(204) nonpar		633,408A	555,241A	
Advance: par		6,000L	5,000L	
(206) nonpar		2,450L	2,200L	
503	$ 7,365,000C	$ 3,310,964A	$ 2,874,071A	$ 7,801,893C

(continued)

Example 3.10 (Continued)

CALCULATION OF INCURRED INCOME YEAR 19B
INSURANCE

	LEDGER	NONLEDGER 19B	NONLEDGER 19A	INCURRED
Death claims: par (107,211) nonpar	625,000D 340,000D	200,000L 85,000L	150,000L 75,000L	
Unreported: par (215) nonpar		42,000L 23,000L	35,000L 21,000L	
510	$ 965,000D	$ 350,000L	$ 281,000L	$ 1,034,000D
Maturity values: par (108,212) nonpar	330,000D 180,000D	50,000L 12,000L	20,000L 10,000L	
511	$ 510,000D	$ 62,000L	$ 30,000L	$ 542,000D
Cash surrender values (109) par Nonpar	1,375,000D 615,000D			
512	$ 1,990,000D			$ 1,990,000D
Disability payments (110) par Nonpar	8,000D 2,700D			
513	$ 10,700D			$ 10,700D
Dividends: cash (114,217) applied (115) reserves (225)	17,530D 1,632,470D	42,500L 1,920,000L	35,000L 1,700,000L	
515	$ 1,650,000D	$ 1,962,500L	$ 1,735,000L	$ 1,877,500D
516 Dividends left (117)	$ 350,000C			$ 350,000C
517 Dividends withdrawn (118)	315,000D			315,000D

(continued)

Example 3.10 (Continued)

CALCULATION OF INCURRED INCOME YEAR 19B INSURANCE

	Ledger	Nonledger 19B	Nonledger 19A	Incurred
Policy reserves: par		$48,788,247L	$44,459,396L	$ 6,697,491D
(222) nonpar		23,534,767L	21,166,127L	153,750D
518		$72,323,014L	$65,625,523L	
519 Increase in dividends on deposit (223)		2,511,250L	2,357,500L	2,610D
Commissions (single): par				
520	1,200D			
(104) nonpar	1,410D			
First year: par				
521	$ 560,000D			864,500D
(105) nonpar	304,500D			
Renewal: par				
522	$ 192,000D			285,500D
(106) nonpar	93,500D			
Income tax: par	$ 175,000D	35,000L	33,000L	
(121,218 nonpar)	165,200D	25,000L	20,000L	
531	$ 340,200D	$ 60,000L	$ 53,000L	347,200D
Other taxes: par	141,500D	30,000L	27,000L	
(122,219) nonpar	72,500D	12,000L	12,000L	
532	$ 214,000D	$ 42,000L	$ 39,000L	217,000D
General expenses: par	1,264,325D	120,000L	110,000L	
(123,220) nonpar	638,510D	59,500L	49,800L	
533	$ 1,902,835D	$ 179,500L	$ 159,800L	$ 1,922,535D

(continued)

Example 3.10 (Continued)

CALCULATION OF INCURRED INCOME YEAR 19B
INSURANCE

	LEDGER	NONLEDGER 19B	NONLEDGER 19A	INCURRED
Increase in loadings				
Due first year: par		24,510L	16,600L	
(207) nonpar		12,687L	9,563L	
Renewal: par		100,640L	90,000L	
(208) nonpar		45,408L	38,350L	
Deferred first year: par		176,309L	168,075L	
(209) nonpar		93,168L	82,918L	
Renewal: par		227,062L	185,405L	
(210) nonpar		74,241L	66,823L	
534		$ 754,025L	$ 657,734L	96,291D
535 Totals (Analysis of operations)	$ 1,086,655C	$74,568,472L	$67,734,636L	$ 5,747,181D
Increase in reserve for unauthorized reins. (226)				
par		356,600L	297,497L	
nonpar		258,227L	215,428L	
530 (Capital and surplus acct.)		614,827L	512,925L	101,902D
Totals (insurance)	$ 1,086,655C	$75,183,299L	$68,247,561L	$ 5,849,083D

Example 3.11

CALCULATION OF INCURRED INCOME YEAR 19B
SUPPLEMENTARY CONTRACTS

	LEDGER	NONLEDGER 19B	NONLEDGER 19A	INCURRED
Considerations (life):				
(112) par	$ 94,000C			
nonpar	41,500C			
516S	$ 135,500C			135,500C
Proceeds left: par	175,000C			
(119) nonpar	78,000C			
516	$ 253,000C			253,000C
Payments (life: 113)				
par	81,000D			
nonpar	37,600D			
517S	$ 118,600D			118,600D
Proceeds withdrawn: par	160,000D			
(120) nonpar	71,000D			
517	$ 231,000D			231,000D
Increases in reserves:				
Life: par		783,497L	736,506L	
(221) nonpar		343,837L	330,894L	
518		$ 1,127,334L	$ 1,067,400L	59,934D

(continued)

Example 3.11 (Continued)

CALCULATION OF INCURRED INCOME YEAR 19B
SUPPLEMENTARY CONTRACTS

	LEDGER	NONLEDGER 19B	NONLEDGER 19A	INCURRED
Certain: par		1,624,625L	1,537,500L	
(224) nonpar		889,700L	840,500L	
519		$ 2,514,325L	$ 2,378,000L	136,325D
Expenses: par	1,015D			
(124) nonpar	650D			
533	$ 1,665D			1,665D
535 Totals	$ 37,235C	$ 3,641,659L	$ 3,445,400L	$ 159,024D
Total insurance	$1,086,655C	$75,183,299L	$68,247,561L	$5,849,083D
Grand totals	$1,123,890C	$78,824,958L	$71,692,961L	$6,008,107D
Totals (125,230):				
Par	479,960C	54,459,534L	49,710,949L	
Nonpar	643,930C	24,365,424L	21,982,012L	
	$1,123,890C	$78,824,958L	$71,692,961L	$6,008,107D

Example 3.12

CALCULATION OF INCURRED INCOME YEAR 19B
ANNUITIES

	LEDGER	NONLEDGER 19B	NONLEDGER 19A	INCURRED
Premiums (single): par	43,000C			
(101) nonpar	5,650,000C			
501	$5,693,000C			$5,693,000C
First year (102) par	137,000C			
Due (201) par		550A	1,190A	
Deferred (203) par		38,415A	42,518A	
502	$ 137,000C	$ 38,965A	$ 43,708A	132,257C
Renewal: par	742,000C			
(103) nonpar	3,850C			
Due (202) par		22,400A	27,700A	
Deferred (204) par		189,715A	180,950A	
503	$ 745,850C	$ 212,115A	$ 208,650A	749,315C
Death claims: par	19,150D	3,600L	5,560L	
(107,211) nonpar	66,700D	11,700L	19,300L	
Surrender values: par	546,527D			
(109) nonpar	497,124D			
Annuity payments: par	80,450D			
(111) nonpar	919,000D			
514	$2,128,951D	$ 15,300L	$ 24,860L	2,119,391D
Dividends: Cash (114)	4,580D			
Applied (115)	121,720D			
Reserves (225)		134,000L	130,000L	
515	$ 126,300D	$ 134,000L	$ 130,000L	130,300D

(continued)

Example 3.12 (Continued)

CALCULATION OF INCURRED INCOME YEAR 19B
ANNUITIES

	LEDGER	NONLEDGER 19B	NONLEDGER 19A	INCURRED
516 Dividends left (117)	117,350C			117,350C
517 Dividends withdrawn (118)	102,758D			102,758D
Policy reserves (222) par nonpar		5,335,971L 22,245,000L	4,980,015L 17,235,000L	
518		$27,580,971L	$22,215,015L	5,365,956D
519 Increase in dividends on deposit (223)		830,700L	782,580L	48,120D
Commissions single par 520 (104) nonpar	1,530D 154,500D $ 156,030D			156,030D
Commissions 521 First year (105) par Renewal: par (106) nonpar	48,200D 34,300D 115D			48,200D
522	34,415D			34,415D
Income tax: par (121) nonpar 531	48,000D 165,000D 213,000D			213,000D

(continued)

Example 3.12 (Continued)

CALCULATION OF INCURRED INCOME YEAR 19B ANNUITIES

	LEDGER	NONLEDGER 19B	NONLEDGER 19A	INCURRED
Other taxes: par	1,400D			
(122) nonpar	3,970D			
532	5,370D			5,370D
General expenses: par	92,894D			
(123) nonpar	166,415D			
533	259,309D			259,309D
Increase in loadings				
Due first year: (207) par		326L	702L	
renewal: (208) par		1,770L	2,216L	
Deferred first year: (209) par		22,742L	25,806L	
renewal: (210) par		14,987L	14,476L	
534		$ 39,825L	$ 43,200L	3,375C
Totals	$3,618,867C	$28,349,716L	$22,943,297L	$1,787,552D
Totals (125,230)				
Par	62,159D	6,093,016L	5,688,997L	
Nonpar	3,681,026C	22,256,700L	17,254,300L	
535	$3,618,867C	$28,349,716L	$22,943,297L	$1,787,552D

Example 3.13

CALCULATION OF INCURRED INCOME YEAR 19B ACCIDENT AND HEALTH

		LEDGER	NONLEDGER 19B	NONLEDGER 19A	INCURRED
502	Premiums: first year (102,201)	$ 82,247C	$ 8,496A	$ 7,969A	$ 82,774C
503	renewal (103,202)	783,508C	80,931A	75,046A	789,393C
	Claims (110)	653,359D	59,573L	46,498L	
	unreported (215)		8,902L	7,750L	
513		$653,359D	$ 68,475L	$ 54,248L	667,586D
	Increase in: reserves (222)		343,505L	317,284L	
	reserves for claims (214)		187,329L	163,864L	
	unreported (216)		30,496L	25,574L	
518			$561,330L	$506,722L	54,608D
532	Taxes, licenses, fees (122,219)	19,242D	1,052L	876L	19,418D
533	General expenses (123,220)	96,042D	2,942L	2,598L	96,386D
	Totals	$ 97,112C	$544,372L	$481,429L	$ 34,169C
	Nonledger totals		$544,372L	$481,429L	
521	Commissions first year (105)	34,362D			34,362D
522	renewal (106)	44,119D			44,119D
531	Income tax paid (121)	40,000D			40,000D
535	Total (125,230)	$ 21,369D	$544,372L	$481,429L	$ 84,312D
	Trial balance total	$ 21,369D			

Example 3.14

INCURRED INVESTMENT INCOME YEAR 19B

	LEDGER	NONLEDGER 19B	NONLEDGER 19A	NONADMITTED	INCURRED
Bond Interest					
U.S. government (01,252)	$ 127,110C	$ 23,211A	$ 19,941A		$
Tax-exempt (02,253)	237,735C	42,792A	36,900A		
Other nonaffiliated					
Accrual of discount	4,349,430C (03)				
	16,303C (05)				
	1,635D				
Amort. (254)	4,364,098C	5,700A	5,000A		
Premium (06)		782,897A	710,259A		
Affiliated (04)	25,000C				
	$4,753,943C	$ 854,600A	$ 772,100A		$4,836,443
Interest on mortgages (09,251,255,305)	3,405,180C	27,465A	25,765A	10,840L	3,432,570
		150,034A	122,256A	8,752A	
	$3,405,180C	$ 177,499A	$ 148,021A	$ 2,088L	
Preferred stocks (07)	60,784C				60,784
Common—unaffiliated (08)	147,966C				147,966
Common—affiliated (08)	250C				250
Real estate—company occupied (12)	315,000C				315,000
Real estate—other (13)	350,000C				350,000
Policy loans (10)	378,000C	188,435A	170,000A		396,435
Cash and bank deposits (11)	20,330C				20,330
550 Gross investment income	$9,431,453C	$1,220,534A	$1,090,121A	$ 2,088L	$9,559,778
Investment expenses					
533 General expenses (26,258)	141,942D	12,430L	11,000L		
533 Real estate expenses (25)	49,250D				
532 Taxes (27)	9,780D				$ 202,402
	$ 200,972D	$ 12,430L	$ 11,000L		

(continued)

Example 3.14 (Continued)

INCURRED INVESTMENT INCOME YEAR 19B

		LEDGER	NONLEDGER 19B	NONLEDGER 19A	NONADMITTED	TOTAL INCURRED
	Depreciation on invested assets					
	Real estate—home office property	$ 75,000D				75,000
	Real estate—other (28,29)	69,000D				69,000
553		$ 144,000D				144,000
	Interest on borrowed	82,400D				82,400
	money (16)	$ 82,400D				82,400
	Total charges	$ 427,372D	$ 12,430L	$ 11,000L		428,802
551	Net investment income (21,259)	$9,004,081C	$1,208,104A	$1,079,121A	$ 2,088L	$9,130,976
552	Interest paid on claims	49,500D	24,742L	22,000L		(52,242)
	Nonledger totals (260)		$1,183,362A	$1,057,121A		
	Cross check	$8,954,581C	$1,183,362A	$1,057,121A	$ 2,088L	$9,078,734

Capital gains and losses on investments

	REALIZED	UNREALIZED		TOTAL
Bonds (14,303)	(125,800D)	(61,292L)		(187,092)
Mortgage loans (304)		23,912A		23,912
Common stocks—unaffiliated (15,302)	243,000C	175,252A		418,252
	$ 117,200C	$ 137,872A		$ 255,072

Dividends to shareholders (20)	250,000D	
Total ledger items	$8,821,781C	
Trial balance total (30)	8,821,781C	
Net investment income	(I) (551)	$ 9,130,976
Cash and invested assets	19A (A)	102,873,857*
	19B (B)	116,957,329*
		$210,700,210
		.08667

$$A + B - I$$
$$2I/(A + B - I)$$

*Including due and accrued investment income (Example 3.24 Assets, items 10A + 19).

Example 3.15

CALCULATION OF MANDATORY SECURITIES VALUATION RESERVE
YEAR 19B

	STATEMENT VALUE	RESERVE $	
Bond and preferred stock component previous year			700,000(A)
Maximum, previous year:			
Total bonds (Ex. 13)	$50,907,520		
Less:			
U.S. government (50)	1,376,420	0	
20% maximum reserve class (310)	1,874,190	374,838	
2% class	$47,656,910	953,138	
Preferred stocks 5%	787,400	39,370	
Maximum bond and preferred stock component Year 19A		$1,367,346	(A.1)
Ratio A/A.1			.512(A.2)

	STATEMENT VALUE	RESERVE INCREASE	
Bonds Year 19B (Ex. 13)	57,570,278		
Less:			
U.S. government (50)	1,563,872	0	
20% maximum reserve class (310)	1,482,916	.02	29,658	(D)
2% maximum reserve class	$54,523,490	.001	54,523	(B)
Preferred stocks	1,053,200	.0025	2,633	(E)
Additional accumulation (A.2 > .500)			86,814	(I)
Realized and unrealized losses	-187,092		0	(I.1)
Less U.S. government bonds (312)	32,016		-155,076	(K)
Total addition			$ -68,262	(M)

(continued)

Example 3.15 (Continued)

CALCULATION OF MANDATORY SECURITIES VALUATION RESERVE
YEAR 19B

	STATEMENT VALUE	RESERVE	
Maximum [20×(B+E) + 10×D]	1,439,700		
Bond and preferred stock component (A+M)		631,738	(O)
Value of common stocks (including affiliate) (Ex. 13)		$3,901,264	(Q)
Reserve increase (1%)		39,013	(R)
Net current year realized and unrealized capital gains (Ex. 8)		418,252	(SG.1)
Increase in common stock component		$ 457,265	(P)
Common stock component previous year		550,000	
Common stock component		$1,007,265	(U,W)
Maximum common stock component 33% of 3,896,264 + 20% of 5,000	1,299,754		
Bond and preferred stock component		631,738	
Total Mandatory Securities Valuation Reserve		$1,639,003	

Example 3.16

STATUTORY

ANALYSIS OF OPERATIONS BY LINE OF BUSINESS YEAR 19B

		TOTAL (SUMMARY OF OPERATIONS)	LIFE INSURANCE	INDIVIDUAL ANNUITIES	SUPP. CONTRACTS	ACCIDENT AND HEALTH
1.	Premiums and considerations for annuities (501-3)	$17,705,635	$10,258,896	$ 6,574,572	$	$ 872,167
2.	Considerations for supplementary contracts (life) (516S)	135,500			135,500	
3.	Considerations for supplementary contracts certain and dividend accumulations (516)	720,350	350,000	117,350	253,000	160,716
4.	Net investment income (551)	9,130,976	6,466,268	2,199,157	304,835	
7.	Totals	$27,692,461	$17,075,164	$ 8,891,079	$ 693,335	$ 1,032,883
8.	Death benefits (510)	1,034,000	1,034,000			
9.	Matured endowments (511)	542,000	542,000			
10.	Annuity payments (514)	2,119,391		2,119,391		
11.	Disability benefits (513)	678,286	10,700			667,586
12.	Surrender values (512)	1,990,000	1,990,000			
14.	Interest on policy funds (552)	52,242	36,470	12,988	1,823	961
15.	Payments on supplementary contracts (life) (517S)	118,600			118,600	
16.	Payments on supplementary contracts, certain and dividend accumulations (517)	648,758	315,000	102,758	231,000	
17.	Increase in policy reserves (518)	12,177,989	6,697,491	5,365,956	59,934	54,608
18.	Increase in reserves for supplementary contracts certain and dividend accumulations (519)	338,195	153,750	48,120	136,325	
20.	Totals	$19,699,461	$10,779,411	$ 7,649,213	$ 547,682	$ 723,155

(continued)

Example 3.16 (Continued)

STATUTORY
ANALYSIS OF OPERATIONS BY LINE OF BUSINESS YEAR 19B

	TOTAL (SUMMARY OF OPERATIONS)	LIFE INSURANCE	INDIVIDUAL ANNUITIES	SUPP. CONTRACTS	ACCIDENT AND HEALTH
21. Commissions (520-2)	1,469,736	1,152,610	238,645		78,481
22. General expenses (533)	2,279,895	1,922,535	259,309	1,665	96,386
23. Taxes, licenses, fees (532)	241,788	217,000	5,370		19,418
24. Increase in loading on due and deferred premiums (534)	92,916	96,291	−3,375		
26. Totals	$23,783,796	$14,167,847	$ 8,149,162	$ 549,347	$ 917,440
27. Net gain before dividends and income tax	3,908,665	2,907,317	741,917	143,988	115,443
28. Dividends paid (515)	2,007,800	1,877,500	130,300		
29. Net gain before income tax	1,900,865	1,029,817	611,617	143,988	115,443
30. Income tax (531)	600,200	347,200	213,000		40,000
31. Net gain after dividends and income tax	$ 1,300,665	$ 682,617	$ 398,617	$ 143,988	$ 75,443

Example 3.17

ALLOCATION OF INVESTMENT INCOME AND INTEREST ON CLAIMS YEAR 19B

ANALYSIS OF OPERATIONS (EX. 3.16)	TOTAL INSURANCE	LIFE	ANNUITIES	SUPPLEMENTARY CONTRACTS	ACCIDENT AND HEALTH
+ 1. Lines 1-3	$ 18,561,485C	$10,608,896C	$ 6,691,922C	$ 388,500C	$ 872,167C
+ 2. Lines 8-12	6,363,677D	3,576,700D	2,119,391D		667,586D
+ 3. Lines 15-16	767,358D	315,000D	102,758D	349,600D	194,285D
+ 4. Lines 21-24	4,084,335D	3,388,436D	499,949D	1,665D	40,000D
+ 5. Lines 28, 30	2,608,000D	2,224,700D	343,300D		
− 6. Increase in reserve for dividends (225)	224,000C	220,000C	4,000C		
= 7. Direct income	$ 4,962,115C	$ 1,324,060C	$ 3,630,524C	$ 37,235C	$ 29,704D
+ 8. One-half direct income	2,481,058C	662,030C	1,815,262C	18,618C	14,852D
+ 9. Funds at beginning of year	106,103,760C	75,142,684C	25,178,422C	3,766,683C	2,015,971C
= 10. Mean funds	$108,584,818C	$75,804,714C	$26,993,684C	$3,785,301C	$2,001,119C
11. Ratio mean funds (A)	100.00%	69.81%	24.86%	3.49%	1.84%
+12. Net investment income (551)	9,130,976C	368,685C	27,750C	304,835C	160,716C
−13. Interest on policy loans (B)	396,435C	6,097,583C	2,171,407C		
=14. Balance (A)	8,734,541C			304,835C	160,716C
Investment income (551) (line 13 + line 14) (552) Interest on claims	$ 9,130,976C	$ 6,466,268C	$ 2,199,157C	$ 304,835C	$ 160,716C
	52,242D	36,470D	12,988D	1,823D	961D
Policy loans 17. 19A (316)	6,200,000	5,757,143	442,857		
18. 19B (317)	7,030,800	6,547,784	483,016		
19. Mean loans	6,615,400	6,152,463	462,937		
Ratio mean loans (B)	100.00%	93.00%	7.00%		

Example 3.18

CAPITAL GAINS AND LOSSES ON INVESTMENTS

	PROFIT ON SALE OR MATURITY	LOSS ON SALE OR MATURITY	NET GAIN OR LOSS FROM CHANGE IN ADMITTED VALUES	NET GAINS OR LOSSES
1. U.S. government bonds (312)	$	$ 32,016	$	$ -32,016
1.1 Tax-exempt bonds (313)		15,974		
1.2 Other bonds (unaffiliated) (314.303)	23,415	101,225	-61,292	-139,102
2.2 Common stocks (315.302)	275,000	32,000	175,252	418,252
3. Mortgage loans (304)			23,912	23,912
10. Totals	$298,415	$181,215	$137,872	$ 255,072

Example 3.19

CAPITAL AND SURPLUS ACCOUNT 19B

32.	Capital and surplus, December 31 of previous year	$7,578,095
33.	Net gain	1,300,665
34.	Net capital gains	255,072
35.	Change in nonadmitted assets and related items	−95,334
36.	Change in liability for reinsurance in unauthorized companies	−101,902
38.	Change in Mandatory Securities Valuation Reserve	−389,003
47.	Dividends to stockholders	−250,000
49.	Net change in capital and surplus for year	719,498
50.	Capital and surplus, December 31 of current year	8,297,593

Example 3.20

EXHIBIT 12 RECONCILIATION OF LEDGER ASSETS

INCREASES IN LEDGER ASSETS

1.	Premiums on life insurance and annuity contracts (501-3)	$ 16,362,850
2.	Accident and health premiums (502-3)	865,755
3.	Considerations for supplementary contracts life (516S)	135,500
4.	Considerations for supplementary contracts certain (516)	253,000
5.	Dividends left to accumulate at interest (516)	467,350
6.	Gross investment income (550)	9,431,453
13.	From sale or maturity of ledger assets (15)	243,000
15.	Total increases in ledger assets	$ 27,758,908

DECREASES IN LEDGER ASSETS

16.	Claims		
16.1	Life (510,511,513)	$1,485,700	
16.2	Accident and health (513)	653,359	
17.	For annuities with life contingencies (514)	2,128,951	
19.	Surrender values (512)	1,990,000	
19B	Interest on policy or contract funds (552)	49,500	
20.	Dividends to policyholders (515)	1,776,300	
21.	Total paid policyholders		$ 8,083,810
22.	Paid for claims on supplementary contracts		
22.1	with life contingencies (517S)	$ 118,600	
22.2	without life contingencies (517)	231,000	349,600
23.	Dividends on deposit disbursed (517)		417,758
26.	Commissions to agents		
26.1	life insurance and annuities (520-22)	$1,391,255	
26.2	accident and health (521-22)	78,481	1,469,736

(continued)

Example 3.20 (Continued)

EXHIBIT 12 RECONCILIATION OF LEDGER ASSETS

DECREASES IN LEDGER ASSETS (Continued)

27. General expenses (533)	2,451,043
28.1 Taxes, licenses and fees (532)	248,392
28.2 Federal income taxes (531)	593,200
30. Paid stockholders for dividends (20)	250,000
32. Interest on borrowed money (16)	82,400
36. From sale or maturity of ledger assets (14)	125,800
37. By adjustment of book values of ledger assets (553)	144,000
38. Total decreases in ledger assets	$ 14,215,739

RECONCILIATION BETWEEN YEARS

39. Amount of ledger assets December 31 of previous year	104,077,020
40. Increase or decrease in ledger assets during the year	13,543,169
41. Total ledger assets December 31 of current year	$117,620,189

Example 3.21

EXHIBIT 13:   YEAR 19A

ASSETS

	LEDGER	NONLEDGER	NONADMITTED	NET
Bonds (50-53,303)	$ 51,660,750	$	$ 753,230	$ 50,907,520
Stocks: preferred (54)	787,400			787,400
common (55-6,302)	2,690,400	344,575		3,034,975
Mortgages first liens (57,304)	35,460,970		107,827	35,353,143
Real estate:				
occupied by company (58)	2,675,000			2,675,000
investment (59)	2,585,426			2,585,426
Policy loans (60)	6,200,000			6,200,000
Cash and bank deposits (61)	249,024			249,024
Other assets				
Agents' balances (64-5) (debit $425,625, credit (145,075)	280,550		280,550	0
Furniture and equipment (62)	237,500		237,500	0
EDP equipment (63)	1,250,000			1,250,000
Deferred and uncollected premiums				
New business (less $303,664				
loading) $71,344 (201-2,207-8)				
Renewal (less $397,270 loading)				
$2,692,651 (203-4,209-10)		2,763,995		2,763,995
Accident and health due and uncollected (201-2)		83,015		83,015
Investment income due and accrued (550,305)		1,090,121	8,752	1,081,369
	$104,077,020	$4,281,706	$1,387,859	$106,970,867

Example 3.22

EXHIBIT 13:   YEAR 19B

ASSETS

	LEDGER	NONLEDGER	NONADMITTED	NET
Bonds	$ 58,384,800	$	$ 814,522	$ 57,570,278
Stocks: preferred	1,053,200			1,053,200
common	3,381,437	519,827		3,901,264
Mortgages first liens	40,959,123		83,915	40,875,208
Real estate:				
occupied by company	2,600,000			2,600,000
investment	2,516,426			2,516,426
Policy loans	7,030,800			7,030,800
Cash and bank deposits	200,459			200,459
Other assets:				
Agents' balances				
Debit $482,659				
Credit $164,515	318,144		318,144	0
Furniture and equipment	275,800		275,800	0
EDP equipment	900,000			900,000
Deferred and uncollected premiums				
First year (less $329,742 loadings) $76,001		3,143,422		3,143,422
Renewal (less $464,108 loadings) $3,067,421		89,427		89,427
Accident and health premiums due and unpaid		1,220,534	10,840	1,209,694
Due and accrued investment income	$117,620,189	$4,973,210	$1,503,221	$121,090,178

Example 3.23

EXHIBIT 14:   YEAR 19B
ANALYSIS OF NONADMITTED ASSETS AND RELATED ITEMS

	END OF PREVIOUS YEAR	END OF CURRENT YEAR	CHANGES
Furniture and equipment	$237,500	$275,800	$−38,300
Agents' balances	280,550	318,144	−37,594
Agents' credit balances	145,075	164,515	−19,440
Totals	$663,125	$758,459	$−95,334

Example 3.24

BALANCE SHEET — STATUTORY BASIS

ASSETS

		YEAR 19B	YEAR 19A
1.	Bonds	$ 57,570,278	$ 50,907,520
2.	Stocks		
	2.1 Preferred	1,053,200	787,400
	2.2 Common	3,901,264	3,034,975
3.	Mortgage loans on real estate	40,875,208	35,353,143
4.	Real estate		
	4.1 Properties owned by the company	2,600,000	2,675,000
	4.3 Investment real estate	2,516,426	2,585,426
5.	Policy loans	7,030,800	6,200,000
8.	Cash on hand and on deposit	200,459	249,024
10 A.	Subtotals, cash and invested assets	115,747,635	101,792,488
12.	Electronic data processing equipment	900,000	1,250,000
17.	Life insurance premiums and annuity considerations, deferred and uncollected	3,143,422	2,763,995
18.	Accident and health premiums due and unpaid	89,427	83,015
19.	Investment income due and accrued	1,209,694	1,081,369
	Totals	$121,090,178	$106,970,867

(continued)

Example 3.24 (Continued)

BALANCE SHEET—STATUTORY BASIS

ASSETS

LIABILITIES, SURPLUS AND OTHER FUNDS

		YEAR 19B	YEAR 19A
1.	Aggregate reserve for life policies and contracts (221,222)	$101,031,319	$ 88,907,938
2.	Aggregate reserve for accident and health policies (214,216,222)	561,330	506,722
3.	Supplementary contracts without life contingencies (224)	2,514,325	2,378,000
4.	Policy and contract claims:		
	4.1 life (211-215)	427,300	335,860
	4.2 accident and health (213,215)	68,475	54,248
5.	Policyholders' dividend accumulations (223)	3,341,950	3,140,080
6.	Policyholders' dividends due and unpaid (217)	42,500	35,000
7.	Provision for policyholders' dividends payable in the following calendar year (225)	2,054,000	1,830,000
9.	Premiums and annuity considerations received in advance (205-6)	10,375	8,650
14.	General expenses due or accrued (220,258)	194,872	173,398
15.	Taxes, licenses and fees due or accrued (219)	43,052	39,876
15 A.	Federal income taxes due or accrued (218)	60,000	53,000
19.	Agents' credit balances (64)	164,515	145,075
25.	Miscellaneous liabilities		
	25.1 Mandatory securities valuation reserve	1,639,003	1,250,000
	25.2 Reserve for reinsurance in unauthorized companies (226)	614,827	512,925
	25.6 Accrued interest on policyholders' funds (259)	24,742	22,000
26.	Total liabilities	112,792,585	99,392,772
27 A.	Capital paid-up	1,500,000	1,500,000
29 B.	Unassigned funds	6,797,593	6,078,095
	Totals	$121,090,178	$106,970,867

LIFE AND ACCIDENT AND HEALTH COMPANIES—ASSOCIATION EDITION

Form 1

ANNUAL STATEMENT

For the Year Ended December 31, 198—
OF THE CONDITION AND AFFAIRS OF THE

NAIC Group Code _____ NAIC Co. Code _____ Employer's ID Number _____

Organized under the Laws of the State of _____, made to the

INSURANCE DEPARTMENT OF THE STATE OF _____

PURSUANT TO THE LAWS THEREOF

Incorporated _____ Commenced Business _____

Home Office _____ , _____
         (Street and Number)   (City or Town, State and Zip Code)

Mail Address _____ , _____
         (Street and Number)   (City or Town, State and Zip Code)

Main Administrative Office _____
         (Area Code)   (Telephone Number)

Contact Person and Phone Number _____

OFFICERS**

President _____

Secretary _____ } Vice-Presidents

Treasurer _____

Actuary _____

DIRECTORS OR TRUSTEES**

State of .... }
County of .... } ss

........................, President, ..., Secretary, ...Treasurer*

of the ...., being duly sworn, each for himself deposes and says that they are the above described officers of the said insurer, and that on the thirty-first day of December last, all of the herein described assets were the absolute property of the said insurer, free and clear from any liens or claims thereon, except as herein stated, and that this annual statement, together with related exhibits, schedules and explanations therein contained, annexed or referred to are a full and true statement of all the assets and liabilities and of the condition and affairs of the said insurer as of the thirty-first day of December last, and of its income and deductions therefrom for the year ended on that date, according to the best of their information, knowledge and belief, respectively.

....
President

....
Secretary

....
Treasurer*

Actuary**

Subscribed and sworn to before me this

.... day of ...., 198—

*Or corresponding person having charge of the accounts and finances of the insurer.
**Show full name (initials not acceptable) and indicate by number sign (#) those officers and directors who did not occupy the indicated position in the previous annual statement.

ANNUAL STATEMENT FOR THE YEAR 198—OF THE   EXAMPLE   (Name)

Form 1

SUMMARY OF OPERATIONS
(Excluding Capital Gains and Losses)

		1 Current Year	2 Previous Year
1	Premiums and annuity considerations (Exhibit 1. Part 1. Line 20d. Col. 1)	17,705,635	
1A	Annuity and other fund deposits		
2	Considerations for supplementary contracts with life contingencies (Exhibit 12. Line 3)	135,500	
3	Considerations for supplementary contracts without life contingencies and dividend accumulations (Exhibit 12. Lines 4 and 5)	720,350	
3A	Coupons° left to accumulate at interest (Exhibit 12. Line 5A)		
4	Net investment income (Exhibit 2. Line 7)	9,130,976	
5	Commissions and expense allowances on reinsurance ceded (Exhibit 1. Part 2. Line 26a, Col. 1)		
5A	Reserve adjustments on reinsurance ceded (Exhibit 12. Line 10A)		
6			
7	Totals (Items 1 to 6)	27,692,461	
8	Death benefits	1,034,000	
9	Matured endowments (excluding guaranteed annual pure endowments)	542,000	
10	Annuity benefits (Exhibit 11. Part 2. Line 6d. Cols. 4 + 8)	2,119,391	
11	Disability benefits and benefits under accident and health policies	678,286	
11A	Coupons, guaranteed annual pure endowments and similar benefits (Exhibit 7. Line 15. Cols. 3 + 4)		
12	Surrender benefits	1,990,000	
13	Group conversions		
14	Interest on policy or contract funds	52,242	
15	Payments on supplementary contracts with life contingencies (Exhibit 12. Line 22.1)	118,600	
16	Payments on supplementary contracts without life contingencies and of dividend accumulations (Exhibit 12. Lines 22.2 + 23)	648,758	
16A	Accumulated coupon° payments (Exhibit 12. Line 23A)		
17	Increase in aggregate reserves for life and accident and health policies and contracts	12,177,989	
18	Increase in reserve for supplementary contracts without life contingencies and for dividend and coupon° accumulations	338,195	
19			
20	Totals (Items 8 to 19)	19,699,461	
21	Commissions on premiums and annuity considerations (direct business only) (Exhibit 1. Part 2. Line 30, Col. 1)	1,469,736	
21A	Commissions and expense allowances on reinsurance assumed (Exhibit 1. Part 2. Line 26b, Col. 1)		
22	General insurance expenses (Exhibit 5. Line 10, Cols. 1 + 2)	2,279,895	
23	Insurance taxes, licenses and fees, excluding federal income taxes (Exhibit 6. Line 7, Cols. 1 and 2)	241,788	
24	Increase in loading on and cost of collection in excess of loading on deferred and uncollected premiums	92,916	
24A	Net transfers to (+) or from (−) Separate Accounts (excluding Variable Life Insurance)		
24B	Net transfers to (+) or from (−) Variable Life Insurance Separate Accounts		

#	Description	Amount
25	Totals (Items 20 to 25)	23,783,796
26	Net gain from operations before dividends to policyholders and federal income taxes (Item 7 minus Item 26)	3,908,665
27	Dividends to policyholders (Exhibit 7. Line 15, Cols 1 and 2)	2,007,800
28	Net gain from operations after dividends to policyholders and before federal income taxes (Item 27 minus Item 28)	1,900,865
29	Federal income taxes incurred (excluding tax on capital gains)	600,200
30	Net gain from operations after dividends to policyholders and federal income taxes	
31	(excluding tax on capital gains) (Item 29 minus Item 30)	1,300,665

CAPITAL AND SURPLUS ACCOUNT

#	Description	Amount
32	Capital and surplus, December 31, previous year (Page 3, Item 30, Col 2)	7,578,095
33	Net gain (Item 31)	1,300,665
34	Net capital gains (Exhibit 4, Line 10 2)	255,072
35	Change in non-admitted assets and related items (Exhibit 14, Item 13, Col 3)	-95,334
36	Change in liability for reinsurance in unauthorized companies, increase (−) or decrease (+) (Page 3, Item 25 2, Col 1 minus 2)	-101,902
37	Change in reserve on account of change in valuation basis, increase (−) or decrease (+) (Exh. 8A, Line 7, Col 4)	
38	Change in mandatory securities valuation reserve, increase (−) or decrease (+) (Page 3, Item 25 1, Col 1 minus 2)	-389,003
39		
40		
41	Change in treasury stock	
42		
43	Change in surplus in Separate Accounts Statement	
44	Change in surplus in Variable Life Insurance Separate Accounts Statement	
45	Capital changes:	
	(a) Paid in	
	(b) Transferred from surplus (Stock Dividend)	
	(c) Transferred to surplus (Exhibit 12, Line 29)	
46	Surplus adjustments:	
	(a) Paid in	
	(b) Transferred to capital (Stock Dividend) (Exhibit 12, Line 30, inside amount for stock $)	-250,000
	(c) Transferred from capital (Exhibit 12, Line 29)	
47	Dividends to stockholders	
48		
49	Net change in capital and surplus for the year (Items 33 through 48)	719,498
50	Capital and surplus, December 31, current year (Items 32 + 49) (Page 3 Item 30)	8,297,593

*Includes coupons, guaranteed annual pure endowments and similar benefits
NOTE: Items 1 to 31 to agree with Page 5, Col 1, Items 1 to 31

Form 1   ANNUAL STATEMENT FOR THE YEAR 190—OF THE . . . . . . EXAMPLE . . . . (Name)   4A

Statement of Changes in Financial Position

FUNDS PROVIDED

	1 Current Year	2 Previous Year
OPERATIONS:		
1. Net gain from operations after dividends to policyholders and federal income taxes (excluding tax on capital gains) (+)	1,300,665	
Charges (+) credits (−) not affecting funds:		
2. Increase (+) in policy reserves	12,177,989	
3. Increase (+) in policy and contract claims	105,667	
4. Increase (+) in other policy or contract liabilities	350,162	
5. Increase in net reinsurance payables (+) receivables (−)		
6. Increase (+) in liability for policyholder dividends, coupons and experience rating refunds	224,000	
7. Increase (+) in commissions, expenses and taxes (other than federal income taxes) due or accrued	24,650	
8. Increase (+) in federal income taxes due or accrued, excluding tax on capital gains	7,000	
9. Increase (−) in premiums receivable	−385,839	
10. Increase in net investment income receivable (−)	−128,325	
11. Depreciation on real estate and other invested assets (+)	144,000	
12. Amortization of premium (+)	1,635	
13. Accrual of discount (−)	−16,303	
14. Increase in net agents' balances	−37,594	
15. Increase in furniture and equipment	−38,300	
16. Depreciation of E.D.P. equipment	350,000	
17. Total funds provided from operations (Items 1 to 16)	14,079,407	
INVESTMENTS SOLD, MATURED OR REPAID:		
18. Bonds	597,830	
19. Stocks	538,297	
20. Mortgage loans	746,673	
21. Real estate		
22. Other invested assets		
23. Net Gains (+) or losses (−) on investments acquired and disposed of during year	117,200	

24.	Tax on capital gains (−)	
25.	Total investments sold, matured or repaid (Items 18 to 24)	2,000,000
	OTHER FUNDS PROVIDED:	
26.	Capital and surplus paid in (+)	
27.	Borrowed money $ ___ less amounts repaid $	
28.		
29.	Total other funds provided (Items 26 to 28)	
30.	Total funds provided (Items 17, 25 and 29)	16,079,407

FUNDS APPLIED

	INVESTMENTS ACQUIRED:	
31.	Bonds	7,307,212
31.1	Net increase (+) decrease (−) in short-term investments	
32.	Stocks	1,495,134
33.	Mortgage loans	6,244,826
34.	Real estate	
35.	Other invested assets	
36.		
37.		
38.	Total investments acquired (Items 31 to 37)	15,047,172
	OTHER FUNDS APPLIED:	
39.	Dividends to stockholders	250,000
40.	Net increase (+) decrease (−) in policy loans	830,800
41.	Other items (net)	
42.		
43.		
44.	Total other funds applied (Items 39 to 43)	1,080,800
45.	Total funds applied (Items 38 and 44)	16,127,972
46.	Increase (+) decrease (−) in cash (Item 30 minus Item 45)	-48,565
	CASH ON HAND AND ON DEPOSIT:	
47.	Beginning of year (Item 48, Column 2)	249,024
48.	End of year (Items 46 + 47)	200,459

2   ANNUAL STATEMENT FOR THE YEAR 198—OF THE .... EXAMPLE .... (Name)

Form 1

ASSETS

	1 Current Year	2 Previous Year
1 Bonds	57,570,278	50,907,520
2 Stocks:		
2.1 Preferred stocks	1,053,200	787,400
2.2 Common stocks	3,901,264	3,034,975
3 Mortgage loans on real estate	40,875,208	35,353,143
4 Real estate:		
4.1 Properties occupied by the company (less $ Nil encumbrances)	2,600,000	2,675,000
4.2 Properties acquired in satisfaction of debt (less $ encumbrances)		
4.3 Investment real estate (less $ Nil encumbrances)	2,516,426	2,585,426
5 Policy loans	7,030,800	6,200,000
6 Premium notes, including $ for first year premiums		
7 Collateral loans		
8.1 Cash on hand and on deposit	200,459	249,024
8.2 Short-term investments		
9		
10 Other invested assets		
10A. Subtotals, cash and invested assets (Items 1 to 10)	115,747,635	101,792,488

11 Reinsurance ceded		
11.1 Amounts recoverable from reinsurers		
11.2 Commissions and expense allowances due		
11.3 Experience rating and other refunds due		
11.4		
12		
13 Electronic data processing equipment	900,000	1,250,000
14 Federal income tax recoverable		
15		
16		
17 Life insurance premiums and annuity considerations deferred and uncollected	3,143,422	2,763,995
18 Accident and health premiums due and unpaid	89,427	83,015
19 Investment income due and accrued	1,209,694	1,081,369
20 Net adjustment in assets and liabilities due to foreign exchange rates		
21		
22		
23		
24		
25		
26 Subtotals (Items 10A to 25)	121,090,178	106,970,867
27A From Separate Accounts Statement		
27B From Variable Life Insurance Separate Accounts Statement		
28 Totals (Items 26 to 27B)	121,090,178	106,970,867

NOTE: The items on this page to agree with Exhibit 13 Col. 4
The Notes to Financial Statements are an integral part of this statement.

Form 1   ANNUAL STATEMENT FOR THE YEAR 196- OF THE .... EXAMPLE .... (Name)

3

LIABILITIES, SURPLUS AND OTHER FUNDS

	1 Current Year	2 Previous Year
1 Aggregate reserve for life policies and contracts $ 101,031,319 (Exh. 8, Line H) less $ Nil included in Item 7.3	101,031,319	88,907,938
2 Aggregate reserve for accident and health policies (Exhibit 9, Line C, Col. 1)	561,330	506,722
3 Supplementary contracts without life contingencies (Exhibit 10, Line 7, Col. 5)	2,514,325	2,378,000
4 Policy and contract claims:		
4.1 Life (Exhibit 11, Part 1, Line 4d, Column 1 less sum of Columns 9, 10 and 11)	427,300	335,860
4.2 Accident and health (Exhibit 11, Part 1, Line 4d, sum of Columns 9, 10 and 11)	68,475	54,248
5 Policyholders' dividend and coupon* accumulations (Exhibit 10, Line 7, Col. 6 plus Col. 7)	3,341,950	3,140,080
6 Policyholders' dividends $ 42,500 and coupons* $ due and unpaid	42,500	35,000
7 Provision for policyholders' dividends and coupons* payable in following calendar year—estimated amounts:		
7.1 Dividends apportioned for payment to Dec. 31 19	2,054,000	1,830,000
7.2 Dividends not yet apportioned		
7.3 Coupons* and similar benefits		
8 Amount provisionally held for deferred dividend policies not included in Item 7		
9 Premiums and annuity considerations received in advance less $ Nil discount; including $ Nil accident and health premiums (Exhibit 1, Part 1, Col. 1, sum of Lines 4 and 14)	10,375	8,650
10 Liability for premium and other deposit funds		
11 Policy and contract liabilities not included elsewhere:		
11.1 Surrender values on cancelled policies		
11.2 Provision for experience rating refunds		
11.3 Other amounts payable on reinsurance assumed		
11.4		
12		
13.† Commissions to agents due or accrued — life and annuity $ accident and health $		
13A Commissions and expense allowances payable on reinsurance assumed		
14 General expenses due or accrued (Exhibit 5, Line 12, Col. 4)	194,872	173,398
14A Transfers to Separate Accounts due or accrued, excluding Variable Life Insurance (net)		
14B Transfers to Variable Life Insurance Separate Accounts due or accrued (net)		
15 Taxes, licenses and fees due or accrued, excluding federal income taxes (Exhibit 6, Line 9, Col. 4)	43,052	39,876
15A Federal income taxes due or accrued, including $ Nil on capital gains (excluding deferred taxes)	60,000	53,000
16 "Cost of collection" on premiums and annuity considerations deferred and uncollected in excess of total loading thereon		

17. Unearned investment income (Exhibit 3, Line 10, Col. 2)		
18. Amounts withheld or retained by company as agent or trustee		
19. Amounts held for agents' account, including $ 164,515 .... agents' credit balances	164,515	145,075
20. Remittances and items not allocated		
21. Net adjustment in assets and liabilities due to foreign exchange rates		
22. Liability for benefits for employees and agents if not included above		
23. Borrowed money $ .... and interest thereon $		
24. Dividends to stockholders declared and unpaid		
25. Miscellaneous liabilities (give items and amounts):		
25.1 Mandatory securities valuation reserve (Page 29A, final Item)	1,639,003	1,250,000
25.2 Reinsurance in unauthorized companies	614,827	512,925
25.3 Funds held under reinsurance treaties with unauthorized reinsurers		
25.4 Unreimbursed expenditures by a parent, affiliate or subsidiary company		
25.5 Drafts Outstanding		
25.6 Accrued interest on policyholder's funds	24,742	22,000
25.7		
25.8		
25.9		
25A. From Separate Accounts Statement		
25B. From Variable Life Insurance Separate Accounts Statement		
26. Total Liabilities (Items 1 to 25B)	112,792,585	99,392,772
27A. Capital paid up	1,500,000	1,500,000
27B.		
28. Gross paid in and contributed surplus (Page 3, Item 28, Col. 2 plus Page 4, Item 46a, Col. 1)	1,000,000	1,000,000
29A. Special surplus funds:		
(a)		
(b)		
(c)		
29B. Unassigned funds (surplus)	5,797,593	5,078,095
29C. Less treasury stock, at cost:		
(1) .... shares common (value included in Item 27A $		
(2) .... shares preferred (value included in Item 27A $		
29D. Surplus (total Items 27B + 28 + 29A + 29B − 29C)	6,797,593	6,078,095
30. Totals of Items 27A and 29D (Page 4, Item 50)	8,297,593	7,578,095
31. Totals of Items 26 and 30 (Page 2, Item 28)	121,090,178	106,970,867

†Direct business only, excluding commissions receivable on reinsurance ceded and payable on reinsurance assumed.

*Includes coupons, guaranteed annual pure endowments and similar benefits.

Form 1   ANNUAL STATEMENT FOR THE YEAR 199— OF THE   EXAMPLE

(Name)

14

EXHIBIT 13—ASSETS

	1 Ledger Assets	2 Non Ledger Assets	3 Assets Not Admitted	4 Net Admitted Assets
1. Bonds (Schedule D, Part 1)	58,384,800		814,522	57,570,278
2. Stocks:				
2.1 Preferred stocks (Schedule D, Part 2, Section 1)	1,053,200			1,053,200
2.2 Common stocks (Schedule D, Part 2, Section 2)	3,381,437	519,827		3,901,264
3. Mortgage loans on real estate (Schedule B, Part 1, Sec. 1):				
3.1 First liens	40,959,123		83,915	40,875,208
3.2 Other than first liens				
4. Real estate (Schedule A, Part 1):				
4.1 Properties occupied by the company (less $ Nil encumbrances)	2,600,000			2,600,000
4.2 Properties acquired in satisfaction of debt (less $ encumbrances)				
4.3 Investment real estate (less $ Nil encumbrances)				
5. Policy loans	2,516,426			2,516,426
	7,030,800			7,030,800
6. Premium notes, including $ for first year premiums				
7. Collateral loans (Schedule C, Part 1)				
8.1 Cash on hand and on deposit:				
a. Cash in company's office				
b. Cash on deposit (Schedule E)				
8.2 Short-term investments (Schedule DA)	200,459			200,459
9.				
10. Other invested assets (Schedule BA, Part 1)				
11. Reinsurance ceded:				
11.1 Amounts recoverable from reinsurers (Schedule S, Part 1)				
11.2 Commissions and expense allowances due				
11.3 Experience rating and other refunds due				
11.4				
12. Other assets (give items and amounts): 482,659 less				
12.1 Agents' balances (gross debit $ Nil for doubtful accounts less				
$ 164,515 credit balances)	318,144		318,144	-0-
12.2 Bills receivable				-0-
12.3 Furniture and equipment	275,800		275,800	-0-
12.4 Cash advanced to or in hands of officers or agents				-0-
12.5 Loans on personal security, endorsed or not				-0-
12.6				
13. Electronic data processing equipment	900,000			900,000
14. Federal income tax recoverable				
15.				
16.				

		End of Previous Year	End of Current Year	
17.	Life insurance premiums and annuity considerations deferred and uncollected on in force Dec. 31st of current year (less premiums on reinsurance ceded and less $793,850 .... loading)		3,143,422	3,143,422
18.	Accident and health premiums due and unpaid		89,427	89,427
19.	Investment income due and accrued		1,220,534	1,209,694
20.	Net adjustment in assets and liabilities due to foreign exchange rates		10,840	
21.				
22.				
23.				
24.				
25.				
26.	Totals (Lines 1 to 25)	117,620,189	4,973,210	121,090,178
27A.	From Separate Accounts Statement			
27B.	From Variable Life Insurance Separate Accounts Statement		1,503,221	
28.	Total (Lines 26 to 27B)			121,090,178

EXHIBIT 14—ANALYSIS OF NON-ADMITTED ASSETS AND RELATED ITEMS
(Excluding Investment Adjustments Not Listed)

	1 End of Previous Year	2 End of Current Year	3 Changes for Year Increase (−) or Decrease (+)
1. Loans on company's stock			
2. Supplies, stationery, printed matter			
3. Furniture and equipment	237,500	275,800	−38,300
4. Commuted commissions			X X X
5. Agents' balances (net)	280,550	318,144	−37,594
6. Cash advanced to or in the hands of officers or agents			
7. Loans on personal security, endorsed or not			
8. Bills receivable			
9. Premium notes, etc., in excess of net value and other policy liabilities on individual policies			X X X
10. Accident and health premiums due and unpaid			
11. Other assets not admitted (itemize):			
11.1			
11.2			
11.3			
12. Agents' credit balances (Page 3 Item 19 inside)	145,075 X X X	164,515 X X X	−19,440
13. Total Change			−95,334

*(Carry to Item 35, Page 4)   Business not exceeding 120 months duration.

Form 1   ANNUAL STATEMENT FOR THE YEAR 198— OF THE   EXAMPLE ....
                                                           (Name)

ANALYSIS OF OPERATIONS BY LINES OF BUSINESS (Gain and Loss Exhibit) (Excluding Capital Gains and Losses)

		1 Total **	2 Industrial Life	Ordinary	
				3 Life Insurance	4 Individual Annuities
1.	Premiums and annuity considerations	17,705,635		10,258,896	6,574,572
1A.	Annuity and other fund deposits				
2.	Considerations for supplementary contracts with life contingencies	135,500		x x x	x x x
3.	Considerations for supplementary contracts without life contingencies and dividend accumulations	720,350		350,000	117,350
3A.	Coupons° left to accumulate at interest				
4.	Net investment income	9,130,976		6,466,268	2,199,157
5.	Commissions and expense allowances on reinsurance ceded				
5A.	Reserve adjustments on reinsurance ceded				
6.					
7.	Totals (Items 1 to 6)	27,692,461		17,075,164	8,891,079
8.	Death benefits	1,034,000		1,034,000	x x x
9.	Matured endowments (excluding guaranteed annual pure endowments)	542,000		542,000	x x x
10.	Annuity benefits	2,119,391		x x x	2,119,391
11.	Disability benefits and benefits under accident and health policies	678,286		10,700	
11A.	Coupons, guaranteed annual pure endowments and similar benefits				
12.	Surrender benefits	1,990,000		1,990,000	x x x
13.	Group conversions				x x x
13A.	Transfers on account of group package policies and contracts	x x x	x x x	x x x	x x x
14.	Interest on policy or contract funds	52,242		36,470	12,988
15.	Payments on supplementary contracts with life contingencies	118,600		x x x	x x x
16.	Payments on supplementary contracts without life contingencies and of dividend accumulations	648,758		315,000	102,758
16A.	Accumulated coupon° payments				
17.	Increase in aggregate reserves for life and accident and health policies and contracts	12,177,989		6,697,491	5,365,956
18.	Increase in reserve for supplementary contracts without life contingencies and for dividend and coupon° accumulations	338,195		153,750	48,120
19.					
20.	Totals (Items 8 to 19)	19,699,461		10,779,411	7,649,213
21.	Commissions on premiums and annuity considerations (direct business only)	1,469,736		1,152,610	238,645
21A.	Commissions and expense allowances on reinsurance assumed				
22.	General insurance expenses	2,279,895		1,922,535	259,309
23.	Insurance taxes, licenses and fees, excluding federal income taxes	241,788		217,000	5,370
24.	Increase in loading on and cost of collection in excess of loading on deferred and uncollected premiums	92,916		96,291	-3,375
24A.	Net transfers to (+) or from (−) Separate Accounts (excluding Variable Life Insurance)				
24B.	Net transfers to (+) or from (−) Variable Life Insurance Separate Accounts				
25.					
26.	Totals (Items 20 to 25)	23,783,796		14,167,847	8,149,162
27.	Net gain from operations before dividends to policyholders and federal income taxes (Item 7 minus Item 26)	3,908,665		2,907,317	741,917
28.	Dividends to policyholders	2,007,800		1,877,500	130,300
29.	Net gain from operations after dividends to policyholders and before federal income taxes (Item 27 minus Item 28)	1,900,865		1,029,817	611,617
30.	Federal income taxes incurred (excluding tax on capital gains)	600,200		347,200	213,000
31.	Net gain from operations after dividends to policyholders and federal income taxes (excluding tax on capital gains) (Item 29 minus Item 30).	1,300,665		682,617	398,617

▲ Business not exceeding 120 months duration.   °Includes coupons, guaranteed annual pure endowments and similar benefits.   ** The items in this column to agree with Page 4, Column 1.
†Includes the following amounts for FEGLI/SGLI: Item 1 .... Item 8 .... Item 13 ....

Item 22 .... , Item 23 ....

5 Supplementary Contracts	6 Credit Life [a] (Group and Individual)	Group		Accident and Health		
		7 Life Insurance†	8 Annuities	9 Group	10 Credit [a] (Group and Individual)	11 Other
X X X						872,167
X X X						
135,500				X X X	X X X	X X X
253,000						
304,835						160,716
693,335						1,032,883
			X X X	X X X	X X X	X X X
			X X X	X X X	X X X	X X X
	X X X	X X X		X X X	X X X	X X X
						667,586
			X X X	X X X	X X X	X X X
			X X X			
X X X						X X X
1,823						961
118,600				X X X	X X X	X X X
231,000						
59,934						54,608
136,325						
547,682						723,155
						78,481
1,665						96,386
						19,418
549,347						917,440
143,988						115,443
143,988						115,443
						40,000
143,988						75,443

Form 1   ANNUAL STATEMENT FOR THE YEAR 19██OF THE   EXAMPLE . . . .
                                                                            (Name)

FORM FOR CALCULATING MANDATORY SECURITIES VALUATION RESERVE
(Section 5(D) of NAIC Valuation Procedures and Instructions for Bonds and Stocks)
DATA FROM ANNUAL STATEMENT OF BONDS AND STOCKS OWNED

Bond and Preferred Stock Reserve Component

Bond and Preferred Stock Component as of December 31, of preceding year . . . . $ 700,000   A

Maximum Bond and Preferred Stock Component as of
  December 31, of preceding year   1,367,346   A.1

Line A ÷ Line A.1, (carried to three decimals) 512   A.2

	Statement Value	Reserve Factor		
Bonds in 2% Maximum Reserve Class	$ 54,523,490,	X .001 =	54,523	B
Bonds in 10% Maximum Reserve Class		X .005 =		C
Bonds in 20% Maximum Reserve Class	1,482,916	X .02 =	29,658	D
Preferred Stocks in 5% Maximum Reserve Class	1,053,200	X .0025 =	2,633	E
Preferred Stocks in 20% Maximum Reserve Class		X .01 =		F
Federally Insured Building and Loan and Savings and Loan Shares carried in Schedule D, Part 2		X .001 =		G
Total Securities in Bond and Preferred Stock Component	$		H	

Total Lines B, C, D, E, F and G . . . . $ 86,814   I

Additional Accumulation. If the ratio shown on Line A.2 is equal to or
  greater than .500 show "0" on this line. If lower than .500,
  show the amount indicated on Line I . . . . $ 0   I.1

Total Lines A, I and I.1 . . . . $ 786,814   J

Net Current Year realized and unrealized capital gains (or losses) permitted in the Bond and Preferred Stock Reserve
  Component (see Section 5(A)(b) Paragraphs (1-4) for limitations) . . . . $ -155,076   K

Voluntary Addition $ _____   (see Section 5(A)(c) for limitation).
  Do not include any amount which would make component greater than maximum . . . . $ None   L

Total Lines J, K (minus K, if loss) and L . . . . $ 631,738   M

Minus adjustment (down to Maximum) if Line M is greater than Maximum
  (Maximum is 20 times Lines B, C, E, F and G, plus 10 times Line D) . . . . $ None   N

  Maximum Bond and Preferred Stock Reserve Component . . . . $ 1,439,700   N.1

Bond and Preferred Stock Reserve Component, December 31, of Current Year (Line M minus Line N; if negative, enter "None") . . . . . $ 631,738   O

Common Stock Reserve Component

Common Stock Reserve Component as of December 31, of preceding year		$ 550,000	P
Statement Value of Common Stocks (including $ 5,000 .... statement value of shares of controlled or affiliated companies valued under Section 4(B), but excluding Federally Insured Building and Loan and Savings and Loan Shares and shares of certain wholly owned life insurance subsidiaries—See Section 5(B))		$ 3,901,264	Q
Enter 1% of Line Q		$ 39,013	R
Net Current Year realized and unrealized capital gain (If company has net realized and unrealized capital loss, report "None" here and report net capital loss on Line SL)	$ 418,252 SG.1		
Excess capital losses not yet restored as of December 31 of preceding year*	$ SL.1		
Line SG.1 less Line SL.1 (if negative, report "None")		$ 418,252	SG
Net Current Year realized and unrealized capital loss (Enter net loss as a positive number. If company has net realized and unrealized capital gain, report "None" here and report the net capital gain on Line SG.1		$ None	SL
Voluntary Addition $ .... (see Section 5(B)(c) for limitation). Do not include any amount which would make component greater than maximum		$ None	T
Total of Lines P, R, SG and T minus Line SL.		$ 1,007,265	U
Minus adjustment (down to Maximum) if Line U is greater than Maximum (Maximum is 20% of shares of controlled or affiliated companies valued under Section 4(B)(a)(i) or 4(B)(a)(iii), and federally chartered banks valued under Section 4(B)(a)(ii) — (book value) — included in Line Q above, plus 33⅓% of the balance of common stocks included in Line Q. above)		$	V
Maximum Common Stock Reserve Component	$ 1,299,754 V.1		
Common Stock Reserve Component, December 31, of Current Year (Line U minus Line V: if negative, enter "None")		$ 1,007,265	W

Excess capital losses not yet restored as of December 31, of Current Year Line SL.1 less Line SG.1; (if negative report "None")	$ W.1	
Absolute value of Line U, if negative (if positive, report "none")	$ W.2	
Sum of Lines W.1 and W.2	$ W.3	

Recapitulation of Reserve Components

Bond and Preferred Stock Reserve Component (Line O above)	$ 631,738
Common Stock Reserve Component (Line W above)	$ 1,007,265
Total Mandatory Securities Valuation Reserve, December 31, of Current Year (Page 3. Item 25.1 of Annual Statement)	$ 1,639,003

*See Section 5(B)(b)(i)(ii).

8
Form 1

ANNUAL STATEMENT FOR THE YEAR 198_ OF THE ...... EXAMPLE ...... (Name)

EXHIBIT 2—NET INVESTMENT INCOME

1. Gross investment income (Exhibit 3, Line 10, Col. 7)	9,559,778
2. Investment expenses (Exhibit 5, Line 10, Col. 3)	192,622 †
3. Investment taxes, licenses and fees, excluding federal income taxes (Exhibit 6, Line 7, Col. 3)	9,780 †
4. Depreciation on real estate and other invested assets	144,000
5. Interest paid on borrowed money	82,400
6. Total (Lines 2 through 5)	428,802
7. Net Investment Income—Line 1 less Line 6 (to Page 4, Item 4)	9,130,976
8. Ratio of net investment income to mean assets (see instructions)	8.67 %

†Includes $ _____ investment expenses and $ _____ investment taxes, licenses and fees, excluding federal income taxes, attributable to Separate Accounts.
These items are not deducted from gross investment income in calculating Item 8.

EXHIBIT 3—GROSS INVESTMENT INCOME

	1 Collected During Year	Current Year 2 Unearned	3 Due	4 Accrued	5 Non-Admitted	6 Previous Year 3 + 4 − 2 − 5	7 Earned During Year 1 − 2 + 3 + 4 − 5 − 6
1. U.S. government bonds	* 127,110			23,211		19,941	130,380
1.1 Bonds exempt from U.S. tax	* 237,735			42,792		36,900	243,627
1.2 Other bonds (unaffiliated)	* 4,364,098		5,700	782,897		715,259	4,437,436
1.3 Bonds of affiliates	‡ 25,000						25,000
2.1 Preferred stocks (unaffiliated)	‡ 60,784						60,784
2.11 Preferred stocks of affiliates							
2.2 Common stocks (unaffiliated)	147,966						147,966
2.21 Common stocks of affiliates	250						250
3. Mortgage loans	** 3,405,180		27,465	150,034	10,840	139,269	3,432,570
4. Real estate	§ 665,000						665,000
5. Premium notes, policy loans and liens	378,000			188,435		170,000	396,435
6. Collateral loans							
7.1 Cash on hand and on deposit	• 20,330						20,330
7.2 Short-term investments							
8. Other invested assets							
9. Options							
9.1							
10. Totals	9,431,453		33,165	1,187,369	10,840	1,081,369	9,559,778

*Includes $ 16,603 accrual of discount less $ 1,635 accrual of discount less $ _____ paid for accrued interest on purchases.
amortization of premium and less $ Nil paid for accrued interest on purchases.
‡Excludes $ _____ paid for accrued dividends on purchases.

**Includes $ _____ accrual of discount less $ _____ paid for accrued interest on purchases.
amortization of premium and less $ _____
§Includes $ 315,000 for company's occupancy of its own buildings; and excludes
$ Nil interest on encumbrances.

*EXHIBIT 4—CAPITAL GAINS AND LOSSES ON INVESTMENTS

	1 Increase in Book Value	2 Profit on Sale or Maturity	3 Decrease in Book Value	4 Loss on Sale or Maturity	5 Net Gain (+) or Loss (−) From Change in Difference Between Book and Admitted Values	6 Net Gains (+) or Losses (−) 1 + 2 − 3 − 4 + 5
1. U.S. government bonds				32,016		−32,016
1.1 Bonds exempt from U.S. tax				15,974		−15,974
1.2 Other bonds (unaffiliated)		23,415		101,225	−61,292	−139,102
1.3 Bonds of affiliates						
2.1 Preferred stocks (unaffiliated)						
2.11 Preferred stocks of affiliates						
2.2 Common stocks (unaffiliated)		275,000		32,000	175,252	418,252
2.21 Common stocks of affiliates			**			
3. Mortgage loans					23,912	23,912
4. Real estate			**			
5. Premium notes, policy loans and liens						
6. Collateral loans						
7.1 Cash on hand and on deposit						
7.2 Short-term investments						
8. Other invested assets	X X X		X X X			
9. Foreign exchange		X X X		X X X		
9.1 Options						
9.2						
10. Totals		298,415		181,215	137,872	255,072

10.1 ﹍s federal income taxes incurred on capital gains

10.2 Balance to Surplus Account, Page 4, Item 34 .... Nil 255,072

Distribution of Line 10.2, Col. 6. (Attach statement or memorandum explaining basis of division.)

Net realized capital gains (+) or losses (−) on assets disposed of during the year $117,200 .... less $ Nil .... reflected in previous years' statements and less $ Nil .... federal income tax incurred on capital gains

11. Net realized capital gains (+) or losses (−) 117,200

12. Net unrealized capital gains (+) or losses (−) of the year 137,872

*Adjustments due to amortization to be reported in Exhibit 3.

**Excluding $ .... depreciation on real estate and $ .... depreciation on other invested assets included in Exhibit 2, Line 4.

Form 1

13   ANNUAL STATEMENT FOR THE YEAR 198— OF THE .... EXAMPLE .... (Name)

EXHIBIT 12—RECONCILIATION OF LEDGER ASSETS

INCREASES IN LEDGER ASSETS

1. Premiums on life policies and annuity considerations	16,362,850
1A. Annuity and other fund deposits	
2. Accident and health cash premiums, including $ .... Nil .... policy, membership and other fees (Schedule T, Line 98, Col. 5)	865,755
3. Considerations for supplementary contracts with life contingencies	135,500
4. Considerations for supplementary contracts without life contingencies, including $ .... Nil .... disability	253,000
5. Dividends left with the company to accumulate at interest	467,350
5A. Coupons* left with the company to accumulate at interest	
6. Gross investment income (Exhibit 3, Line 10, Col. 1)	9,431,453
7. Increase of paid up capital during the year	
8. From other sources (give items and amounts):	
8.1.	
8.2.	
8.3.	
9. Borrowed money gross $ .... less amount repaid $	
10. Commissions and expense allowances on reinsurance ceded	
10A. Reserve adjustments on reinsurance ceded	
11.	
12.	
13. From sale or maturity of ledger assets (Exhibit 4, Line 10, Column 2)	243,000
14. By adjustment in book value of ledger assets (Exhibit 4, Line 10, Column 1)	
15. Total Increases in Ledger Assets	27,758,908

DECREASES IN LEDGER ASSETS

16. Policy and contract claims (Exhibit 11, Part 2):	
16.1 Life	1,485,700
16.2 Accident and health	653,359
17. For annuities with life contingencies, excluding payments on supplementary contracts (including cash refund payments)	2,128,951
18. Premium notes and liens voided by lapse, less $ .... restorations	
19. Surrender values	1,990,000
19A. Group conversions	
19B. Interest on policy or contract funds	49,500

20.	Dividends to policyholders:	
	20.1 Life insurance and annuities (Exhibit 7, Line 9, Col. 1)	1,776,300
	20.2 Accident and health (Exhibit 7, Line 9, Col. 2)	
20A.	Coupons, guaranteed annual pure endowments and similar benefits (Exhibit 7, Line 9, Cols. 3 + 4)	
21.	Total Paid Policyholders	8,083,810
22.	Paid for claims on supplementary contracts:	
	22.1 With life contingencies	118,600
	22.2 Without life contingencies	231,000
23.	Dividends and interest thereon held on deposit disbursed during the year	349,600
23A.	Coupons* and interest thereon held on deposit disbursed during the year	417,758
24.		
25.		
26.	Commissions to agents (direct business only):	
	26.1 Life insurance and annuities, including $ Nil commuted commissions	1,391,255
	26.2 Accident and health, including $ Nil commuted commissions	78,481
	26.3 Policy, membership and other fees retained by agents	
26A.	Commissions and expense allowances on reinsurance assumed	
27.	General expenses (Exhibit 5, Line 13, Col. 4)	2,451,043
28.1	Taxes, licenses and fees, excluding federal income taxes (Exhibit 6, Line 10, Col. 4)	248,392
28.2	Federal income taxes, including $ Nil on capital gains	593,200
29.	Decrease of paid up capital during the year	
30.	Paid stockholders for dividends (cash $ 250,000 stock $ Nil	250,000
31.	Borrowed money repaid gross $ less amount borrowed $	
32.	Interest on borrowed money	82,400
32A.	Net transfers to (+) or from (−) Separate Accounts (excluding Variable Life Insurance)	
32B.	Net transfers to (+) or from (−) Variable Life Insurance Separate Accounts	
33.		
34.		
35.		
36.	From sale or maturity of ledger assets (Exhibit 4, Line 10, Column 4)	125,300
37.	By adjustment in book value of ledger assets (Exhibit 4, Line 10, Column 3 and Exhibit 2, Line 4)	144,000
38.	Total Decreases in Ledger Assets	14,215,739
	RECONCILIATION BETWEEN YEARS	
39.	Amount of ledger assets December 31st of previous year	104,077,020
40.	Increase (+) or decrease (−) in ledger assets during the year (Line 15 minus Line 38)	13,543,169
41.	Total — Ledger Assets December 31st of Current Year (Exhibit 13, Line 26, Col. 1)	117,620,189

*Includes coupons, guaranteed annual pure endowments and similar benefits.

Review questions

1. May officers of U.S. life insurance companies use their own judgment in setting asset values for statutory statements? Explain your answer.
(**Answer:** See section 3.1.)

2. What are the prescribed values for the following types of investments, assuming that the security is not in default?
    a) bonds
    b) mortgage loans (first liens)
    c) preferred stocks
    d) common stocks
    e) real estate
    f) collateral loans
(**Answer:** See section 3.2.)

3. At the end of 1980 the agents' debit and credit balances of a U.S. life insurance company are:

Debit balances	$635,000
Credit balances	215,000

What entries should appear in the NAIC balance sheet?
(**Answer:** Agents' credit balances of $215,000 are included in "other liabilities." The agents' debit balances will be treated as a nonadmitted asset and will not appear in the balance sheet. See section 3.2.)

4. A U.S. life insurance company has Canadian dollar assets of US$18,456,972 and liabilities of US$17,546,839 using book exchange rates of Can$1 = US$.85. The current value of the Canadian dollar at the date of the statement is US$.835. What entry is required in the balance sheet?
(**Answer:** Revalued assets = $18,456,972 × .835/.85 = $18,131,261
liabilities = 17,546,839 × .835/.85 = 17,237,189
                                   $ 910,133 $ 894,072
The reduction in excess of assets over liabilities ($910,133 − $894,072) = $16,061 must be entered in item 14 of the liabilities. (See sections 3.2, 20.)

5. What is the purpose of the mandatory securities valuation reserve?
(**Answer:** See sections 3.3, 25.1.)

6. What additions must be made to each of the components of the MSVR?
(**Answer:** See sections 3.3, 25.1.)

7. What deductions may be made from each of the components of the MSVR?
(**Answer:** See sections 3.3, 25.1.)

8. Why is the change in agents' credit balances not included in the reconciliation of ledger accounts?
(**Answer:** See section 3.5.)

9. The following items are taken from the 1980 and 1981 balance sheets of a life insurance company. If the net investment income for 1981 is $5,942,850, calculate the ratio of net investment income to mean invested assets.

	1980	1981
Bonds	$22,835,000	$24,748,000
Stocks	1,936,054	2,611,700
Mortgages	48,250,000	50,275,000
Policy loans	5,214,000	5,725,500
Real estate	2,475,000	2,241,000
Cash	1,302,000	1,963,000
Investment income due and accrued	804,000	875,182
Borrowed money	2,500,000	3,200,000
(**Answer:** Total invested assets (including investment income due and accrued)	$82,816,054	$88,439,382
Less borrowed money	2,500,000	3,200,000
Net invested assets	$80,316,054	$85,239,382
	(A)	(B)

$I = \$5,942,850$

$$\frac{2I}{A + B - I} = \frac{11,885,700}{159,612,556} = .0745)$$

Chapter 4: Preparing Life Insurance Financial Statements According to U.S. GAAP

Statutory accounting practices for U.S. companies / differences between SAP and GAAP / 1974 changes in SEC requirements for stock life insurance company statements / GAAP principles / application to life insurance companies / AICPA Audit Guide principles / premium revenue / recognition of costs / amortization of deferred acquisition costs / reserve increases / recommendations of Academy of Actuaries / policy dividends / investments / reinsurance ceded / purchase accounting / deferred income taxes / SEC statements / examples.

4.1 Introduction

To ensure the solvency of life insurance companies, regulatory authorities in the United States have required that company statements submitted to them be prepared using specified practices, which are now termed Statutory Accounting Practices (SAP).

These practices have led to the establishment of rules for the valuation of assets which are, in some cases, more conservative than prudent management would require. For instance, furniture and equipment (except for EDP equipment) and unsecured amounts owing, such as agents' debit balances, cannot be included in assets, even though the furniture and equipment usually has some value, and at least a portion of the amounts owing is likely to be collected.

Mortgage loans that are not first liens or that exceed a certain percentage of the market value of the property are prohibited in some states. If a life insurer has mortgages which violate statutory requirements, all or a portion of the principal must be treated as a "nonadmitted asset" and excluded from assets in the balance sheet. Collectability of the loan is not considered.

The statutory practices also prescribe minimum standards for policy reserves which specify mortality tables and maximum interest rates. Also, reserves for policies must at least equal cash surrender values. General contingency reserves, such as the Mandatory Securities Valuation Reserve, are treated as liabilities, instead of as allocations of surplus.

While such practices protect the solvency of life insurance companies, they tend to distort the income statement, which measures the results of a company's operations. To enable investors to better judge the earnings of stock life insurance companies, a demand arose for the use of generally accepted accounting principles (GAAP) designed to provide a more reliable income statement.

In 1974 the Securities and Exchange Commission (SEC), which

previously had accepted statements based on statutory accounting practices from life insurance companies, required that statements filed by stock life insurance companies be prepared according to GAAP and audited by independent public accountants. [The form and content of the statements was also prescribed, (4.3).]

Generally accepted accounting principles provide that financial statements should be prepared on the "going-concern" basis, rather than on the assumption that all assets might have to be sold at the date of the statement. Values of assets and liabilities should be conservative but realistic.

According to GAAP, costs of producing revenue should be matched against the resulting revenue. The statutory life insurance practice of charging expenses as they are incurred, instead of amortizing them against premiums, is unacceptable.

Furthermore, financial statements should be objective and should provide full disclosure of all relevant information. There should be no anticipation of revenue or accrual of losses.

Statements prepared under GAAP must follow these general principles. In addition, principles especially applicable to life insurance company statements have been published in "Audits of Stock Life Insurance Companies," an industry audit guide produced by the American Institute of Certified Public Accountants. (See Chapter 2, section 2.5, pages 37-38.)

4.2 Key principles of the Audit Guide

The following paragraphs describe the more important provisions of the Audit Guide.

1. Recognition of premium revenue. The matching of revenues and costs in life insurance is a difficult problem. For example, for level premium individual life insurance policies, revenues are premiums received in level amounts during the premium-paying period. Investment income, on the other hand, is normally received in increasing amounts as the reserve increases. Costs, consisting of commissions, acquisition expenses, maintenance expenses, overhead, increases in reserves and claims, also vary from year to year.

However, the net level premium reserve method results in uniform charges to premiums for claims and increases in reserves. If acquisition costs are deferred, it is reasonable to consider premiums on such contracts as revenue when due, so that, over the life of the contract, premiums for annual and single premium life and endowment insurance should be recognized as earned when due.

Premiums for term insurance on a single premium or limited payment basis (such as credit life insurance) should be recognized as earned each year that a policy is in force. This recognition should be based on the ratio of the amount of insurance in force each year to the total of the annual amounts in force over the life of the policy.

2. Recognition of costs. Costs include acquisition expenses, other expenses and reserve increases. Each type of cost is described below.

a) **Acquisition expenses,** such as sales and issue expenses, vary with and are primarily related to the production and issue of new business. They should be capitalized and amortized in proportion to the premium revenues recognized. The Audit Guide describes three methods of amortizing initial expenses.

The first method, known as the static worksheet method, requires the preparer to:

1) estimate the premiums to be received each year from a block of business using mortality and withdrawal rates,

2) calculate the ratio of acquisition expenses to be deferred to the estimated total premiums to be received, and

3) set the amount to be amortized each year as that ratio of the premiums estimated to be received in the year.

It should be noted, however, that if the actual premiums received differ from the estimates, due to different actual termination rates, the amortized amount in any year will not be in proportion to the premium revenue. In such a case, making periodic adjustments to the ratios to take this into account may make the method impractical.

The second method (dynamic worksheet) is to determine the ratios of the unamortized expenses at the end of each year to the estimated amount of insurance in force at that time. Applying these factors to the actual amount of insurance in force at the end of a year determines the unamortized cost at that time. The amount amortized during the year will be the sum of the unamortized cost at the end of the previous year and the unamortized costs incurred during the year and capitalized, less the unamortized cost at the end of the year. This method automatically corrects for errors in estimates. For instance, if actual termination rates in the year are higher than estimated, the amount of business in force—and therefore of unamortized cost at the end of the year—will be lower, and the amount amortized during the year will be higher.

The third method (the factor method, which is consistent with actuarial reserve calculations) takes interest into account, so that the factors applied to amounts of insurance in force are annuities based on interest, mortality and terminations.

In the latter two methods, the amount of unamortized expense per $1,000 is divided by the factor at issue to determine the amount required for amortization of initial expense out of each premium. Gross premiums must be sufficient to provide for the net valuation premium, the expenses chargeable to each premium (commissions, taxes, administrative expenses and the amount required to amortize initial expenses). If the gross premium is insufficient, one may capitalize only as much initial expense as can be amortized by the amount available.

If the amortization factors are calculated using interest, the amount required from each premium will be higher. The amounts amortized each year will be lower in the earlier years and higher in the later years than would be the case if interest were not used, although the total amount amortized will be the same.

Although the Audit Guide states that actual expenses should be used as long as gross premiums are sufficient to provide for their amortization, estimates of expenses used in the calculation of gross premiums may be used if they do not vary significantly from actual expenses.

Traditionally, there has been reluctance to show unamortized acquisition expenses as assets in life insurance statements because they are not assets in the sense that bonds and mortgages, which can be converted into cash, are. The same effect has been achieved by deducting them in the calculation of policy reserves. Although the Audit Guide concedes this, it states that "the magnitude of deferred acquisition expenses and their effect on reported earnings will be of significant interest to users of insurance company financial statements." As a result, complete disclosure is considered to require separate presentation, which, in turn, requires classification as a deferred charge. However, it is important to note that an asset for unamortized acquisition expenses may only be set up if the expenses included are recoverable; that is, if the gross premium is sufficient to provide the valuation premium for future costs, ongoing renewal expenses and the amount required to amortize deferred acquisition costs.

The actual determination of acquisition expenses subject to deferment is a difficult problem which depends on many factors, including the sales operations of the company, e.g., general agents, branch sales organizations, mail-order, etc. The Audit Guide contains these general guidelines:

> Only those acquisition expenses which both vary with, and are primarily related to, the production of new business should be deferred. These should include renewal commissions based on a descending commission scale even though such expenses are incurred subsequent to issue. The inclusion of any indirect expenses in acquisition expenses requires judgment on the part of both the company and the auditor, with overriding considerations being those of reasonable conservatism, consistency, and recoverability.

Example of amortization of deferred acquisition costs

As an example of the three methods of amortization, envision a 10-payment life policy issued at age 35 with a gross premium of $49.17 per M. Of this amount, $33.24 is the acquisition cost to be deferred. On a block of $100,000 worth of insurance issued in a calendar year, the total premium will be $4,917 and the deferred acquisition cost $3,324. The mortality and lapse rates are assumed to be 1955 Basic Select Male and LIMRA Select Lapse Rates by amount (TSA XXVII, pages 244 and 275 respectively, Table 4.2). If all premiums are payable annually, mortality equals the assumptions and lapses are 10 percent greater, the assumed and actual amounts in force at the beginning of each year and premiums received will be as in Table 4.1.

Table 4.1

YEAR	ASSUMED		ACTUAL	
	SUM INSURED	PREMIUMS	SUM INSURED	PREMIUMS
1	$100,000	$ 4,917	$100,000	$ 4,917
2	87,592	4,307	86,360	4,246
3	82,594	4,061	80,947	3,980
4	78,413	3,856	76,450	3,759
5	74,853	3,681	72,642	3,572
6	71,666	3,524	69,251	3,405
7	69,071	3,396	66,505	3,270
8	66,745	3,282	64,056	3,150
9	64,657	3,179	61,866	3,042
10	62,786	3,087	59,914	2,946
Total premiums		$37,290		$36,287

Using the first (static worksheet) method, the total estimated premiums amount to $37,290 and the amount to be amortized per dollar of premium is $3,324/$37,290 = .08914. The amounts amortized each year, based on estimated premium collections, are shown in Table 4.3. It is evident that the amortization is not in proportion to actual premiums collected. (For example, in the first year the ratio is $438/$4917 = 8.9 percent, and in the tenth it is $275/$2946 = 9.3 percent.)

To use the second (dynamic worksheet) and third (factor) methods (assuming an interest rate of six percent for the factor method), one must calculate annuity values based on the assumed mortality and withdrawal rates for each year. The values are:

Table 4.2

ANNUITY VALUES FOR AMORTIZATION OF ACQUISITION COSTS

YEAR	MORTALITY RATES	WITHDRAWAL RATES	ANNUITY VALUES	
			NO INTEREST	6%
0	.00077	.1233	7.583	6.056
1	.00097	.0561	7.516	6.119
2	.00122	.0494	6.910	5.754
3	.00140	.0440	6.225	5.308
4	.00158	.0410	5.474	4.784
5	.00181	.0344	4.673	4.190
6	.00208	.0316	3.811	3.508
7	.00238	.0289	2.909	2.751
8	.00273	.0262	1.971	1.916
9	.00315	.0239	1.000	1.000

The annuity values may be calculated by starting at the last value, 1.000 (the value of 1 payable immediately). This value is multipled by 1 minus the sum of the death and withdrawal rates for the preceding year (e.g., 1 − .00273 − .0262 = .97107) and divided by 1 plus the interest rate (1.06 for the last column). 1 is added to give the preceding annuity value. All preceding values may be calculated in the same way.

E.g., 1.000 × .97107 / 1.06 + 1 = 1.916
1.916 × .96872 / 1.06 + 1 = 2.751

The annual amortization per $1,000 of insurance in force without interest will be $33.24/7.583 = $4.383. At six percent, it will be $33.24/6.056 = $5.489. Applying these factors, multiplied by annuity values, to the actual amounts in force each year will yield the unamortized acquisition costs, and the annual decreases in the latter will be the amounts amortized, as shown in Table 4.3.

Table 4.3

	METHOD 1 STATIC WORKSHEET		METHOD 2 DYNAMIC WORKSHEET		METHOD 3 FACTOR METHOD	
YEAR	(a)	(b)	(a)	(b)	(a)	(b)
0	$3,324		$3,324		$3,324	
1	2,886	$ 438	2,845	$ 479	2,900	$ 424
2	2,502	384	2,452	393	2,556	344
3	2,140	362	2,086	366	2,227	329
4	1,796	344	1,743	343	1,907	320
5	1,468	328	1,419	324	1,593	314
6	1,154	314	1,111	308	1,281	312
7	851	303	817	294	967	314
8	558	293	535	282	651	316
9	275	283	263	272	329	322
10	0	275	0	263	0	329
		$3,324		$3,324		$3,324

a) Unamortized acquisition costs at end of year
b) Amount amortized in year

b) **Other expenses.** If an expenditure has substantial future utility and is clearly associated with and recoverable from future revenue, it may be considered for separate deferral in line with practices followed in other industries.

Expenses which are not incurred regularly during the life of a policy, such as those connected with terminations and claims, and regular expenses incurred after the premium-paying period, must be provided for during the premium-paying period. This may be done by including them in the reserve calculation.

Some life insurance company expenses, such as policy maintenance and general overhead, are not associated directly with acquiring new business, nor are they appropriate for separate deferral. As in the case of other business enterprises, such expenses should be charged to operations in the period in which they are incurred. Therefore, level renewal expenses in the premium-paying period do not require a reserve, but the expense portion of the gross premium must be adequate to cover such expenses as well as deferred costs. In addition, all renewal expense assumptions should take into account the possible effect of inflation on these expenses.

c) **Reserve increases.** Reserves should take into account reasonable assumptions of interest, mortality and withdrawal at the time the policies are issued. These assumptions should be based on realistic estimates of the rates to be experienced, with a provision for adverse deviations. If underwriting is adequate, a select mortality table should be used.

These reserves may be less than cash values because, employing the going concern concept, it is unreasonable to assume that all policies will be surrendered at the same time.

Periodically, the reserve (less the deferred expense asset for each block of business, valued on the same valuation basis) should be checked against a gross premium valuation based on realistic assumptions of mortality, interest, withdrawals, and maintenance expense. As long as the reserve is sufficient, no change in assumptions should be made. However, if the reserve is insufficient, the possibility of loss should be recognized immediately by changing the valuation assumptions to more realistic bases and making a charge to earnings in the current period to increase reserves or reduce unamortized acquisition expenses.

It should be noted that the above provision results in establishing minimum levels of reserves. The reserves may never be less than those set up when the policies were issued, based on the assumptions appropriate at the time of issue. If future losses are expected, the reserves may be increased by using less favourable assumptions, but such reserves then become the minimum level for subsequent years. The Audit Guide points out that this procedure means that variances from the original estimates are recognized in the periods in which they occur, as long as reserves are maintained at levels sufficient to provide for future benefits and expense.

The assumptions are the professional responsibility of the actuary, who must be able to demonstrate to the auditor that they are "reasonably conservative." Moreover, in determining methods and assumptions used in calculating actuarial reserves and unamortized acquisition expenses, the actuary must take into consideration the Financial Reporting Recommendations and Interpretations (FRRI) of the Academy of Actuaries. An actuary who uses an assumption or a method which conflicts with one of these recommendations should be prepared to justify its use.

FRRI Recommendation 1 deals with actuarial methods and assumptions for use in financial statements of stock life insurance companies prepared in accordance with generally accepted accounting principles. Other recommendations include:

"2. Such actuarial assumptions (a) should be appropriate to the specific circumstances of the company, (b) should be based on experience or estimated experience which is reasonably applicable to the specific business in the light of all the characteristics of that business and the trends of experience which may be reasonably expected in the future, and (c) should be so selected that no portion of the actual gross premium would be available as a specific loading for profit unless the risks of adverse deviation are duly provided for in the valuation premium.

"3. The following should be among the elements considered by the actuary in choosing such actuarial assumptions:

"(a) The character and magnitude of the company's business, the types of business it writes, the age of the company, and its rate of growth.

"(b) Prior experience of the company to the extent that the actuary considers it a valid basis for current assumptions, with due regard for the probable consequences of any significant changes in the method of operation or plans for the future.

"(c) Trends in experience results, economic and investment conditions, governmental or other external influences, and medical and social developments affecting costs and financial requirements.

"4. For non-participating ordinary and industrial life insurance the range of such actuarial assumptions should be constrained by the relationship, *for an entire line of business,* of actual gross premiums to three theoretical valuation premiums:

"Type 1: A Type 1 valuation premium is a premium based on assumptions selected as of the acquisition date which include provisions, selected without regard to the level of the gross premium, for the risks of adverse deviations from the most likely assumptions.

The following example illustrates the rules for determining the valuation premiums and corresponding assumptions. For simplicity, we compare valuation and gross premiums for a single plan and age. In practice, the comparison would be based on data for an entire line or a major block of business.

Assume a 10-year term policy issued at age 35. If the most likely assumptions are those used in the example of the amortization of deferred acquisition costs (Table 4.2), with $3.00 per $1,000 acquisition costs, of which $2.00 is deferrable, $.30 per $1,000 maintenance expenses, 60% first year commission and 5% renewal, the valuation premium (Type 2) will be $2.54 per thousand.

If we provide for adverse deviations by using 105 percent of mortality and withdrawal rates, 5.5 percent interest, and maintenance expenses of $.32 per thousand, the Type 1 valuation premium will be $2.67 per thousand.

If the valuation assumptions which reproduce a gross premium of $2.65 per thousand are 95 percent of mortality rates, 105 percent of withdrawal rates, and 7 percent interest, the valuation premium on that basis (Type 3) will be $2.48 per thousand (since only $2.00 of the acquisition expenses can be deferred). We can set out the following valuation premiums and assumptions to be used for different levels of gross premiums:

GROSS PREMIUM	VALUATION PREMIUM	ASSUMPTIONS
$2.84	$2.67	105% mortality 105% lapse, 5.5%, .32 maintenance
2.65	2.48	95% mortality 105% lapse, 7%, .30 maintenance
2.50	2.50	100% mortality 100% lapse, 6%, .30 maintenance

"Type 2: A Type 2 valuation premium is a premium based on most likely assumptions (i.e., without provision for the risks of adverse deviations) selected as of the acquisition date.

"Type 3: A Type 3 valuation premium is a premium based on assumptions selected as of the acquisition date which substantially reproduce the actual gross premium.

"5. The assumptions for Type 1 valuation premiums and for Type 3 valuation premiums should be so chosen that a reasonable balance is maintained with respect to the provisions for each type of adverse deviation."

Since Type 1 valuation premiums include provisions for the risks of adverse deviations while Type 2 valuation premiums do not, Type 1 valuation premiums will be greater than Type 2 valuation premiums.

The valuation premiums and assumptions to be used depend on the relative level of gross premiums and are specified in items 6, 7 and 8. The specifications may be summarized as follows:

CONDITION	VALUATION PREMIUM	ASSUMPTIONS
6. Gross $>$ = Type 1	Type 1	Type 1
7. Type 1 $>$ Gross $>$ = Type 2	Type 3	Type 3
8. Type 2 $>$ Gross	Gross	Type 2

"9. Assumptions selected as of the acquisition date should be used in computing the reserves for use in all subsequent financial statements prepared by the company in accordance with generally accepted accounting principles unless, at a subsequent valuation date, reserve strengthening is required to recognize future losses. Reserve strengthening is required on a valuation date whenever:

a) The then present value of future benefits and expenses exceeds the sum of

(i) the then present value of future gross premiums and

(ii) the current reserve on the existing valuation basis

for an entire line of business or a major block of business, using most likely assumptions selected as of the valuation date. Reserves on the strengthened basis are the excess of the present value of future costs over the present value of future gross premiums, valued on current most likely assumptions. Reserves on subsequent dates should continue to be valued on those assumptions, unless at a later date further strengthening is required to recognize future losses. It should be noted that, if most likely assumptions are used in the valuation process, there will be a need for frequent review to determine whether additional reserve strengthening becomes necessary as a result of deterioration in the expected experience.

"10. When reserves are calculated according to item 8 or strengthened according to item 9, and when the negative element of the total reserve arising from acquisition expenses is separated and shown as an asset (often labeled 'unamortized acquisition expense'), the effect of the deficiency should be recognized first by reducing the 'unamortized acquisition expense'."

FRRI interpretation 1-A discusses the underlying theory of GAAP accounting, pointing out that one of its main purposes is the matching of cost and revenue through the use of a reserve system which encompasses all elements of cost and presumes the use of actuarial assumptions characterized by reasonable, realistic conservatism.

The interpretation states further:

"3. Accounting theory takes into consideration, among other concerns, the effect of accounting practice on the emergence of profits. Insurance operating profit (or loss, if negative) will, in general, arise from three sources, the three being combined algebraically:

a) The effect of expected experience i.e., most likely assumptions more (or less) favorable than valuation assumptions; plus

b) The effect of actual experience more (or less) favorable than expected experience; plus

c) A specific loading for profit (which may be zero).*

"4. The choice of actuarial assumptions affects the distribution of profit among these sources. The general theory underlying the disciplining of actuarial assumptions for GAAP reserves has been called, by the Joint Actuarial Committee on Financial Reporting, 'the intermediate form of release from risk reserving method'. That form of the release from risk reserving method has the effect of applying the following specific disciplines to the actuarial assumptions and to the relationship between the actual gross premium and the valuation premium based on those assumptions:

a) Each actuarial assumption underlying GAAP reserves should be chosen with regard to providing for the risk of adverse deviation, over and above the most likely assumption,

b) There should be a reasonable balance among the provisions for risk of adverse deviation, both by type of assumption and by policy year,

c) Any specific loading for profit in the actual gross premium is limited to the excess, if any, of the gross premium over the valuation premium based on actuarial assumptions which include appropriate provisions for risks of adverse deviation, and

d) Measures to avoid deferring the recognition of loss should be taken if the actual gross premiums are inadequate."

(Margins should be added only when they tend to defer the reporting of GAAP profit.)

---

*Other sources of profits are items such as interest on GAAP capital and surplus, while losses may be caused by acquisition expenses not eligible for deferment.

"5. With these disciplines, profit from the first source should be positive and will emerge substantially in proportion to release from risk; profit or loss from the second source will emerge each accounting period to the extent that actual experience is more favorable or less favorable than expected experience; and any profit from the third source will emerge substantially in proportion to the receipt of premiums.

"7. The determination of actual gross premiums is the responsibility and prerogative of the company. If the gross premiums so established make relatively small provision for the risk of adverse deviation, the GAAP reserves will be based on actuarial assumptions which produce a valuation premium substantially equal to the actual gross premium, with no specific loading for profit."

Concerning the treatment of expenses, Interpretation 1-C points out:

"2. The Audit Guide's requirement that the negative reserve component reflecting prepaid and amortized acquisition expenses be shown separately as a deferred charge is based on accounting principles, not on actuarial principles. The choice of methods for determining the amount of such deferred charge is not necessarily governed by actuarial principles, but actuarial techniques may be employed in such determination and must be employed to test recoverability of the amount of unamortized acquisition expense. To be consistent with actuarial principles, the difference between the amount carried on the balance sheet as reserve liability and the amount carried as deferred charge on account of unamortized acquisition expense must be substantially equal to the present value of future costs less the present value of future valuation premiums, based on actuarial assumptions determined in accordance with Recommendation 1.

"3. Sound actuarial practice takes account of all elements of future cost, including all maintenance expenses, when testing the adequacy of premiums and reserves to carry policies to completion, and it is good actuarial practice to include actuarial assumptions for level maintenance expenses in reserve computations. For those policies for which level premiums are payable throughout the term of the policy, it is true, as the Audit Guide suggests, that the actuarial assumption for level maintenance expense does not affect the reserve. The reserve for other types of policies may be affected, however, and any maintenance expense assumption which is not level will always affect the reserve. Similarly, unlevel renewal commissions will affect either the reserve or the amount of unamortized expenses."

3. Policy dividends. Many stock companies restrict the amount of earnings on participating business which can inure to the benefit of shareholders. The Audit Guide requires that undistributed earnings on participating business which may not be credited to shareholders not be included in unassigned surplus.

This may be accomplished either by treating future dividends as planned contractual benefits in computing reserves, or by excluding the portion of earnings which cannot be expected to inure to shareholders by a charge to earnings and a credit to an appropriate liability account. If the second method is used, dividends to policyholders declared or paid should be charged to the liability account and any excess charged to operations.

4. Valuation of investments and resulting gains and losses. In 1979, the AICPA issued Statement of Position 793 dealing with accounting for investments for stock life insurance companies. It requires that bonds be carried at amortized cost if the company has both the intent and the ability to hold the bonds until maturity and there is no decline in the market value of the bonds (other than a temporary decline). Common and nonredeemable preferred shares should be carried at market, and mortgages at unpaid principal, or amortized cost if purchased at a discount or premium, unless collectability is uncertain. Real estate investments should be accounted for at depreciated cost unless their value is impaired. (Except for preferred shares, for which admitted values are at cost, these values correspond with admitted values in the United States.)

Investments in unconsolidated subsidiaries should be included at the equity value (under which the paid-in value of stocks is increased or decreased by an appropriate share of the surplus or deficit of the subsidiary) and shown separately.

Realized gains and losses on all assets held for investment are included in the statement of net income, below operating income and net of applicable income taxes. Unrealized investment gains and losses should be recognized in stockholders' equity, net of applicable income taxes. They may not be included in net income.

Real estate is classified as either an investment or property used in the business, based on its primary use. Depreciation and other real estate operating expense are classified as investment expense or operating expense consistent with the balance sheet classification of the related asset. With regard to real estate used in the business (e.g., home office property) an imputed rent should not be charged as an expense and treated as investment income. (This differs from the treatment of property used in the business in the statutory statement.)

5. Reinsurance ceded. The principal recommendations for reinsurance ceded are those contained in Recommendation 4 of the financial reporting recommendations and interpretations of the Academy of Actuaries, which deal with the treatment of reinsurance ceded in financial statements of a stock life insurance company to be presented as having been prepared in accordance with GAAP. Paragraphs 2, 3 and 4 specify:

"2. When reserves are computed according to generally accepted accounting principles, the cost of reinsurance ceded should be taken into consideration in the same manner as other costs. An equivalent alternative to recognizing the cost directly in the reserve calculation is to calculate the reserves without consideration of reinsurance and calculate an adjustment to this reserve for the ceded reinsurance. Although this adjustment is frequently referred to as a "reinsurance credit", it is important to keep in mind that it is actually an adjustment of the basic reserve and has no special independent significance. In particular, there is no necessary relationship between the reinsurance reserve adjustment of the reinsured company and the reserve for reinsurance accepted established by the reinsurer (except in the case of affiliated companies filing consolidated statements).

"3. In determining the reinsurance cost, it is appropriate to take into consideration the expected value of all transactions between the reinsurer and the reinsured including reinsurance premiums, claim reimbursements, experience refunds, and any other benefits or expenses reimbursed by the reinsurer. Because the reinsurance reserve adjustment relates to the reserves for the basic policy, it is important that the assumptions for the reinsurance adjustment be consistent with the original assumptions. When testing for recoverability of acquisition expenses or when testing for the necessity of reserve strengthening to recognize future losses, the expected cost of reinsurance must be taken into consideration.

"4. In practice, the degree of materiality of reinsurance adjustments is such that most companies will be able to use simplified approaches without distorting their financial statements. For example, for YRT, most companies will find it convenient to calculate, as the reinsurance adjustment, the statutory reserve credit, the unearned reinsurance premium, or, possibly, no adjustment at all. For coinsurance where the conditions of reinsurance parallel those of the original insurance, the adjustment to the benefit reserve would usually be proportional to the benefit computed prior to the adjustment for reinsurance, and the expense reserve would need to be adjusted to reflect the amount and incidence of expenses reimbursed by the reinsurer. The same approach would be appropriate for modified coinsurance whenever the interest component of the reinsurance transfer reserve is computed in a manner consistent with the interest assumption in the benefit reserves. The resulting benefit reserve must then be increased by the amount of the reinsurance reserves transferred to the company under the reinsurance arrangement. Special consideration must be given to those reinsurance arrangements which do not parallel those of the original insurance.

Interpretation 4A points out, however, that there will be situations when special care should be given to the assessment of the materiality of a "simplified approach."

"When the amount of reinsurance ceded is a substantial proportion of insurance in force with the ceding company, or when 'special' reinsurance arrangements are in effect, it is incumbent on the actuary to use the approximations suggested in paragraph 4 only

after extensive tests have satisfied him or her that such approximations do not introduce material distortion into the ceding company's
financial statements."

In some cases companies enter into reinsurance arrangements to
improve their surplus position or to minimize income taxes payable.
These agreements frequently provide for a large provisional commission
and accomplish the desired payback through subsequent adjustments of
the provisional commissions, based on experience. Unless there is a
significant transfer of economic risk between the companies, the Audit
Guide warns that the transactions under such agreements should be
regarded as financial arrangements, and net credits arising from this type
of reinsurance treated as a deferred credit or liability by the ceding
company.

6. Purchase accounting. When a life insurance company purchases
another company, subsequent statements of the purchaser must include
the purchased business. GAAP provide two methods of accounting for
such business: the "pooling method" under which the acquired assets and
liabilities are merged with those of the purchaser, and "purchase
accounting" under which the acquired assets and liabilities are accounted
for using special rules.

The pooling method is restricted, by Opinion No. 16 of the Accounting
Principles Board (APB), to cases in which the proprietary interests of
previously independent organizations are merged by the exchange of
common stock. In addition, its use is generally straightforward because
the same rules apply to both purchased and other business. Therefore, the
following discussion will concentrate on purchase accounting.

When one corporation is purchased by another, any excess of the
purchase price over the fair market value of the purchased assets minus
that of the purchased liabilities is assumed to be paid to obtain future
earnings. For this reason, the assets and liabilities purchased must be
entered into the balance sheet of the purchasing corporation at fair market
values, and the excess set up as an intangible asset, "goodwill," to be
written down by systematic charges against earnings in future years.
Under this procedure, the purchase causes neither a gain nor a loss in the
year of purchase and the excess paid over fair market value is disclosed.
If future earnings realized from the purchase are greater (or less) than the
charges to goodwill, earnings will be increased (decreased) until the
goodwill is written off. (The length of the period over which the goodwill
is to be written off is obviously important, and most accountants would
recommend a period well under the maximum of 40 years.)

Corbett (TSA XXVII, p. 313) points out that three types of assets are
usually acquired in the purchase of a life insurance company: an adjusted
statutory surplus, a block of in-force business and intangibles such as
agency organization, charter and management. The restated fair value of
statutory surplus requires that invested assets be revalued at market; that
nonadmitted assets and reserves such as the mandatory securities
valuation reserve be added back, and that claims liabilities and accounts
payable be fairly stated.

The value of the block of in-force policies may be taken as the present value of estimated future profits using "best estimate" assumptions of mortality, investment income, withdrawals and expenses, and using a reasonable rate of return. If the value was calculated in good faith before the purchase, it may be taken as the amount of the purchase price allocated to this asset. If the value has not been previously calculated, it is necessary to arrive at a value based on realistic assumptions.

The excess of the purchase price over the amounts allocated to the preceding assets will be taken as the value of intangibles, or goodwill, which must be amortized over the future periods estimated to be benefited by the intangibles in question.

The determination of policy reserves for the in-force business is dealt with an Interpretation 1-D of the FRRI:

"1. It is stated in Recommendation 1 that reserves computed under "Purchase Accounting" situations should be based on assumptions which are chosen as of the date of purchase. Several methods of computing reserves in these situations have been developed. The following two methods are recognized as producing results consistent with the application of Recommendation 1 to other business.

"a) Defined Initial Reserve Method. The initial reserve is taken as a predetermined amount. Using this initial reserve and actuarial assumptions appropriate to the business which include provisions for adverse deviations, valuation premiums are computed which may be used in subsequent valuations. If the resulting valuation premiums exceed the gross premiums, the provisions for adverse deviations may be reduced to the extent necessary to avoid this deficiency, except that in no event may the valuation assumptions be less conservative than most likely assumptions.

"If valuation premiums exceed gross premiums under most likely assumptions, the gross premiums should be used as valuation premiums and reserves should be computed using most likely assumptions. The excess of the reserves over the predetermined amount may be treated as goodwill.

"If the resulting valuation premiums are negative, reserves should be taken as the present value of future benefits and expenses, and the excess of the predetermined amount over the reserves may be treated as negative goodwill. Such a situation could occur if a large portion of the business is paid up.

"Although, under the Defined Initial Reserve Method, the initial reserve is taken as a predetermined amount, the total reserve must then be allocated to each plan, issue year and issue age cell.

"In arriving at the predetermined amount, it would be appropriate to use the amount determined by the purchaser in establishing the purchase price, so long as elements of the purchase price were bargained for in good faith and the predetermined amount gave due consideration to appropriate provisions of APB Opinion No. 16 relating to the allocation of the purchase price and the subsequent accounting thereof. If the purchase price has been determined by a method which uses book values for the assets of the purchased company, the Defined Initial Reserve Method is not appropriate for determining the reserves for the individual business.

"b) Defined Valuation Premium Method. Valuation premiums for the acquired business are taken as the gross premiums less a reasonable profit allowance for the risk assumed by the acquiring corporation. Reserves are then computed as the present value of future benefits and maintenance expenses less the present value of future valuation premiums, using assumptions appropriate to the business which include provision for adverse deviations.

"In applying the Defined Valuation Premium Method a determination of a reasonable profit allowance must be made. The profit allowance and the provision for adverse deviation used in determining the reserves should be consistent with those which apply to current new business issued by the company which will be assuming the future risk on the acquired business. This may be either the acquiring company or the purchased company, depending whether or not the purchased company is continued as a separate entity or merged with the purchaser.

"2. Under both methods, assumptions for experience after the date of purchase are to be chosen as of the purchase date. The interest assumptions should be chosen with due consideration to the investment income which will be generated by the assets attibutable to the business, which will have been revalued to market at the time of purchase. Mortality, expense and lapse assumptions should reflect current experience rather than the historical assumptions appropriate at the time the policies were originally issued by the purchased company. Assumptions for future maintenance expenses should be appropriate for the company which will be maintaining the business in the future, which may be either the acquiring company or the purchased company.

"3. In applying either of the above methods, the actuary should consider the reasonableness of the results. The reasonableness of the Defined Initial Reserve Method may be judged by examining the relation of valuation premiums to gross premiums. The reasonableness of the Defined Valuation Premium Method may be judged by comparing the amount of goodwill to other items in the financial statement.

[Douglas A. Eckley has criticized both the defined initial reserve method and the defined valuation premium method, maintaining that the use of a gross premium reserve with provision for adverse deviations in the assumptions is the most practical approach and most consistent with GAAP. If the use of the gross premium reserve would result in an immediate profit or loss, the reserve should be adjusted to eliminate the profit or loss by adjusting the margins for adverse deviation or, in the case of a profit, by an arbitrary adjustment, and in the case of a loss, by recognizing the loss immediately. (TSA XXXIV, p. 449.)]

"4. It is required for purposes of presentation of the financial statement to divide the reserve into an asset item and a liability item. One technique for accomplishing the division is to calculate valuation premiums, using the assumptions adopted in accordance with paragraph 2, which have a present value equal to the deferred acquisition cost carried by the purchased company at the date of purchase. This amount could then be added to both assets and liabilities so as to produce a deferred acquisition cost and increase the benefit reserve. Another technique would be to determine the additional valuation premiums necessary to make the benefit reserve equal to the benefit reserves carried by the purchased company at the purchase date, and to add the present value of these additional premiums to both assets and liabilities, so as to produce a deferred acquisition cost asset. A third technique would be to split the valuation premium into an expense valuation premium and a benefit valuation premium in the same proportion as the valuation premium is split on new issues.

"5. When, because of purchase accounting rules, cumulative deferred tax credits are eliminated from the balance sheet, reserves for the insurance then in force should be sufficient to provide for future Federal Income Taxes which are expected to be generated by such business.

"6. If the cost of the purchased company exceeds net assets (assets less liabilities) acquired, the excess should be amortized in accordance with the requirements of prevailing accounting rules. If the excess arises only in connection with the acquisition of existing individual life insurance business, the actuary may, for example, compute an amortization method which is proportionate to the GAAP profits expected to emerge from the business, based on the revised valuation assumptions. If the excess arises from other lines of insurance or from business to be generated in the future by the existing management and agency plant, the actuary may compute an amortization method which is proportionate to the projected GAAP profits from all sources.

"7. If the net assets of the purchased company exceed the cost, it may be appropriate to reduce valuation net premiums for the existing insurance in force, so as to increase future profit margins. The reduction should first be applied to the portion of the premiums representing deferred acquisition costs."

7. Deferred income taxes. Because the accounting treatment of taxable income is based on rules which, in some respects, differ from both statutory and GAAP accounting, differences between accounting income and taxable income often arise. If these differences concern the time of inclusion of items of revenue and expense in the computation of taxable income, generally accepted accounting principles provide that the incidence of taxes on specific transactions be recorded in the period in which the transactions are recognized for accounting purposes. This means that the income tax charged in published statements will differ from that actually paid, requiring the establishment of an asset or liability for deferred income taxes.

The Audit Guide requires that this practice be followed for life insurance companies, pointing out that the most significant timing differences concern increases in GAAP reserves and those used for tax purposes, and the deferral and amortization of acquisition costs, which affect gain from operations. (Therefore, only companies taxed on gain from operations need be concerned with these timing differences.)

For example, suppose the increase in reserves allowed for income tax (based on statutory reserves) is $12,000,000, while the increase in GAAP reserves is $11,000,000 and the increase in deferred policy acquisition expenses is $500,000, a net difference of $1,500,000. Income presented according to GAAP will therefore be increased over taxable gain from operations by this amount. Since increases in reserves are eventually decreased as the policies involved terminate, the position will be reversed in future years. Thus, to charge GAAP income with the tax actually paid will distort after-tax income for current and future years. Therefore, the correct procedure is to charge GAAP income with income tax based on it, and credit the excess over the tax paid to deferred taxes.

Although differences in reserves and the deferral and amortization of acquisition costs will also affect taxable investment income (due to differences in interest amounts required to maintain reserves), the differences affect only total assets or aggregate reserves. These amounts will always be greater or less than comparable amounts for tax purposes. Accordingly, amounts of such differences do not reverse in subsequent periods, making tax adjustments unnecessary.

8. Nonadmitted assets. Nonadmitted assets should be restored to the balance sheet where appropriate. Receivables, however, must be reviewed to determine collectability, and appropriate valuation reserves established by a charge to income.

4.3 SEC statements

Financial statements filed with the Securities and Exchange Commission must conform with Regulation S-X, which spells out the requirements for their form and content. In addition to providing that statements of stock life insurance companies be prepared according to GAAP, the regulation specifies that the presentation of certain items be different from that in statutory statements (Rules 7a-01 to 7a-06). The SEC-required treatment of each of these items is listed below.

Balance Sheet

1. Investments in affiliates must be shown separately from other investments
2. For accounts receivable, the balance of the allowance for doubtful accounts which was deducted must be shown.
3. That portion of deferred and uncollected premiums which represents the adjustment of future policy benefits must be deducted from the

liability for future policy benefits, and that portion which represents the adjustment of acquisition costs must be added to deferred acquisition costs.

4. Deferred acquisition costs shall not be deducted from future policy benefits.

5. The depreciated cost of real estate, furniture and equipment used in the conduct of the insurance business and not considered an investment must be included in property and equipment.

Income statement

1. Considerations for supplementary contracts shall be reduced by the related amounts of death and other benefits and increases in future policy benefits.

2. The amount of deferred acquisition costs amortized to income during the period shall be stated separately.

3. Other operating costs and expenses should include all selling, general and administrative expenses not deferred as policy acquisition costs.

4. Equity in unconsolidated subsidiaries should be stated separately net of any applicable tax provisions.

Schedules

In addition to the financial statements, a number of schedules must be submitted, including summaries of the different classes of assets, policy liabilities and insurance in force. Details of deferred acquisition costs, reinsurance ceded, and the calculation of the liability for income tax must also be provided.

4.4 Examples of GAAP statements

In order to illustrate the preparation of GAAP statements, a set of adjustments (e.g., policy reserves on an assumed GAAP basis, deferred income tax amounts, etc.) has been prepared and listed in Example 4.1. GAAP statements are then prepared, showing the adjustments made to the statutory statements in Chapter 3, pages 118-137 to produce GAAP figures. (See Examples 4.2 and 4.3.)

This procedure has been followed to illustrate the differences between the GAAP statements and the NAIC statements. However, while this method is followed by some companies in preparing GAAP statements, others use a separate procedure, independent of the preparation of NAIC statements.

For easier reference, all items in the list of adjustments have been numbered, so that adjustments in the various statements may be traced back. Items in the balance sheet referred to in the income statement and capital and surplus account are indicated by single capital letters. Items in the income statement whose presentation differs from that in the statutory statement of operations are indicated by double capitals.

For example, the item "increase in statutory loadings on due and deferred premiums" does not appear in the GAAP income statement. The increase in loadings on deferred premiums (DD) is added to the increase in liabilities for future policy benefits, while the increase in loadings on due premiums (AA) is deducted from premium income.

Balance Sheet (Example 4.4)

Bonds. Since investments in affiliates must be shown separately, and bonds are listed at amortized cost, the bond value is decreased by the transfer of bonds of affiliates to a separate category and increased by nonadmitted bond values.

Mortgages. Statutory values are increased by nonadmitted assets.

Preferred stocks. Valued at market instead of cost.

Investments in affiliates. The value of stocks includes a share of the unappropriated surplus of the affiliate. (In the statutory statement investments in affiliates are combined with and valued in the same manner as similar investments.)

Due and accrued investment income. Increased by the amount nonadmitted in the statutory statement.

Amounts receivable. Agents' debit balances are included at the ledger values less an allowance for uncollectable amounts.

Property and equipment. Includes home office real estate and furniture and equipment at depreciated values. Original cost (calculated by adding the accumulated depreciation to the depreciated values) is shown less accumulated depreciation.

Unamortized acquisition costs. The amount calculated assuming annual premiums is increased by the deferred expense portion of deferred premiums.

Due and uncollected premiums life. Net deferred premiums are deducted from the amount in the statutory statement since they are to be treated as deductions from policy reserves; the change in the basis of policy reserves for GAAP results in changes in net due premiums.

Policy reserves. Policy reserves are valued on assumptions of interest, mortality and withdrawal considered reasonable when the policies were issued. Individual reserves may be less than cash values. Net deferred premiums (on GAAP bases) are deducted from policy reserves. If reserves are not calculated on the assumption that the annual premium is paid on the policy anniversary, this deduction is not necessary. (See Statement of Income below, under Premiums.)

Provision for policyholders' dividends payable in the following calendar year. Not required since policy reserves include reserves for future policy dividends.

Deferred income tax. Required by GAAP.

MSVR and reserve for unauthorized reinsurance. These reserves are not considered as liabilities for the GAAP statement, although it would be correct to set up a reserve for business reinsured with a company whose financial position is questionable.

Stockholders' Equity. This is a new category of the balance sheet required by GAAP. It includes capital, contributed surplus, unrealized capital gains or losses on investments, appropriations of surplus and unappropriated surplus.

Reserve for mortgage loans. A reserve for mortgage loans which may prove to be uncollectable is set up as an allocation of surplus. If necessary, reserves for other investments or other contingencies could also be set up as allocations of surplus.

Unappropriated surplus. Net increases in asset values and decreases in liabilities increase unappropriated surplus, while increases in appropriated surplus decrease it.

Statement of income (Example 4.5)

Premiums. In the statutory statement of operations, the increase in gross due and uncollected premiums, and in gross deferred premiums, are added to premiums collected, and the increase in premiums in advance is deducted. For GAAP statements, Recommendation 5 of the Academy of Actuaries provides that premiums may be recognized either when due and paid; when due, or continuously throughout the policy year. (This does not imply a contradiction with the requirements of the Audit Guide (4.2,1), which call for the recognition of premiums throughout the term of the contract, not during a single policy year.) The second method is commonly used in life insurance and the third in accident and health insurance.

In the first case, the increase in premiums paid in advance must be deducted from premiums collected; in the second, the increase in due and uncollected premiums must be added and the increase in advance premiums deducted. In both cases, if the policy reserves are calculated on the assumption that an annual premium is paid on the anniversary, net deferred premiums must be deducted from the liability for future policy benefits.

In the third case, the increases in advance premiums and unearned premiums must be deducted from premiums collected, and the increase in due and uncollected premiums added to the result. If reserves have been calculated assuming continuous payment of premiums (for instance, by using mid-terminal reserves), no adjustment for deferred premiums is to be used.

The example assumes that premiums are recognized when due, so that the increase in due and uncollected premiums and the increase in the deferred acquisition expense portion of deferred premiums are added to premiums collected, and the increase in advance premiums deducted. Net deferred premiums are deducted from the liability for future policy benefits.

The increase in the loadings on due premiums is shown in the example in two parts: 1) the increase in statutory loadings, and 2) the excess of the increase in GAAP loadings over the increase in statutory loadings, since the former refers to an item in the statutory statement of operations, and the latter to the list of adjustments and the balance sheet.

Increase in policy reserves. The amount in the statutory statement is reduced by adjustments in policy reserves resulting from changes in valuation bases, and by the increase in net GAAP deferred premiums. The increase in net deferred premiums is broken down into the increase in gross deferred premiums; the increase in statutory loadings, and the change from statutory net premiums to GAAP net premiums.

In accordance with Regulation S-X, the payments on supplementary contracts and the increase in reserve have been netted against considerations. However, since this results in a negative item, it has been included in the increase in policy reserves. It would be possible to show it as a separate disbursement item.

Dividends to policyholders. The statutory amount has been reduced by the increase in reserves for dividends payable in the following policy year, which was eliminated from the liabilities.

Amortization of deferred acquisition costs. Shown separately as required by Regulation S-X.

Other operating costs and expenses. Includes commissions, general expenses and taxes, licenses and fees. Reduced by deferred acquisition expenses capitalized and by home office rent less real estate expenses.

Increase in loading on due and deferred premiums. The calculation of actuarial reserves and deferred policy acquisition expense on the assumption that premiums are collected and expenses incurred annually on the policy anniversary requires adjustments for due and uncollected premiums. The assumption that premiums are recognized when due requires that premium income include the increase in nct due and uncollected premiums plus the deferred policy acquisition expense portion of those premiums. Thus, no item for increases in loadings on due and deferred premiums is required in GAAP income statements, since the increase in net due and uncollected premiums plus the DPAE portion is included in premium income, while the increase in net deferred premiums is deducted from actuarial reserves.

In the example, the transfers of statutory loadings are shown separately from the adjustments due to the change in net premiums from statutory to GAAP treatment.

Income tax. Statutory income tax is increased by the increase in deferred income taxes.

Realized investment gains. Statutory net investment gains include both realized and unrealized gains, as well as changes in nonadmitted invested assets. Unrealized investment gains from the statutory statement are deducted to leave realized investment gains.

Unrealized investment gains (Example 4.7). The changes in nonadmitted assets must be excluded from statutory unrealized investment gains to obtain the amount for the GAAP statement. The increase of $178,297 can also be obtained as the sum of the unrealized gain on common stocks of $175,252 plus that on preferred stocks of $3,045.

The example assumes that there are no statutory or other restrictions on the amount of profits earned on participating business that may be credited to stockholders. The policyholders' interest was determined by setting up a reserve for future dividends according to the dividend scale at the date of issue as though they were guaranteed benefits.

For a company to which such restrictions apply, no reserve for future dividends is required, but the profit earned on participating business must be calculated each year (allocating expenses, investment income and other items using some reasonable method). The portion of the profit to which stockholders are not entitled must be charged to operations and credited to a special liability account. Dividends declared or paid must be charged to this liability account. Any dividends paid in excess of the credits to the liability account must be charged to operations.

4.5 General considerations

It is apparent that the use of GAAP produces financial statements which differ considerably from statutory statements and eliminates many of the distortions which SAP create in the income statement. However, it is not surprising that some proponents of GAAP were somewhat disappointed with the results.

Even the most informative financial statements are limited in their ability to convey to a reader the strengths and weaknesses of a corporation. Moreover, one year is an extremely short period in which to measure the profitability of a long-term business, such as life insurance. The significance of policy reserves and deferred acquisition costs makes a comparison between companies very much dependent on the relative conservatism of the valuation assumptions underlying the calculation of those amounts, and there is still considerable variation in such assumptions. (For example, in a 1980 survey of 65 U.S. companies, the interest assumptions proposed to be used for GAAP reserves on current nonparticipating issues ranged from 5.5 percent to 10 percent with a mean of 7.5 percent for the first five years, and from 3.5 percent to 7 percent with a mean of 5.5 percent for durations after 30.) While the inclusion of a description of the assumptions used in the notes to the financial statements can give a reader of the statements some indication of the relative conservatism of the assumptions, it is not possible for the reader to determine the financial effect of the use of one set of assumptions instead of another.

Example 4.1

To illustrate the differences between SAP and GAAP, data required for the GAAP statement have been prepared for the example used in Chapter 3 to illustrate the NAIC life and health annual statement. These data are listed below with references to the paragraphs above in which the requirements are described.

2(a) Deferred acquisition costs. Since mortality, interest and withdrawal assumptions must be used in the amortization of deferred acquisition costs, a method similar to that used for the calculation of policy reserves has been used, preparing factors for unamortized costs per $1,000 in force by duration for each major category of business and applying the appropriate factors to amounts in force at the valuation date.

1.	Unamortized acquisition costs 19A	$3,768,935
2.	Commissions deferred 19B	775,795
3.	General expenses deferred 19B	134,000
4.		$4,678,730
5.	Less amount amortized 19B	491,024*
6.	Unamortized acquisition costs 19B	$4,187,706

*Items 1 and 6 are determined using the calculated factors; this amount is the balancing item.

2(c) Policy reserves. Policy reserves are calculated using assumptions of interest, mortality and withdrawal considered reasonable at the time the policies were issued. Since, for this example, it is assumed that there are no restrictions on the amount of profits from participating business which may be credited to stockholders, a reserve for future dividends according to the scale at the date of issue is included.

The change in valuation bases results in changes in the net due and deferred premiums. Since a portion of the gross premiums is required to amortize deferred acquisition expenses, the amount of this expense allowance included in deferred premiums must be calculated and included in the deferred acquisition expense asset value.

		GAAP	SAP	DIFFERENCE
Policy reserves life 19A				
7.	Guaranteed benefits	$ 76,626,006	$ 88,907,938	
8.	Future dividends	7,211,629		
9.		$ 83,837,635	$ 88,907,938	$ −5,070,303
10.	Gross deferred premiums	2,509,789	2,509,789	
11.	loadings	832,142	543,503	288,639
12.	Net deferred premiums	$ 1,677,647	$ 1,966,286	$ −288,639
13.	Due premiums: gross	955,140	955,140	
14.	loading	190,674	157,431	33,243
15.	net	$ 764,466	$ 797,709	$ −33,243

Policy reserve life 19B

16.	Guaranteed benefits	87,388,144	101,031,319	
17.	Future dividends	7,623,902		
18.		$ 95,012,046	$101,031,319	−6,019,273
19.	Deferred premiums: gross	2,837,822	2,837,822	
20.	loading	961,201	608,509	352,692
21.	net	$ 1,876,621	$ 2,229,313	−352,692
22.	Due and uncollected: gross	1,099,450	1,099,450	
23.	loading	225,683	185,341	40,342
24.	net	$ 873,767	$ 914,109	−40,342

Acquisition expenses included
in deferred premiums

25.	19A	$	489,505
26.	19B		593,108

4. Investments

Preferred stocks are carried at market and investments in affiliates at their equity value.

Year 19A

27.	Preferred stocks	$ 848,540	787,400	61,140
28.	Stocks of affiliates	6,417	5,000	1,417

Year 19B

29.	Preferred stocks	$ 1,117,385	1,053,200	64,185
30.	Stocks of affiliates	7,385	5,000	2,385

Imputed investment income and real estate expenses for home office property are not in investment income and expenses.

Year 19B

31.	Home office rent	$	315,000
32.	Home office real estate expenses		−49,250
33.	Depreciation of home office property		−75,000
34.	Net adjustment	$	190,750

Unrealized investment gains, less applicable income tax, are shown as a separate item in stockholders' equity.

35.	Unrealized capital gains 19A	$	405,715
36.	19B		584,012
37.	Increase	$	178,297

5. Deferred income taxes

38.	Deferred income tax 19A		517,000
39.	19B		859,000

6. Nonadmitted assets

Nonadmitted assets are included in the balance sheet, but reserves for accounts receivable such as agents' debit balances are deducted from the assets, and a reasonable reserve for mortgages which may prove to be uncollectable is set up as an appropriation of surplus.

		19B	19A	INCREASE
40.	Bonds	$814,522	$753,230	$ 61,292
41.	Mortgages	83,915	107,827	-23,912
42.	Reserve for mortgages	35,000	03,500	31,500
43.	Furniture and equipment*	275,800	237,500	38,300
44.	Agents' debit balances	482,659	425,625	57,034
45.	Reserve for uncollectable			
	agents' debit balances	195,817	175,415	20,402
46.	Mortgage interest due	10,840		2,088

*Depreciated values

Under GAAP, the presentation of depreciable assets requires that the original cost and accumulated depreciation be shown; the accumulated depreciation amounts for such assets are listed below.

Accumulated depreciation				
47.	Investment real estate	276,000	207,000	69,000
48.	Home office real estate	875,000	800,000	75,000
49.	EDP equipment	1,050,000	700,000	350,000
50.	Furniture and equipment	314,215	279,590	34,625
51.		$2,239,215	$1,779,590	$459,625

Example 4.2

BALANCE SHEET—STATUTORY BASIS

ASSETS

		YEAR 19B	YEAR 19A
1.	Bonds	$ 57,570,278	$ 50,907,520
2.	Stocks:		
	2.1 preferred	1,053,200	787,400
	2.2 common	3,901,264	3,034,975
3.	Mortgage loans on real estate	40,875,208	35,353,143
4.	Real estate:		
	4.1 properties occupied by the company	2,600,000	2,675,000
	4.3 investment real estate	2,516,426	2,585,426
5.	Policy loans	7,030,800	6,200,000
8.	Cash on hand and on deposit	200,459	249,024
10 A	Subtotals, cash and invested assets	115,747,635	101,792,488
12.	Electronic data processing equipment	900,000	1,250,000
17.	Life insurance premiums and annuity considerations deferred and uncollected	3,143,422	2,763,995
18.	Accident and health premiums due and unpaid	89,427	83,015
19.	Investment income due and accrued	1,209,694	1,081,369
	Totals	$121,090,178	$106,970,867

LIABILITIES, SURPLUS AND OTHER FUNDS

1.	Aggregate reserve of life policies and contracts	$101,031,319	$ 88,907,938
2.	Aggregate reserve for accident and health policies	561,330	506,722
3.	Supplementary contracts without life contingencies	2,514,325	2,378,000
4.	Policy and contract claims:		
	4.1 life	427,300	335,860
	4.2 accident and health	68,475	54,248
5.	Policyholders' dividend accumulations	3,341,950	3,140,080
6.	Policyholders' dividends due and unpaid	42,500	35,000
7.	Provision for policyholders' dividends payable in the following calendar year	2,054,000	1,830,000
9.	Premiums and annuity considerations received in advance	10,375	8,650
14.	General expenses due or accrued	194,872	173,398
15.	Taxes, licenses and fees due or accrued	43,052	39,876
15 A	Federal income taxes due or accrued	60,000	53,000
19.	Agents' credit balances	164,515	145,075
25.	Miscellaneous liabilities		
	25.1 Mandatory securities valuation reserve	1,639,003	1,250,000
	25.2 Reinsurance in unauthorized companies	614,827	512,925
	25.6 Accrued interest on policyholders' funds	24,742	22,000
26.	Total liabilities	112,792,585	99,392,772
27 A	Paid-up capital	1,500,000	1,500,000
29 B	Unassigned funds	6,797,593	6,078,095
		$121,090,178	$106,970,867

Example 4.3

SUMMARY OF OPERATIONS (STATUTORY) 19B

Premiums and considerations for annuities: life	$16,833,468
accident and health	872,167
Consideration for settlement annuities: life	135,500
certain and dividend accumulations	720,350
Net investment income	9,130,976
Total	$27,692,461
Death benefits	$ 1,034,000
Matured endowments	542,000
Annuity payments	2,119,391
Accident and health benefits	678,286
Surrender values	1,990,000
Interest on policy or contract funds	52,242
Payments on settlement annuities: life	118,600
certain and dividend accumulations	648,758
Increase in policy reserve	12,177,989
Increase in reserves for supplementary contracts certain and dividend accumulations	338,195
Commissions	1,469,736
General expenses	2,279,895
Taxes, licenses and fees	241,788
Increase in loading on due and deferred premiums	92,916
Total	$23,783,796
Net gain before dividends and income tax	3,908,665
Dividends paid	2,007,800
Net gain before income tax	1,900,865
Income tax	600,200
Net gain after dividends and income tax	$ 1,300,665

Example 4.4
BALANCE SHEET GAAP BASIS
ASSETS

	ADJUSTMENTS	19B	19A	ADJUSTMENTS	INCREASE IN ADJUSTMENTS
Cash and investments	$	$	$	$	$
Cash		200,459	249,024		
Bonds amortized cost (statutory)					
in affiliates	−250,000	57,570,278	50,907,520	−250,000	
non-admitted (40)	814,522	564,522	503,230	753,230	61,292 A
Mortgages amortized cost (statutory)		$ 58,134,800	$ 51,410,750		
		40,875,208	35,353,143		
non-admitted (41)	83,915	83,915	107,827	107,827	−23,912 B
Preferred stocks at cost (statutory)		$ 40,959,123	$ 35,460,970		
excess market over		1,053,200	787,400		
cost (27,29)	64,185	64,185	61,140	61,140	3,045 C
Common stocks market (statutory)		$ 1,117,385	848,540		
		3,901,264	3,034,975		
affiliated (28,30)	−5,000	−5,000	−5,000	−5,000	
		$ 3,896,264	$ 3,029,975		
Policy loans		7,030,800	6,200,000		
Real estate (less accumulated depreciation $276,000)		2,516,426	2,585,426		
Investments in affiliates equity basis (28,30)	7,385			6,417	968 D
bonds	250,000	257,385	256,417	250,000	
Total		$ 257,385	$ 256,417		
		$114,112,642	$100,041,102		
Due and accrued investment income (statutory)		1,209,694	1,081,369		
non-admitted (46)	10,840	10,840	8,752	8,752	2,088 E
		$ 1,220,534	$ 1,090,121		

(continued)

Example 4.4 (Continued)

BALANCE SHEET GAAP BASIS

ASSETS

	ADJUSTMENTS	19B	19A	ADJUSTMENTS	INCREASE IN ADJUSTMENTS
Accounts receivable and agents' balances (net of $195,817 allowance for doubtful accounts)					
(44)	482,659	286,842	250,210	425,625	57,034 F
(45)	–195,817			–175,415	–20,402 G
Property and equipment at cost					
Land		500,000	500,000		
Buildings		2,975,000	2,975,000		
Furniture and equipment		2,540,015	2,467,090		
		$ 6,015,015	$ 5,942,090		
		2,239,215	1,779,590		
Less accumulated depreciation (51)	275,800	$ 3,775,800	$ 4,162,500	237,500	$ 38,300 H
Unamortized acquisition costs (1,6) included in deferred premiums (25,26)	4,187,706	4,780,814	4,258,440	3,768,935	418,771 I
	593,108			489,505	103,603 J
Due and uncollected premiums					
life (statutory) net deferred (12,21)	3,143,422		2,763,995		
	–2,229,313	–2,269,655	–1,999,529	–1,966,286	–263,027 *
increase in loading on due (15,23)	–40,342			–33,243	
		$ 873,767	764,466		–7,099 K
accident and health		89,427	83,015		
Total assets	$4,049,648	$125,139,826	$110,649,854	$3,678,987	$ 370,661

*This amount does not appear as a single adjustment in the statement of income but as the net sum of three adjustments of the increase in liability for future policy benefits:

Gross deferred premiums 19B	–$2,837,822
19A	2,509,789
Statutory increase in loadings (20-11)	65,006
	–$ 263,027

(continued)

Example 4.4 (Continued)
BALANCE SHEET GAAP BASIS

LIABILITIES

	ADJUSTMENTS	19B	19A	ADJUSTMENTS	INCREASE IN ADJUSTMENTS
Policy liabilities					
Future policy benefits					
Life and annuity (statutory)		$101,031,319	$ 88,907,938	$	$
decrease in reserves*	-6,019,273	-7,895,894	-6,747,950	-5,070,303	-948,970 M
deferred premiums**	-1,876,621			-1,677,647	-198,974 N
		$ 93,135,425	$ 82,159,988		
Accident and health		561,330	506,722		
Supplementary contracts certain		2,514,325	2,378,000		
Dividend deposits		3,341,950	3,140,080		
		$ 5,856,275	$ 5,518,080		
Unpaid claims		495,775	390,108		
Dividends		42,500	35,000		
Total		$100,091,305	$ 88,609,898		
Income tax		60,000	53,000		
Accrued expenses		237,924	213,274		
Other: Agents' credit balances		164,515	145,075		
Accrued interest on policyholder funds		24,742	22,000		
Premiums received in advance		10,375	8,650		
Reserve for dividends (statutory)	-2,054,000	2,054,000	1,830,000	-1,830,000	-224,000 O
		-2,054,000	-1,830,000		
		0	0		
Deferred income taxes (38,39)	859,000	859,000	517,000	517,000	342,000 P
(M.S.V.R.) (statutory)	-1,639,003	1,639,003	1,250,000	-1,250,000	-389,003 Q
		-1,639,003	-1,250,000		
		0	0		

(continued)

Example 4.4 (Continued)

BALANCE SHEET GAAP BASIS

LIABILITIES

	ADJUSTMENTS	19B	19A	ADJUSTMENTS	INCREASE IN ADJUSTMENTS
Reserve for reinsurance in unlicensed companies (statutory)	-614,827	614,827 / -614,827 / 0	512,925 / -512,925 / 0	-512,925	-101,902 R
Total liabilities	-$11,344,724	$101,447,861	$ 89,568,897	$-9,823,875	$ -1,520,849

*(9,18)
**(12,21)

STOCKHOLDER'S EQUITY

	ADJUSTMENTS	19B	19A	ADJUSTMENTS	INCREASE IN ADJUSTMENTS
Capital stock	$	$ 1,500,000	$ 1,500,000	$	$
Net unrealized investment gains (35,36)	584,012	584,012	405,715	405,715	178,297 S
Appropriations of surplus Reserve for mortgage loans (42)	235,000	235,000	203,500	203,500	31,500 T
Unappropriated surplus (statutory)	$ 819,012	6,797,593	6,078,095	$ 609,215	
Plus adjustments to assets	4,049,648			3,678,987	
Plus adjustments to liabilities	11,344,724			9,823,875	
Less adjustments above	-819,012			-609,215	
Unappropriated surplus (GAAP)		$ 21,372,953	$ 18,971,742		
Total stockholders' equity		$ 23,691,965	$ 21,080,957		
Total liabilities		101,447,861	89,568,897		
Total liabilities and stockholders' equity		$125,139,826	$110,649,854		

Example 4.5

STATEMENT OF INCOME GAAP BASIS 19B

Revenue:
Premiums:

life and annuity (statutory)	$ 16,833,468
less increase in deferred gross (19)	-2,837,822
(10)	2,509,789
increase in statutory loading on due (AA)	-27,910
change from statutory to GAAP on due (K)	-7,099
plus increase in deferred expense loading (J)	103,603
	$ 16,574,029

Premiums:

accident and health	872,167
Considerations for supplementary contracts life	135,500
less deduction from reserve increase (FF)	-135,500
Considerations for supplementary contracts certain and dividend accumulations	720,350
less deduction from reserve increase (BB)	-720,350
	0
Net investment income (statutory)	9,130,976
plus increase in nonadmitted due (E)	2,088
less home office rent minus real estate expenses (34)	-190,750
	8,942,314
Total revenue	$ 26,388,510

Benefits and expenses:

Death benefits	1,034,000
Annuity benefits	2,119,391
Endowment and surrender benefits	2,532,000
Accident and health benefits	678,286
Increase in liability for future policy benefits:	
Life and accident and health (statutory)	12,118,055
Supplementary contracts life (statutory)	59,934
less difference in reserve increase (M)	-948,970
increase in deferred gross (19)	-2,837,822
(10)	2,509,789
plus statutory increase in deferred loading (DD)	65,006
change from statutory to GAAP (20)	352,692
(12)	-288,639
less considerations for supplementary contracts (FF)	-135,500
plus supplementary contract payments (GG)	118,600
	$ 11,013,145
Increase in reserve for supplementary contracts certain and dividend accumulations (statutory)	$ 338,195
less considerations and deposits (BB)	-720,350
plus payments and withdrawals (CC)	648,758
	$ 266,603
Dividends to policyholders (statutory)	2,007,800
less increase in reserve (O)	-224,000
	$ 1,783,800
Payments on settlement annuities certain and dividend deposits (statutory)	648,758
less added to increase in reserve (CC)	-648,758
	0

Interest on policy or contract funds	52,242
Payments on supplementary contracts life (statutory)	118,600
less added to increase in reserve (GG)	–118,600
	0
Amortization of deferred acquisition costs (5)	491,024
General expenses (statutory)	2,279,895
Commissions (statutory)	1,469,736
Taxes, licenses and fees (statutory)	241,788
less: H.O. rent minus real estate expenses (34)	–190,750
commissions deferred (2)	–775,795
general expenses deferred (3)	–134,000
plus increase in allowance for uncollectable agents' debit balances (G)	20,402
Other operating cost and expenses	$ 2,911,276
Increase in loading on due and deferred premiums	
Deferred (statutory)	65,006
less adjustment to reserve increase (DD)	–65,006
Due (statutory)	27,910
less adjustment to premiums (AA)	–27,910
	0
Total benefits and expenses	$-22,881,767
Equity in increase in undistributed earnings of subsidiaries (D)	968
Income before income tax	$ 3,507,711
Income tax paid	600,200
Increase in deferred income tax (P)	342,000
Income after income tax, before net investment gains	$ 2,565,511
Net investment gains (total statutory)	255,072
less unrealized (EE)	–137,872
Net realized investment gains	$ 117,200
Net income	$ 2,682,711

Example 4.6

CAPITAL AND SURPLUS ACCOUNT
GAAP BASIS

Capital and unappropriated surplus 19A	$ 20,471,742
Net income	2,682,711
Dividends to stockholders	−250,000
Appropriations of surplus (T)	−31,500
Capital and unappropriated surplus 19B	$ 22,872,953

Example 4.7

NET UNREALIZED INVESTMENT GAINS

Net unrealized investment gains 19A (35)	$	405,715
plus unrealized statutory (EE)		137,872
plus: increase in unrealized gain on preferred stocks (C)		3,045
increase in nonadmitted bond values (A)		61,292
less decrease in nonadmitted mortgage values (B)		−23,912
Net unrealized investment gains 19B (36)	$	584,012

Review questions

1. Show that if experience mortality and lapses are equal to the assumptions, the amortizations of deferred acquisition costs using methods 1 and 2 are identical.

Answer: (If experience is the same as assumptions, the amounts in force at the end of each year will be the assumed amounts in Table 4.1. The unamortized and amortized amounts will therefore be:

YEAR		UNAMORTIZED	AMORTIZED
0	$100.000 \times 4.383 \times 7.583 =$	3,324	
1	$87.592 \times 4.383 \times 7.516 =$	2,886	438
2	$82.594 \times 4.383 \times 6.910 =$	2,501	385
3	$78.413 \times 4.383 \times 6.225 =$	2,139	362
etc.			

2. List five general principles of GAAP.

(Answer:

1. Financial statements should be prepared on a going-concern basis.

2. Values of assets should be conservative but realistic.

3. Cost of producing revenue should be matched against resulting revenues.

4. Financial statements should be objective and provide full disclosure of all relevant information.

5. There should be no anticipation of revenue or accrual of losses. (See section 4.1)

3. Why does the Audit Guide require unamortized acquisition costs to be shown as an asset?

(Answer: See section 4.2a.)

4. What changes should be made in GAAP actuarial reserves and unamortized acquisition costs if recent experience and current estimates of future experience are more favorable than the assumptions made at the time a block of policies was issued?

(Answer: None. See section 4.2c.)

5. Describe the two methods of accounting for dividends when there are restrictions on the portion of profits of participating policies which may be credited to shareholders.

(Answer: See section 4.2, 3.)

6. Summarize the responsibilities of the actuary and the auditor with respect to actuarial assumptions in a GAAP statement?

(Answer: The actuary's responsibility is to use adequate and appropriate assumptions. The auditor may expect the actuary to be able to demonstrate that the assumptions used meet such standards. (4.1)

7. For what investments do SAP and GAAP values differ?
(**Answer:** See section 4.2, 4.)

8. Describe the treatment of real estate expenses on property used in the business using SAP and GAAP.
(**Answer:** Under SAP the real estate expenses are classed as investment expenses and are offset by an imputed rent income charged as an operating expense. Under GAAP such real estate expenses are classed as operating expenses and there is no imputed rent income. See section 4.2, 4)

9. Why will GAAP statements usually include amounts for deferred income taxes?
(**Answer:** See section 4.2, 7.)

10. Describe the treatment of nonadmitted assets in the GAAP statement.
(**Answer:** See section 4.2, 8.)

11. Describe the treatment of deferred premiums in GAAP statements filed with the SEC.
(**Answer:** See section 4.3.)

Chapter 5:
Canadian Life and Accident and Sickness Statement (Form INS-54)

Purpose of 1978 and 1981 revisions of Canadian statement / special requirements of Canadian and British Insurance Companies Act / fund accounting / principal statements of annual report / presentation of life and accident and sickness data / balance sheet / asset values / amortization of gains and losses on debt securities / formula adjustment reserve on shares / actuarial reserves shown in statement / four parts of income statement / reconciliation of unappropriated earned surplus / statement of changes in financial position / changes in reserves / analysis of income by fund and line of business / reconciliation of funds / summary of funds and amounts owing / test of compliance with Section 103 / investment valuation and currency reserves / exhibits / out-of-Canada business / examples.

5.1 Principal provisions of the Canadian statement

As a result of revisions in 1978 and 1981 (see Chapter 2), life insurance companies incorporated in Canada now complete one statement for life insurance and accident and sickness insurance (Form INS-54) and one for segregated fund business (Form INS-85). Companies incorporated outside Canada file a different statement showing assets and liabilities in Canada and reporting on Canadian transactions (Form INS-55), along with the general business statement required by their home jurisdiction (see Chapter 6, 6.11). (However, companies which maintain separate assets, accounts and surplus for Canadian business may obtain permission from the Minister of Finance to report their Canadian business on the form required for Canadian companies.)

The current statement form is designed, in the words of the Superintendent of Insurance quoted earlier (Chapter 2, 2.7), "to bring the annual statement form more in line with financial statements prepared using generally accepted accounting principles. It continues to be our objective to have the statement filed with the Department report a balance sheet and income statement identical to those contained in the report to the company's members."

This is accomplished by using the reconciliation of surplus as a buffer between the income statement and the balance sheet. Normally, conservative values for assets and liabilities produce an income statement which reports a smaller income than would be reported if less conservative values were used. The current Canadian statement allows the use of GAAP to prepare the income statement. However, if this approach produces less conservative asset and liability values than the Department of Insurance considers necessary, certain reserves, treated as appropriations of surplus, must be set up.

For example, a company may include in its balance sheet nonadmitted assets, (such as depreciated values of furniture and equipment; debit balances owed by agents, and investments not permitted by the Insurance Act) if it sets aside corresponding amounts as appropriations of surplus. Similarly, actuarial reserves may include negative reserves and reserves less than cash surrender values, but the sum of negative reserves and deficiencies from cash values must be included in appropriated surplus. Thus the income statement is not distorted, although a portion of surplus is earmarked as appropriated or "required by the Department", and unappropriated surplus is not increased.

This is in accordance with the recommendations of the CICA on accounting and auditing practices which state that "reserves" are amounts "that have been appropriated from retained earnings or other surplus: a) at the discretion of management, or b) pursuant to the requirements of a statute" (*CICA Handbook,* December 1968, p. 1571).

At present (1985) the accounting profession in Canada has not set up generally accepted accounting principles for life insurance companies. Although many practices now permitted by the Department of Insurance (e.g., treatment of formerly nonadmitted assets, deferred policy acquisition expenses, deferred income taxes) conform to recommendations of the CICA research study, some (e.g., treatment of realized and unrealized gains and losses on investments) are still different. However, it is hoped that ongoing discussion among representatives of the CICA and CIA and the Department of Insurance will eventually resolve these differences.

In addition to customary accounting practices followed in the format of the Canadian statutory statement, life insurance companies follow practices arising out of the requirements of the Insurance Act and the policies of the Department of Insurance:

1. The Insurance Act provides that life insurance companies which issue accident and sickness insurance and/or segregated fund policies (policies whose reserves may vary according to the market values of the assets in the fund) must maintain separate funds and separate assets for life insurance and annuities; accident and sickness insurance, and segregated fund policies. Hence the combined life and accident and sickness statement has a balance sheet and income statement of the total business and separate analyses by life and by accident and sickness. The total assets and liabilities in segregated funds are shown as single items in both versions of the balance sheet.

2. Another provision of the Insurance Act is that, in the life insurance and annuity fund, separate accounts must be maintained for participating policies, nonparticipating policies and shareholders' interest. The Act also

stipulates that a minimum percentage of participating profits (ranging from 90 percent to 97.5 percent, depending on the size of the participating fund) be distributed to participating policyholders. Thus, if $800,000 were distributed to participating policyholders in a year, it would be illegal to transfer $100,000 to the shareholders' account.

To monitor compliance with these provisions, the statement of income is analyzed by fund, and, at the end of the year of account, the funds (the shares of the assets of the company arising out of transactions with the members of the fund) must be reconciled with those held at the end of the previous year. The statement also requires details as to the method of allocation of investment income and expenses among the various funds and lines of business. (In addition to the participating, nonparticipating and shareholders' funds, the company may maintain an investment reserve fund and staff pension and insurance funds. However, the separation of funds in the life insurance branch does not require a separation of assets.)

The aim of displaying the financial status of the company as a whole is reconciled with the statutory requirements of separation of assets and accounts by the presentation of three total statements—I (assets), II (liabilities, capital and surplus) and III (income)—in the first section of the annual statement, followed by an analysis of each of these statements. The following table summarizes the principal statements and the methods of presentation. Apart from minor differences, which will be cited as the statements are described, items in the combined statements are the totals of similar items in the analyses.

Table 5.1

CANADIAN ANNUAL STATEMENT (FORM INS-54)
PRINCIPAL STATEMENTS

	COMBINED	ANALYSIS
Assets	I*	XI Life, A&S
Liabilities, capital and surplus	II*	XII Life, A&S
Income	III*(a)	XIII Fund (b)
		XVI Line (b)
Reconciliation of surplus	IV*	
Changes in financial position		V* Life, A&S
Changes in capital and contributed surplus		IX Life, A&S
Changes in reserves		VIII Life, A&S
Reconciliation of funds		XIV Fund
Summary of funds and amounts owing		XV Fund

(a) Includes normal income, unusual and extraordinary income and income from subsidiaries and ancillary operations.
(b) Includes only normal income.
*Life insurance companies in Canada must include an audit certificate from an independent auditor with their annual reports to the Department of Insurance. The statements marked with an asterisk are those to which the audit certificate must refer.

The statements of assets, liabilities capital and surplus, and income are summary statements. Most of the items in these statements are shown in greater detail in subsequent exhibits and schedules. For instance, details of bonds and shares owned are listed in Schedules A and B respectively, while investment income is shown by class of investment in Exhibit 6.

5.2 I: Statement of assets

Invested assets are shown by category at book values prescribed by government regulation. Investments in subsidiaries must be shown as a separate category of assets. A minimum prescribed investment valuation reserve must be held as an appropriation of surplus.

Debt securities. Book values for debt securities (bonds, mortgages, etc.) are amortized values for securities not in default and market values for others.

In the life branch, gains and losses on the sale of debt securities must be amortized over the remaining term of the security sold, but not more than 20 years (but see 1984 amendments, Section 5.20), and the net unamortized gains (losses) subtracted from (added to) the book values in total. (Since a gain on sale increases assets, and therefore surplus, the unamortized gain must be subtracted from the assets if surplus is only to increase by the amount amortized.) An example of the amortization procedure is given in Example 5.1.

In the accident and sickness branch, gains and losses on both debt and equity securities must be included in income in the year they are realized.

Equity securities. Statement values for equity securities (preferred and common stocks) are cost values.

However, in the life branch, since 1978, gains (losses) on the sale of shares must be subtracted from (added to) an adjustment reserve as they are realized. At the end of each year, if total market values exceed adjusted book values (book values plus the adjustment reserve, at the beginning of the year, minus current year net capital gains), seven percent* of the excess is included in income and added to the adjustment reserve. If market values are less than adjusted book values, seven percent (now 15 percent) of the deficiency must be charged to income and deducted from the adjustment reserve. (See Example 5.2.)

Since the only transactions in the adjustment reserve account are the addition (subtraction) of net realized and unrealized gains (losses) taken into income and the subtraction (addition) of realized gains (losses) incurred, the adjustment reserve at any time will be the sum of the net capital gains and losses taken into income minus the net capital gains realized since 1977. If, at any time, the net realized and unrealized capital gains taken into income since 1977 equal the net realized capital gains since 1977, the adjustment account will be zero.

---

*Increased to 15% in 1984.

In the accident and sickness branch, realized capital gains and losses on shares must be included in income as they are incurred. Unrealized gains and losses are ignored, except in the calculation of the investment reserve and in the determination of market values used in the Section 103 test. (See Example 5.10.)

For both debt and equity securities in the life branch, the analyses of assets show book values, adjustment reserve and total; the combined statement shows only the net totals.

Real estate. Real estate is normally included at cost, plus improvements, minus depreciation (minus encumbrances, i.e., debts secured by the property, e.g. mortgages). The Superintendent may allow appraised values to be used, but there is no provision for regular reappraisals. Ground rents (land owned and rented to tenants for building) are shown similarly.

Policy loans. Policy loans are shown at book values, except for loans in excess of the policy reserve, for which the excess must be deducted. This differs from the way other assets are shown, in which the full value is listed in the assets and a reserve held for any unsecured portion. This method is probably used because the amounts involved are usually small and the reserve would require a special category, because policy loans are neither miscellaneous assets nor other investments. (Note that in the computation of taxable income, policy loans are deducted from actuarial liabilities.)

Other investments. Term deposits and guaranteed investment certificates are shown separately from cash and demand deposits in view of the difference in liquidity. All other invested assets except investments in subsidiaries, which are shown by category in the analysis of assets and in total in the combined statement, must be included in "other investments" and listed in a separate schedule along with any reserves held.

Common and preferred shares in subsidiaries must be shown at "equity values," i.e., cost plus a share of the retained earnings of the corporation equal to the ratio of shares owned to total shares outstanding. Changes in equity values during the year must be shown in the income statement.

The remaining items require little explanation. Miscellaneous assets include both those, such as furniture and equipment and agents' debit balances, which require a full reserve as an appropriation of surplus, and others, such as EDP equipment, which may not need such a reserve. They are also listed in a schedule along with any reserve required. Depreciation may be charged to miscellaneous assets such as furniture and equipment, and reserves for uncollectable accounts may be set up for accounts receivable such as agents' debit balances. In such cases the reserve required would be for the net balance in the account. The total assets in segregated funds are shown as a single item (at market values) so that the total assets in the combined statement will be the assets owned by the company.

5.3 II: Liabilities, capital and surplus

Net actuarial reserve. The amount of the net actuarial reserve included in the liabilities is the responsibility of the valuation actuary, who must be an actuary appointed by the board of directors with notification to the Superintendent. (The Insurance Act defines an actuary as a fellow of the Canadian Institute of Actuaries.)

A life insurance company must attach a report by the valuation actuary to its annual statement. This report must state, with respect to the reserve included in the liabilities shown in the annual statement, that, in his or her opinion,

a) the rate or rates of interest and the rate or rates of mortality, sickness or other contingencies used in calculating the reserve are appropriate to the circumstances of the company and the policies in force;

b) the method used to calculate the reserve produces a reserve in respect of each policy that is not less than the reserve produced by the minimum method described in the Insurance Act, and

c) the reserve makes good and sufficient provision for all the unmatured obligations guaranteed under the terms of the policies in force.

In the report, the actuary is also required to specify the nature of any prospective changes in dividend scales that he or she has taken into consideration in stating the above opinions and to include the aggregate total of negative reserves and deficiencies from cash values included in the reserves.

The actuary must explain, for each valuation assumption having a significant effect on the valuation liabilities, why he or she believes the assumption to be appropriate. He or she must provide sufficient detail to support the valuation so that it may be used by the Department to verify the inventory of in-force policies and the actuarial reserve.

An insurance company transacting accident and sickness insurance business must attach to its annual statement a report by the valuation actuary with respect to the reserve shown in the annual statement for noncancellable accident and sickness policies (including any unearned premium reserve held on such policies) and for claims under accident and sickness policies payable in installments. The requirements for the report are similar to corresponding ones for life policies, with the exception of paragraph b) above, since no method is specified for the calculation of reserves on accident and sickness policies.

Reserve methods. The 1978 Insurance Act amendments provided for a new minimum reserve method—the 1978 Canadian method. Under this method, the deduction from the first net level annual premium for the policy is the least of three values:

1) 150 percent of the net level premium,

2) actual acquisition expenses as determined by the valuation actuary or

3) the present value of expenses that will be recoverable in the second

or later years; namely, an amount for which the required renewal valuation premiums will not exceed the premium available to pay for the benefits guaranteed under the policies, i.e., the gross premium less provision for commissions, premium tax, administrative expenses and dividends.

Valuation assumptions. Although the requirement that the assumptions be appropriate to the circumstances of the company and the policies in force has replaced the specification of interest rates and tables of mortality in the Insurance Act, the assumptions used must be acceptable to the Superintendent. However, at present, prior approval is not required, and the Superintendent regards as acceptable any valuation basis considered appropriate by the valuation actuary, reserving the right to question any basis which seems to produce inadequate reserves. Normally, if a reserve is to be questioned, it is questioned within four weeks of the receipt of the statement and the report of the valuation actuary.

The valuation actuary must review all assumptions each year. Those which are no longer appropriate must be changed. Any decrease (increase) in actuarial liabilities due to changes in assumptions is normally classed as positive (negative) unusual income.

Professional responsibility of the valuation actuary. In view of the greater responsibilities for determination of appropriate actuarial reserves now placed on the valuation actuary, the Canadian Institute of Actuaries has approved an opinion (CIA-6) on the actuarial principles and practices for the valuation actuary which interprets and amplifies sections of the Institute's guides to professional conduct addressed to the appointed valuation actuary of an insurance company.

Paragraph 5 of the opinion states:

> "It is the opinion of Council that Guide 4 requires that the valuation actuary take into consideration the Recommendations for Insurance Financial Reporting of the Canadian Institute of Actuaries. A member whose conduct does not conform to these Recommendations should be prepared to justify his departure from them to the members of the Institute appointed by Council to consider his conduct."

The recommendations deal with the verification of data, the selection of assumptions, methods of valuation and the content of the valuation actuary's reports in both the published and statutory statements. It is likely that the recommendations will be amended and expanded on the basis of experience and "in order to take into account the advances in actuarial science, the evolution of the insurance business and changes in the environment of that business."

Reserves listed in the annual statement. The analysis of liabilities must show the "actuarial reserve before deduction of deferred policy acquisition expenses" (the net level premium reserve calculated using the same assumptions as are used in the calculation of the net actuarial reserve in the statement); the "deduction in respect of deferred policy acquisition expenses" (the difference between the net level premium reserve and the net actuarial reserve), and the net actuarial reserve. In addition, the minimum reserve required by the Insurance Act for life insurance policies, calculated on the same assumptions as are used in the net actuarial reserve, must be shown in a footnote. However, instead of calculating the minimum reserve using withdrawal rates, a company may calculate the reserve assuming withdrawal rates of zero and substituting zeros for negative reserves and cash surrender values for reserves less than the cash surrender value (using a "cash value floor"). The actuary therefore has a choice of minimum reserves.

If the net actuarial reserve is different from both the net level premium reserve and the minimum reserve, approximate methods may be used for the calculation of the latter reserves. The report of the valuation actuary "need only contain as much detail concerning such reserves as the actuary deems appropriate," according to Opinion CIA-6.

The net actuarial reserve in the life branch includes reserves on life insurance and annuities, including supplementary benefits such as waiver and income disability, as well as settlement annuities with and without life contingencies. However, proceeds of policies left on deposit are not included but rather are combined with similar items, e.g., dividends left on deposit and premium deposit funds.

In the accident and sickness branch, the net actuarial reserve includes gross unearned premiums less deferred policy acquisition expenses, actuarial reserves on noncancellable policies, and reserves for installment benefits on both reported and unreported claims (the latter may include an explicit provision for claims adjustment expenses). If deferred policy acquisition expenses exceed 30 percent of gross unearned premiums, a reserve for the excess must be held as an appropriation of surplus. However, if actuarial reserves on noncancellable policies are calculated on a preliminary term method, the "deduction in respect of deferred policy acquisition expenses" will include the difference between the net level premium reserve and the net actuarial reserve. The required reserve for deferred policy acquisition expenses, however, only applies to the deduction from gross unearned premiums on other than noncancellable policies.

In the combined statement of liabilities, capital and surplus, only the net actuarial reserve is shown.

Outstanding claims. The provision for outstanding claims includes amounts due but unpaid on reported claims and an estimate of unreported claims at the statement date. However, installment benefits on unreported claims in the accident and sickness branch are excluded from this item because they are included in the net actuarial reserve in the line above.

The remaining liability items are self-explanatory, with a few exceptions:

Other contract liabilities. Other liabilities on insurance contracts are listed separately in an exhibit. They include premiums received in advance of the due date (credited to the premium account), payments under settlement annuities due but unpaid, and dividends to policyholders and experience rating refunds due but unpaid.

Details of the provision for dividends and experience rating refunds are also shown separately in an exhibit. If the valuation actuary includes an explicit or implicit provision for future dividends to policyholders in the net actuarial reserve, this provision may be reduced by the amount so included for the years for which the provision is held.

Miscellaneous liabilities. Details of this item are also shown in an exhibit. It includes commissions on due and unpaid premiums; investment income received in advance; accrued interest on outstanding claims; dividends to shareholders declared but unpaid, and amounts received but not allocated.

The liability for deferred income taxes is not required by the Department of Insurance, but may be shown to conform with generally accepted accounting practices. It is not included in the total liabilities but is treated as a special liability not part of appropriated surplus.

Capital and surplus. The surplus funds are split into appropriated earned surplus, unappropriated earned surplus and contributed surplus. Appropriated earned surplus includes reserves required by the Department of Insurance (investment valuation and currency reserves; reserves for negative reserves and cash value deficiencies; reserves for reinsurance ceded to unregistered companies, and the valuation reserve for miscellaneous assets and other investments). (For the accident and sickness branch, the Department of Insurance also requires a reserve for deferred policy acquisition expenses in excess of 30 percent of the gross unearned premiums.) Finally, appropriated earned surplus includes reserves required by foreign jurisdictions and additional reserves set up voluntarily by management.

5.4 III: Income statement

The income statement is divided into four parts:

1) normal income from insurance operations; that is, the income from normal insurance operations comparable with that of other periods and of other similar companies.

2) unusual income from insurance operations: "gains, losses and provision for losses resulting from normal business operations which are both abnormal in size and caused by rare or unusual circumstances" (*CICA Handbook*). Such income includes capital gains and losses in the life insurance branch from investments other than bonds, mortgages and shares, changes in actuarial reserves due to changes in assumptions as to future conditions, etc.

3) extraordinary items: "gains, losses and provision for losses which, by their nature, are not typical of the normal business activities of the enterprise, are not expected to occur regularly over a period of years, and are not considered as recurring factors in any evaluation of the ordinary

operations of the enterprise" (*CICA Handbook*). An example would be gains or losses on sale of subsidiaries.

4) income from subsidiaries and ancillary operations. Life insurance companies may carry on any business that is reasonably ancillary to the life insurance business, but only to a limited extent. For instance, management services may be provided to a subsidiary insurance corporation.

1. Normal income from insurance operations

Insurance premiums and annuity considerations. This item includes amounts received in connection with segregated funds, which are deemed to be received by the insurance funds and then transferred to the appropriate segregated fund. (The amount transferred is often the net amount, after deduction of provision for commissions and administrative expenses, and appears in the analyses of income by fund and by line of business as part of the net transfer of policy liabilities (to) from segregated funds.)

Net investment income. Net investment income includes gross investment income less interest on borrowed money, less investment expenses and taxes. It includes investment income on staff pension and insurance funds but not investment income on segregated funds.

Net investment gain (loss) on segregated fund assets. This item includes regular investment income as well as any net realized and unrealized capital gain or loss on the assets, which are included in the statement at market values.

Reserve adjustments on reinsurance ceded. Reinsurance on the "modified co-insurance" plan provides that the reinsuring company will lend the increase in reserves to the ceding company. The inclusion of these amounts in income avoids the distortion which would otherwise occur in the normal increase in actuarial reserves.

Claims incurred. Claims incurred does *not* include payments under settlement annuities, claims paid directly from segregated funds and payments from staff pension and insurance funds. These payments must be shown as separate items.

Normal increase in actuarial reserves. The normal increase is the increase in the actuarial reserve at the end of the year over that at the beginning calculated on the same method and using the same assumptions. (Changes in reserves for the current year due to changes in methods or assumptions must be shown as items of unusual income. Changes in reserves of prior years must be shown as adjustments of earned surplus.) In the combined statement, this item is subdivided into the mandatory provision, the increase in minimum reserves and the additional provision (the excess of the increase in the net actuarial reserve over the mandatory provision). Thus, combining the additional provision with net income will yield net income on the basis of minimum reserves.

Interest credited to amounts on deposit. Only the interest credited is shown, instead of including amounts deposited as income and amounts withdrawn (and the corresponding increase in reserve) as disbursements. It is calculated by deducting the net amount deposited from the increase in liability.

An example will make this clearer. If we assume the amount on deposit at the end of the year is $100,000 and interest is credited at 6%, with all transactions taking place at midyear, the account may be as follows:

	AMOUNT ON DEPOSIT	ACCRUED INTEREST	LIABILITY*
On deposit January 1	$100,000	$3,000	$103,000
Interest capitalized	6,000		
Deposits	50,000		
Withdrawals	−20,000		
On deposit December 31	$136,000	$4,080	$140,080

*Amount on deposit plus accrued interest.

The interest actually credited is the amount capitalized ($6,000) plus the increase in accrued interest ($1,080), or $7,080. This amount is calculated for the statement by subtracting the amount deposited from the sum of the amounts withdrawn and the increase in liability.

Amount withdrawn	$20,000
Increase in liability	37,080
Sum	$57,080
Less amount deposited	−50,000
Interest credited	$ 7,080

The increase in the fund is the excess of deposits over withdrawals, or $30,000. The increase in liability is the excess of deposits over withdrawals plus the interest credited. Therefore, in order to get the increase in funds for the reconciliation of funds, the increase in liability ($37,080) is added to the income transferred from the income statement which includes the interest credited (−$7,080).

Dividends and experience rating refunds. In the combined statement and the analysis by line of business, the amount incurred in the year for each of these benefits is shown, as is the increase in the provision for future benefits. In the analysis by fund the amount shown is the sum of the incurred amount and the increase in provision.

Income taxes. The last item is income tax charged, separated into current and deferred. The Department does not require that provision be made for deferred income taxes, but permits that provision in order to enable companies to comply with generally accepted accounting principles for other corporations.

2. Unusual income from insurance operations

Changes in current actuarial reserves due to changes in valuation bases or

methods. However, changes to reserves of prior years may not be included here. Instead, they must be entered in the reconciliation of unappropriated earned surplus as prior period adjustments.

Net capital gains and losses from invested assets in the life insurance fund. Reductions in book values due to anticipated losses are also included. Note: in this context, invested assets do not include bonds, mortgages or shares.

Gains or losses due to changes in book rates of exchange. Companies with business in other currencies normally convert all assets, liabilities and transactions to Canadian dollars, using a standard exchange rate (the book rate of exchange). If management considers the book rate of exchange unrealistic, in view of current exchange rates, a rate may be substituted closer to the current rate. The change in surplus arising from the revaluation of assets and liabilities in foreign currencies is entered as an unusual item of income.

3. Extraordinary income from insurance operations

This will include such infrequent items as gains and losses on the sale of subsidiary, etc. Only the net total is shown, with details listed in the notes to financial statements.

4. Income from subsidiaries and ancillary operations

This section includes dividends from subsidiaries, as well as the increase or decrease in the equity values of shares, and income from ancillary operations. Details of the latter must be shown in an exhibit.

Analyses of income. The analyses of income by fund and by line of business include all the items of normal income from insurance operations, plus transfers between funds and lines of business resulting from transfers of liabilities, e.g., premiums for segregated fund contracts received in the life insurance funds and transferred; asset values of policies transferred between participating and nonparticipating or insurance and annuities, and expense charges and mortality costs incurred on behalf of segregated funds.

The remainder of the income transferred to the reconciliation of unappropriated earned surplus must be allocated by fund in the reconciliation of funds.

5.5 IV: Reconciliation of unappropriated earned surplus

This statement reconciles the unappropriated earned surplus at the end of the year with that at the end of the previous year, adding to the latter the net income for the year and any other special adjustments to the surplus, and subtracting (adding) increases (decreases) in appropriated surplus and dividends to shareholders. Special adjustments to surplus include adjustments relating to prior years, such as tax adjustments and changes in actuarial reserves.

5.6 V: Statement of changes in financial position

The statement of changes in financial position is essentially a cash flow statement, separated by life and accident and sickness which reconciles the amounts of cash at the end of the year with those at the end of the previous year.

This statement was added in 1982 and is one of the statements included in the certificate of the external auditor. The inclusion of this statement conforms with generally accepted accounting practices. Moreover, it was considered necessary by the Superintendent of Insurance because of the cash flow problems encountered by some companies due to high and fluctuating interest rates.

The format of the statement is as follows:

A. Sources of cash

I. From operations:

- Net income carried to reconciliation of surplus.
- Charges (credits) not involving cash, such as changes in assets and liabilities such as actuarial reserves, outstanding claims, taxes and expenses due and unpaid, outstanding premiums and due and accrued investment income.

II. Principal payments on disposition of invested assets.

III. Other sources:

- Changes in borrowed money.
- Capital and contributed surplus paid in.
- Inter-fund transfers.

B. Application of funds generated

I. Acquisition of income-producing assets.

II. Other dispositions of cash:

- Dividends to shareholders.
- Acquisitions of miscellaneous assets.

A − B = net change in cash (a)

C. Reconciliation of cash
- Cash at beginning of year (b)
- Cash at end of year (equal to (a) + (b)).

The items in A I are principally noncash items included in income. Examples are the increase in premiums receivable, which increases incurred premiums, and the increase in outstanding claims, which increases incurred claims and thus decreases income. Hence, increases in assets must be deducted from net income and increases in liabilities added to net income.

One difficulty encountered in balancing this statement is that it includes data, e.g., principal repayments on investments and new investments made, which are not shown elsewhere in the statement. However, if the initial draft of this statement is out of balance, errors can be located fairly quickly if the theory underlying the statement is kept in mind.

Because earned surplus, both appropriated and unappropriated, is the difference between assets and the sum of liabilities, capital and contributed surplus, if we let

S = appropriated and unappropriated earned surplus,
L = total liabilities,
A = total assets excluding cash,
B = cash,
C = capital and
R = contributed surplus.

$$S = A + B - (L + C + R) \tag{1}$$

Subtracting this equation for year A from the equation for year B, we have

$$S_B - S_A = (A_B - A_A) + (B_B - B_A) - (L_B - L_A) \quad (C_B - C_A) - R_B - R_A) \tag{2}$$

and, transposing,

$$B_B - B_A = (S_B - S_A) + (L_B - L_A) + (C_B - C_A) + (R_B - R_A) - (A_B - A_A) \tag{3}$$

and, because $S_B - S_A$ = increase in earned surplus
= net income carried to
reconciliation of surplus (R of S)
+ increase in assets in R of S
− increase in liabilities in R of S

Increase in cash
= net income carried to R of S
+ increases in assets in R of S
− increases in liabilities in R of S
+ increases in liabilities in balance sheet
+ increases in capital
+ increases in contributed surplus
− increases in other assets in balance sheet.

If net increases during the year in assets and liabilities in the balance sheet are listed, these increases, along with the net income transferred to the reconciliation of surplus and asset and liability changes in the reconciliation, should account for all items in the statement of changes in financial position. Increases in balance sheet assets will be negative, increases in balance sheet liabilities positive, and increases in assets and liabilities in the reconciliation of surplus positive and negative respectively.

Many items in the listing of net increases in assets and liabilities will be entered directly in the statement of changes, e.g., investment income due and accrued; outstanding premiums, and due and unpaid expenses and taxes. Others will check with the sum of two or more items in the statement. For example, the net increase in book values of real estate will equal the sum of depreciation on real estate and the decrease in book values of real estate sold minus the cost of real estate acquired. (Note that the decrease in book values on the sale of invested assets is equal to the proceeds of sale minus the net profit on sale.)

As an example:

Book value of real estate year 19A	$550,000
Decrease in book values on disposition	
(proceeds $155,000, profit $30,000)	–125,000
Depreciation	–48,500
Purchase of real estate	300,000
Book value year 19B	$676,500
Increase in book value	$126,500
Items in statement of changes 19B	
Depreciation of real estate	$ 48,500
Decrease in book value	125,000
Cost of acquisition of real estate	–300,000
Net sum	–126,500

The $30,000 profit on real estate is not entered in the statement of changes because it is included in the net income, which includes unusual and extraordinary income.

5.7 VIII: Changes in reserves

This statement shows, for life and accident and sickness separately, the changes in reserves set up as appropriations of surplus in the current year. It conforms with generally accepted accounting practices for other corporations. The reserves are listed in three categories:

1) Reserves required by the Department of Insurance.
2) Reserves required by other jurisdictions.
3) Additional reserves, set up at the discretion of management.

The reserves required by the Department of Insurance for both branches include the investment valuation and currency reserve; the reserve for negative reserves and cash value deficiencies; the reserves for reinsurance ceded to unregistered companies; the valuation reserves for miscellaneous assets and other investments, and, for the accident and sickness branch only, the reserve for deferred policy acquisition expenses in excess of 30 percent of gross unearned premiums.

The statement shows the reserves at the end of the current and preceding years and the increase or decrease. The total for each category appears in the statement of liabilities, capital and surplus, while the net increase or decrease is entered in the reconciliation of unappropriated earned surplus.

5.8 IX: Changes in capital and contributed surplus

This statement shows, for life and accident and sickness separately, the changes in capital stock and surplus contributed by shareholders. It includes amounts of surplus transferred between the life and accident and sickness branches, but since such amounts are treated as contributed surplus, they do not appear in the reconciliation of unappropriated earned surplus.

5.9 XIII, XIV: Analysis of income by fund and reconciliation of funds (Example 5.8)

As stated previously, the net income before unusual or extraordinary items is split by fund and by line of business. The analysis by fund includes all the items in the combined statement plus transfers between funds representing normal transactions, such as premiums transferred to segregated funds and assets transferred in connection with changes of policies from, say, nonparticipating to participating. Data are shown for all the funds in the life branch (including totals for segregated funds). For the shareholders' fund, totals are shown for the life branch, while the accident and sickness fund is split between policyholders and shareholders.

Most of the entries (e.g., premiums, claims, increases in reserves, etc.) are available from normal accounting records. Others, such as net investment income, profits or losses on currency exchange, expenses and taxes, may have to be allocated among the various funds using appropriate formulas (Example 5.7). While no method is prescribed by the Department of Insurance, the methods used for this allocation, as well as the allocation by lines of business, must be described in the statement and may be challenged if the Superintendent considers them inappropriate. As a specific example, the allocation of investment income on the basis of actuarial reserves is normally not an appropriate method.

The reconciliation of funds reconciles the amounts in each fund at the end of the current and previous years. The net income before unusual or extraordinary items is added to the amount of the funds at the beginning of the year. Next, since the amounts in the funds represent shares of the assets of the company, the net income must be corrected for charges which do not represent reductions in assets. These adjustments include the normal increase in actuarial reserves and staff pension and insurance funds; increases in provisions for dividends and experience rating refunds, and the increase in amounts on deposit. (Note that special increases in actuarial reserves, since they appear either as items of unusual income or in the reconciliation of unappropriated earned surplus, need not be added back.)

In addition, unusual and extraordinary items of income; income from subsidiaries and ancillary operations, and items from the reconciliation of unappropriated earned surplus which affect assets, must be allocated by fund and included in the reconciliation. These items include capital gains and losses not subject to amortization; currency adjustments due to changes in book rates of exchange; changes in asset values of subsidiaries, and dividends to shareholders. Other items which must be included are transfers of surplus between funds, including the shareholders' fund, and income taxes on unusual items of income.

Transfer of surplus from insurance funds to other funds are limited by the provisions of the Insurance Act. For instance, as noted earlier, the participating policyholders are entitled to a share in the profits of participating business ranging from 90 percent to 97.5 percent, depending on the size of the fund, and these restrictions must be observed in the transfers of funds. There are also restrictions on the amount which may be transferred from life insurance funds to the accident and sickness fund. In addition, such transfers must be authorized by a bylaw passed by the board of directors and approved at a special general meeting of the company. Transfers from life insurance funds to segregated funds are also limited by amount and must be authorized by bylaw.

5.10 XV: Summary of funds and amounts owing (Example 5.8)

This statement is a summary of the various funds. In addition to showing liabilities and surplus, it can be used to check the accuracy of the total funds. Since the assets of the company are derived from the net contributions of policyholders and shareholders, plus amounts due to others (e.g., borrowed money, amounts due but unpaid, taxes withheld, etc.), the sum of the funds plus amounts owing must equal the total assets.

The policyholders' funds are shown first, split into participating, nonparticipating and accident and sickness, with the totals for life and accident and sickness. The liabilities to policyholders (actuarial reserves, amounts on deposit, provision for dividends and experience rating refunds), are entered in total, followed by deferred income taxes, if any, and amounts of appropriated surplus. Then the unappropriated surplus, and the total amount of each fund, are shown. (In practice, the totals of the funds are taken from the reconciliation of funds, and the unappropriated surplus is the balancing item.)

The amounts in other funds—shareholders' (including capital) staff pension and insurance funds and segregated funds—are then added to give the total funds. When the total amounts owed by the company (outstanding claims, taxes and expenses due, borrowed money, etc.) are added, the final total must equal the total assets.

A summary of the figures in the first part of the statement for the previous year is listed at the bottom of the page for comparison.

5.11 XVI: Analysis of income by line of business

The principles followed in completion of the analysis of income by line of business are the same as for the analysis by fund. The totals of the various items by fund must agree with the items in the fund analysis statement.

In the life branch, the lines of business are all eight combinations of participating and nonparticipating, individual and group, insurance and annuities. In practice, many companies maintain funds by line of business and allocate first by line of business, obtaining the fund allocation from the results.

5.12 XIX: Test of compliance with Section 103

Section 103 of the Insurance Act requires companies writing insurance other than life (including accident and sickness branches of life insurance companies) to hold a minimum amount of surplus. This amount is:

 Capital
+ Appropriated surplus
+ Unappropriated surplus
+ Excess of market value of assets over book value
− Reserves required by Department (see 5.7 above)
− A percentage of unearned premiums on other than noncancellable policies
− 15 percent of unpaid claims and adjustment expenses other than installment claims.

The percentage referred to above is a maximum of 15 percent, but, if the expected ratio of claims and adjustment expenses to earned premiums is less than 95 percent, the company may use the difference between a ratio not less than the expected claims ratio on the business in force (the selected claims ratio) and 80 percent, using zero if the selected claims ratio is less than 80 percent. The expected claims ratio must be certified by an actuary or an officer of the company acceptable to the Superintendent. Also, the selected claims ratio must not be less than the actual claims ratio for the most recent calendar year.

This statement is a worksheet to calculate the margin between the assets available according to the provisions of the Act and the required assets. Unearned premiums on other than noncancellable policies are listed, followed by the required increment (expressed as a percentage). The same is done for unpaid claims and adjustment expenses. The total of other liabilities (total liabilities from the analysis of liabilities, capital and surplus minus the liabilities entered above) along with reserves required by the Department (other than the investment valuation and currency reserve and the reserve for miscellaneous assets, which are deducted from the total assets below). The total is the amount of required assets.

To determine the assets available, the total of the assets is listed; the investment valuation and currency reserve and the reserve for miscellaneous assets are deducted, and any excess of market values over book values is added. The net total is the amount of required assets. The difference between the amount available and the amount required is the margin.

The margin can be checked by taking the total capital, surplus and reserves from the analysis of liabilities, capital and surplus, subtracting the reserves required by the Department and the required percentage of unearned premiums and unpaid claims and adjustment expenses, and adding any net excess of market values of assets over book values (Example 5.10).

5.13 Schedule K: investment valuation and currency reserve

The investment valuation reserve and the currency reserve are calculated separately. The investment valuation and currency reserve is the net sum.

The currency reserve (Example 5.3) is the change in the excess of assets in foreign currencies over the corresponding liabilities, when Canadian dollar values are calculated at current exchange rates instead of book rates. For simplicity, it is calculated using total assets, liabilities and appropriated surplus, since the book values of Canadian currency assets and liabilities will not change. (The reserve for miscellaneous assets and other investments is deducted from assets and excluded from appropriated surplus.) Since the investment valuation and currency reserve is to be calculated, that reserve, which is in Canadian dollars and has no effect on the calculation, is excluded from appropriated surplus. If the change in surplus is negative, it is added to the investment valuation reserve and, if positive, subtracted.

Book values of assets (minus the reserve for miscellaneous assets and other investments), and book values of liabilities and appropriated surplus (minus the reserve for miscellaneous assets and other investments and the investment valuation and currency reserve), are listed in total by currency. The reserve for unamortized gains or losses on debt securities and the formula adjustment for shares are listed separately. Values at current exchange rates are calculated by multiplying the book values by the ratio of current to book rates for each currency, except for the reserve for unamortized gains and losses on debt securities and the adjustment reserve for shares. For the former, since the amount shown in the exhibit is not broken down by currency, the conversion must be made using data from working papers, while the value of the latter at current rates is shown in the schedule from which the book values are taken. (See Example 5.1 and Example 5.2.)

Investment valuation reserve (life)

Since cost values are the statement values of equity securities and real estate, and amortized values are the statement values of debt securities, an investment valuation reserve is required to protect the company against fluctuations in market values. Reserves are set up for each class of assets separately, based on the residual market deficiency for that class of asset, i.e., the net deficiency reduced by any net excess on the other classes. For debt securities, recognizing the fact that only a small percentage of the portfolio may have to be sold on a depressed market, the reserve is the greater of 10 percent of the residual deficiency and 1.5 percent of the total book value (Example 5.4).

It is important to note that the book value of debt securities used in calculating the market excess or deficiency *excludes* unamortized realized capital gains and losses. The book value of shares *includes* the formula adjustment reserve.

For equity securities, the reserve is the residual market deficiency for the current year or the average of the deficiencies for the current and previous two years, if less.

For real estate the reserve is the residual market deficiency.

The unadjusted reserve is the smaller of 1) the sum of the three separate reserves and 2) the greater of a) the total net market deficiency and b) 1.5 percent of the book values of debt securities.

Since the minimum reserve for debt securities is 1.5 percent of the total book value, this is the minimum unadjusted reserve, since the sum of three separate reserves cannot be less than the minimum of one of them, nor can it be less than 1.5 percent of the book value.

If book values of securities have been written down in accordance with the regulations, due to threatened or actual default, the amount written down (less any reduction in the reserve arising from the write-down) may be spread over three years by deducting two-thirds of the unadjusted reserve at the end of the year the security was written down and deducting one-third the following year. (In the first year, the charge to surplus is reduced by the two-thirds by which the reserve is adjusted, and one-third is charged in each of the following two years as the adjustment is reduced to zero.)

The currency reserve is then added to or subtracted from the investment reserve to obtain the investment valuation and currency reserve.

Investment valuation reserve (accident and sickness)

Although the currency reserve is calculated for the accident and sickness branch in the same manner as for the life branch, the investment reserve is calculated according to different principles, in view of the shorter average term of accident and sickness liabilities (Example 5.4).

Debt securities are split into short-term (maturing in five years or less from the date of the statement) and long-term. No reserve is required for the market deficiency on short-term securities (except for short-term mortgages if total mortgages constitute more than 80 percent of the book value of assets), but full reserves for the residual market deficiencies of long-term debt securities, equity securities and real estate are required with two qualifications. They are:

1. The average of the net deficiency of equity securities for the current year and the previous year may be used.

2. To take into account long term liabilities, the ratio (T) of long-term liabilities, defined as the reserve on noncancellable policies plus reserves on installment claims, (i.e., those liabilities covered by the actuary's certificate (see 5.3)) to total liabilities, may be used in a formula to reduce the reserve.

The unadjusted reserve is the least of:

1. The net deficiency of long-term securities, equities, and real estate, plus that of short-term mortgages, if required.

2. The net market deficiency for total debt securities, equity assets and real estate.

3. The sum of the total market deficiencies for long-term bonds,

long-term mortgages, equities, and real estate, and, if mortgages exceed 80 percent of the total book value of assets, the excess of the market deficiency on short-term mortgages over any market excess on short-term bonds.

The adjusted reserve is the unadjusted reserve multiplied by $1.1 \times (1 - .5T)$, so that, for instance, if T is .25, the factor is .9625; if T is .5, it is .825, and if T is .75, it is .6875. The minimum factor, with $T = 1$, would be .55. The rationale is that, on the average, long-term liabilities reduce to about one-half in five years, so that if all liabilities and all assets were long-term, the 55 percent reserve would represent 100 percent of the deficiency on 50 percent of the assets and 10 percent of the deficiency on the other 50 percent.

Again, any currency reserve is added to or subtracted from the investment reserve to obtain the investment valuation and currency reserve.

5.14 Exhibit 6: Net investment income (Example 5.6)

Net investment income includes gross investment income less investment expenses and taxes and interest paid on borrowed money. For the life branch, gross investment income includes the amortization of gains and losses on debt securities and of the realized and unrealized gains and losses on equity assets. For the accident and sickness branch, realized gains on all invested assets are included.

The average net rate of interest earned is calculated by the formula $2I/(A + B - I)$, where I is the net investment income and A and B are the book values of invested assets (including the unamortized gains and losses on debt securities and the adjustment reserve on equity assets in the life branch) less borrowed money, at the end of the current and previous years, respectively.

5.15 Exhibit 3: Accident and sickness premiums and claims

A summary comparison of accident and sickness premiums and claims is required, split by individual cancellable, individual noncancellable and group. Direct premiums written, premiums earned and claims are shown by major classes of benefit (income replacement, creditor disability, accidental death and dismemberment, medical care and all other) and in total. Claims liabilities and reserves are then shown for the current and previous years to obtain the direct incurred claims. Premiums and claims on reinsurance assumed are added to direct premiums and claims incurred, and those on reinsurance ceded are subtracted. The ratios of net incurred claims to net premiums are then calculated for individual cancellable and group, and for total direct and total net.

The total claims incurred (net) should balance with the total accident and sickness claims in the analysis of income plus the increase in the net reserve for installment claims in the summary of actuarial reserves between the preceding and current years.

5.16 Exhibit 5: Review of net claims

The review of net claims consists of analyzing the adequacy of claims reserves for the preceding three years for installment claims and claims other than installment claims.

For each prior year, the unpaid claims at the end of the preceding year (including reserves for unreported claims) are compared with the amounts paid during the year for claims from previous years plus the reserves for unpaid claims at the end of the year. For installment claims, the excess or deficiency is shown; for other claims the ratios of the excess or deficiency to the unpaid amounts at the beginning of the first year reported are also shown. (A small deficiency is normal for installment claims because interest on the reserve is not taken into account.)

5.17 Exhibit 15: Net actuarial reserves

The net actuarial reserves on gross business in force in the life branch must be listed by valuation basis within each line of business, showing the gross amount in force, the reserve and the percentage of the total reserve for that valuation basis. Reserves on settlement annuities and disability annuities must be shown separately.

The summary shows the participating and non-participating totals for each category and the grand totals. Reserves on reinsurance ceded and deferred premiums less loadings are then deducted to give the net actuarial reserve carried in the liabilities.

For the accident and sickness branch, reserves are split into individual cancellable, individual noncancellable and group. For each category, unearned premiums, mid-terminal reserves and reserves for claims and adjustment expenses on claims payable in installments are shown, with reserves on direct written, reinsurance assumed and reinsurance ceded listed in separate columns. The summary shows the unearned premiums on other than noncancellable policies, unearned premiums and mid-terminal reserves on noncancellable policies, and the total reserves for claims payable in installments, with gross reserves, reserves on reinsurance ceded and net reserves in separate columns. The total net reserve is the reserve carried in the liabilities.

5.18 Exhibit A: Movement of policies (life)

The exhibit of movement of policies (gross) reconciles the amount of life insurance in force at the end of the previous year with that in force at the end of the current year. It is split into individual (direct and reinsurance assumed) and group. (Only the amount held by the company is shown on shared groups.)

The exhibit starts with the number of policies and amount in force at the beginning of the year, followed by any adjustments in amounts due to currency revaluation, and by movements in (new issues, revivals, increases, etc.) and the total. Terminations are then shown by category, followed by total terminations, any reductions due to currency revaluation and the gross amount in force at the end of the year.

Similar data are shown for annuities, separated into deferred and vested, with separate columns for settlement annuities and disability annuities.

5.19 Out of Canada business

For business written out of Canada, the following additional statements and exhibits for this business only are required:
1. Analysis of assets.
2. Analysis of liabilities.
3. Premiums (life).
4. Dividends to policyholders (life).
5. Claims (life).
6. Premiums and claims (A&S).
7. Claims liabilities (A&S).
8. Review of net claims (other than monthly income).
9. Review of net claims (monthly income).
10. Movement of life insurance policies.
11. Movement of annuities.
12. Summary of net actuarial reserves (life and A&S).

5.20 1984 Amendments

In 1984 amendments were made to the regulations under the Canadian and British Insurance Companies Act liberalizing certain provisions regarding the annual statement.

(a) In addition to changing the percentage of realized and unrealized gains and losses on equity securities from 7 percent to 15 percent as referred to in Section 5.2 above, provision was made for writing off the stock adjustment account if a company liquidates its equity portfolio. Beginning in the third year after all equities have been disposed of, the adjustment account will be written off to income in three equal annual installments.

(b) A company may, at its option, amortize the gains and losses on all debt securities sold thereafter by calculating the amount of gain or loss on a security in any year as the difference between the amortized value of the security at the sale yield rate and the amortized value at the purchase yield rate.

(c) In calculating the Investment Valuation Reserve (Accident and Sickness), the market deficiency on short term mortgages must be included only if mortgages amount to at least 80 percent of assets, instead of 40 percent.

(d) Instead of calculating the Investment Valuation Reserve (Accident and Sickness), as described in Section 5.13 above, the company may hold the greater of
(i) 1.5 percent of the book value of debt securities and

(ii) the reserve calculated as for the Investment Valuation Reserve (Life) multiplied by $(1 - A/B)$ where

A is the discounted value of such unmatured obligations on accident and sickness policies minus the discounted value of such unmatured obligations arising within five years of the statement date, and

B is the book value of all long-term debt securities minus the discounted value of all amounts expected to be received from those securities in the five years following the statement date, using the yield rates of the securities.

Example 5.0

EXAMPLE OF COMPLETION OF CANADIAN STATEMENT (INS-54)
INDEX TO DATA FOR ANNUAL STATEMENT

	DESCRIPTION OF DATA	REFERENCE NOS.	EXAMPLE
Additional data	Accident and sickness	350-372	5.19
	Investment	367-371	5.19
	Life	301-330	5.19
Incurred income	Line of business	510-526	5.21
	Miscellaneous accident and sickness	500-503	5.20
	Miscellaneous life	500-506	5.20
Nonledger accounts	Investment 19A, 19B	250-260	5.18
	Line of business 19A	210-228	5.16
	Line of business 19B	210-228	5.17
Trial balance	Assets and liabilities	50-99	5.15
	Miscellaneous income	01-29	5.14
	Line of business 19A	101-126	5.12
	Line of business 19B	101-126	5.13

This example of completion of the Canadian Life and Accident and Health Statement has been included to give students a better understanding of the text material. It is important that students work through the example, as many matters will only be thoroughly understood if the arithmetical work is done. Although every possible situation cannot be included in a single example, an attempt has been made to include enough to help students understand the principles involved.

Ledger and nonledger accounts for two successive years are supplied, along with additional data required for completion of the statement, such as details of actuarial reserves and market values of investments. (See Examples 5.12 to 5.19.) The assembly of the data into the various statements is shown (Examples 5.20 to 5.23), followed by copies of the principal statements from the annual statement form, with the data inserted. Appended to the descriptions are references to the items included on each line.

Except for the main asset schedules, wherein dollar amounts may be shown, and the exhibit of premiums, cash values and dividends, all financial statements must be completed to rounded thousands of dollars. Because the total of a number of lines should be the sum of the items entered, it may be necessary, in some cases, to round figures to the nearest thousand. The most satisfactory method is to enter nonledger items already rounded and to round ledger balances in the trial balance, correcting any balance error by adjusting income or disbursement accounts which will appear as lowest level items in exhibits.

The sample company is assumed to issue only individual participating and nonparticipating insurance and annuities and nonparticipating accident and health policies. The example shows trial balances and nonledger assets and liabilities for two successive years, 19A and 19B, as well as additional data, such as market values of investments, required for completion of the statement for year 19B. In the trial balances, items marked D are debits; those marked C are credits. Nonledger assets are identified with A, appended and nonledger liabilities with L. (The example assumes that the ledger is on a cash basis and therefore includes nonledger assets and liabilities since that is still a common procedure and is the more difficult case.) Ledger accounts are numbered 01 to 199, nonledger accounts 200 to 299, additional data items 300 to 399, and items from the calculation of incurred income 500 to 599. In the completed statements, the reference numbers of the accounts whose total is entered are listed in parentheses after the description.

In the trial balance for year 19B some items are shown twice: the first listing is for the balance prior to year-end entries and the second for the balance after those entries have been made. It will be seen that the balance account for year 19B before year-end entries is equal to the net sum of nonledger assets and liabilities plus unappropriated surplus for the year 19A.

Trial Balance Year 19B

Par insurance	$ 469,834C
annuities	63,251D
Nonpar insurance	637,805C
annuities	3,678,997C
Accident and sickness	22,399D
Miscellaneous income life	8,603,057C
accident and sickness	143,250C
Assets and liabilities life	112,301,499D
accident and sickness	611,689D
Total	99,465,895D
Balance account	99,465,895C

Nonledger Assets and Liabilities Year 19A

Par insurance	$ 47,650,071L
annuities	5,606,021L
Nonpar insurance	21,647,565L
annuities	16,564,900L
Accident and sickness	494,492L
Investments life	1,049,257A
accident and sickness	21,759A
Net sum	90,892,033L
Unappropriated earned surplus 19A	
Life	8,555,757L
Accident and sickness	18,105L
Net sum of nonledger assets and liabilities plus unappropriated surplus	$ 99,465,895L

We first calculate the incurred income for year 19B, using the ledger items for year 19B plus the nonledger assets and liabilities for 19B minus those for 19A (see Example 5.20, Example 5.21). In order to check the accuracy of the work, the net sum of ledger and nonledger accounts (checked against the totals in the source data) is balanced against the incurred total. (In practice, the columnar format used for the miscellaneous income is easier to check than the method used for income from policyholders, which was used to enable readers to find the source of the various items more easily.)

It is important to check the totals, because errors will cause the unappropriated earned surplus calculated in the reconciliation of unappropriated earned surplus to differ from that shown in the balance sheet.

After this is done we calculate the amortization of gains and losses on debt securities, the formula adjustment on shares, and the current year investment valuation and currency reserves.

Example 5.1

AMORTIZATION OF GAINS AND LOSSES ON DEBT SECURITIES

In this case the amortization is calculated on the basis of years to maturity rather than months (both methods are permissible). For both methods, the period includes the month or year of sale, so that the amortization factor is the difference between the maturity year and the current year plus 1. The securities are grouped by currency within maturity year for ease of calculation and listing in the statement.

The data required are taken from the additional data shown in Example 5.19, 315-317, and are entered as follows, using book rates of exchange and entering gains as negative and losses as positive:

CURRENCY	YEAR OF MATURITY	UNAMORTIZED PREVIOUS YR.	INCURRED CURRENT BOOK VALUES AT BOOK RATES ($000)	AMOUNT AMORTIZED	UNAMORTIZED END OF YR. BOOK	CURRENT
Can. $	19B+7	225		28	197	197
U.S. $	19B+8		36	4	32	34
Can. $	19B+9		87	9	78	78
Totals		225	123	41	307	309

(Example 5.22 shows the data in dollars for ledger entries.)

Example 5.2

FORMULA ADJUSTMENT ON SHARES

The previous year balances of the formula adjustment and the book values and market values of shares by currency are taken from Additional Data (Example 5.19, 311, 312, 321, 322). The market values of shares at book rates of exchange are found by multiplying the market values by the ratios of book to market rates.

The allocation of the formula adjustment amount to current revenue (investment income) as well as the net balance of the formula adjustment at the end of the year are calculated for the shares in each currency separately. The following items enter into the calculation:

a) book value of shares at book rates (311A,312A),
b) market value at book rates (311B,312B),
c) opening balance of formula adjustment (322) and
d) net gain or loss incurred in current year (321).

The interim balance of the formula adjustment account in each currency in this case is found by subtracting the gain on Canadian securities from the account at the beginning of the year and adding the loss on U.S. securities. The amount allocated to revenue is seven percent (increased to 15 percent in 1984) of the difference between the market value at book rates and the sum of the book values and the adjustment account. For Canadian currency, this is $.07 \times (4{,}522 - 4{,}052 - 66 = 404) = 28$ and, for U.S. currency, $.07 \times (387 - 359 - 23 = 5) = 0$. The amount allocated is added to the interim adjustment account to obtain the formula adjustment at the end of the year. The formula adjustments in foreign currencies are then converted to current rates for use in the calculation of the currency reserve. (In this case, $23 \times 1.22/1.15 = 24.4$, which is rounded up to 25 so that the total will be correct.)

FORMULA ADJUSTMENT ($000)

CURRENCY	BALANCE PREVIOUS YEAR	NET (GAIN)/LOSS	INTERIM BALANCE	ALLOCATED CURRENT YEAR	FORMULA ADJUSTMENT BOOK	FORMULA ADJUSTMENT CURRENT
Can. $	309	−243	66	28	94	94
U.S. $	18	5	23	0	23	25
Totals	327	−238	89	28	117	119

The market excess or deficiency at current exchange rates is the market value minus the sum of the book value and the formula adjustment, all taken at current exchange rates.

Book value 19B at current rates	$4,434
Formula adjustment	119
Adjusted book value	4,553
Market value	4,933
Deficiency (excess)	(380)

(Example 5.23 shows the data in dollars for ledger entries.)

Assets and Liabilities

In order to calculate the currency reserve we require the total assets and total liabilities, so it is convenient to enter the items in those statements at this time. Most of the asset items come from the trial balance, with a few from nonledger assets and liabilities. For example, item 01, bonds, is taken from item 50. Item 17, shares in subsidiary, is the sum of 56 (shares, affiliated) and 260 (equity in subsidiary).

Item 27, miscellaneous assets, consists of:

62	Furniture and equipment	$ 275,800D
63	EDP equipment	900,000D
65	Agents' debit balances	482,659D
68	Provision for uncollectable balances	195,817C
	Miscellaneous assets	$1,462,642D

The only items from other sources are the reserve for unamortized losses on bonds and the formula adjustment, which were calculated in the previous section.

Most of the liability items are taken from the nonledger assets and liabilities, with a few from the trial balance. Other liabilities include:

64	Agents' credit balances	$ 164,515C
205	Commissions on due premiums	37,523C
206		$ 147,818C
		$ 349,856C

Appropriated surplus (except for the investment valuation and currency reserve), which is also required for the calculation of the currency reserve, may be taken from the nonledger liabilities and the trial balance, using the asset total for miscellaneous assets and the previous year figure for additional reserves.

226	Reserve for unlicensed reinsurance	$ 614,827C
227	Reserve for cash value deficiencies	1,948,679C
72	Additional reserve	647,247C
	Appropriated surplus*	$3,210,753C

*Excluding investment valuation and currency reserve and reserve for miscellaneous assets

Example 5.3

CALCULATION OF CURRENCY RESERVE

ASSETS IN CANADIAN ($000)

Total assets (life)		$118,538
Less:		
Reserve for miscellaneous assets*	563	
Assets in U.S. currency (307,312,319)	11,958	
Unamortized losses on bonds	307	
Formula adjustment on shares	117	12,945
		105,593

*Accounts 62, 65, 68 from trial balance.

LIABILITIES AND APPROPRIATED SURPLUS CANADIAN $

Total liabilities (life)	$102,343
Plus:	
Appropriated surplus excluding investment valuation and currency reserve and reserve for misc. assets	3,211
Less U.S. currency liabilities (320)	−10,845
Total required for currency reserve	$ 94,709

CURRENCY RESERVE (LIFE) ($000)

ASSETS	BOOK RATES	CURRENT RATES
$Canadian	$105,593	$105,593
$U.S.	11,958	12,685
Unamortized losses on bonds*	307	309
Formula adjustment on shares#	117	119
Total assets	$117,975	$118,706
Liabilities and appropriated surplus		
$Canadian	94,709	94,709
$U.S.	10,845	11,505
Total liabilities	$105,554	$106,214
Excess of assets over liabilities	12,421	12,492

Currency reserve = excess book − excess current = −71.

*See Example 5.1.
#See Example 5.2.

It can easily be seen that the currency reserve may be calculated by including only assets, liabilities and appropriated surplus in foreign currencies, plus the unamortized losses on debt securities and the formula adjustment on shares, which include foreign currency amounts.

	ASSETS		LIABILITIES AND APPROPRIATED SURPLUS	
	BOOK (A)	CURRENT (B)	BOOK (C)	CURRENT (D)
		($000)		
U.S.$	$11,958	$12,685	$10,845	$11,505
Unamortized losses	307	309		
Formula adjustment	117	119		
Totals	$12,382	$13,113	$10,845	$11,505
A – C	$ 1,537			
B – D	$ 1,608			
Difference	–$ 71			

Any items of appropriated surplus in foreign currencies, such as reserves required by foreign jurisdictions, should be included with the foreign currency liabilities and appropriated surplus.

Example 5.4

CALCULATION OF INVESTMENT RESERVES

Investment reserve life ($000)

The reserve for debt securities is the greater of 1.5 percent of the book values of the securities (310) (excluding unamortized losses) at current rates = .015 × $98,026 = $1,470 and 10 percent of the residual market deficiency on debt securities (310) and equity securities (313) (since in this case there is neither an excess or deficiency on real estate) at current rates = .1 × ($5,867 − $499) = $537. The reserve is therefore $1,470.

There are no reserves for equity securities or real estate because there are no market deficiencies.

The maximum reserve is the greater of 1.5 percent of the book values of bonds ($1,470) and the total net market deficiency ($5,368), or $5,368.

The unadjusted reserve is the lesser of the sum of the three separate reserves ($1,470) and the maximum reserve ($5,368). Thus the unadjusted reserve is $1,470.

The reduction in book values of bonds in Year 19B was $75 (318). Because this reduced the reserve by 1.5 percent, the net reduction was $74. The adjustment in the current year reserve is two-thirds of this, or $49. The gross reduction in book values in Year 19A was $63 (318) and the net $62 so that the one-third allowance is $21 and the total adjustment is $49 + $21 = $70. The final calculation is:

Unadjusted reserve	$1,470
Less adjustment	70
Investment valuation reserve	$1,400
Plus currency reserve	(71)
Investment valuation and currency reserve	$1,329

At this point, the additional reserve may be adjusted. In this case, we assume that the management of the company considers $1,900 to be an adequate reserve so that the additional reserve is the excess over $1,329 or $571.

In preparing the statement for filing, the updated investment valuation and currency and additional reserves should be used to calculate the currency reserve. This will not change the result since the former reserves are in Canadian currency.

Investment valuation reserve accident and sickness ($000)
For the accident and sickness investment valuation reserve, debt securities are split into short-term and long-term, and the market excess or deficiency calculated for each group separately. (See additional data, items 361-366.)

The reserve for equity securities is the residual deficiency for the current year (365) ($16 − $18 = $2) or the average of the residual deficiencies for the current and previous years (372) (1), if less.

Because mortgages comprise less than 80 percent of the book values of assets, no reserve for short-term mortgages is required.

The unadjusted reserve is the smallest of three items:

Q, the sum of the deficiencies for long-term debt securities, equities, real estate and short-term mortgages, if required, $= 42 + 9 + 1 + 0 = 52$, (Example 5.19, 363-365).*

R, the residual deficiency for all debt securities and equity assets, $= -10 + 2 + 42 + 9 + 1 = 44$ (Example 5.19, 361-5,372), and

S, the residual deficiency for long-term debt securities, equity assets and real estate $= 42 + 9 + 1 + 0 = 52$.

The unadjusted reserve is therefore 44.

T is the ratio of the reserve on noncancellable policies (295) plus the reserves for installment claims (187 + 31) 513 (Example 5.19, 350,352-3), to total liabilities (634) $= .809$

The adjusted reserve is therefore:

$1.1 \times (1 - .5 \times .809) \times 44 = 1.1 \times .595 \times 44 = 29$.

Because all assets and liabilities in the accident and sickness branch are in Canadian currency, there is no currency reserve to be calculated. In this case, since we are assuming that the total of the required and additional investment reserves is to be unchanged, the additional reserve is the difference between 100 and 29 = 71.

We are now in a position to make the yearend entries and prepare the statement of increases in reserves.

---

*Since the book value of mortgages ($204,000) is under 80 percent of total assets, the deficiency for short-term mortgages may be ignored.

Example 5.5

YEAREND ENTRIES

1. Portions of the net gains and losses on bonds and shares (the amounts allocated to current investment income) are transferred to the income accounts, and the remainders are transferred to adjust the reserve for unamortized gains and losses on bonds and the formula adjustment reserve, respectively.

2. The investment valuation and currency reserves and the additional reserves are adjusted to the new totals, and the reserve for miscellaneous assets is increased to equal the total of miscellaneous assets (furniture and equipment less depreciation and agents' debit balances minus the reserve for uncollectable amounts) which require a 100 percent reserve.

The net difference in debits and credits is charged to the balance account.

For ledger entries, the calculation of gains and losses on bonds; the formula adjustment account, and the investment valuation and currency reserves are calculated to the dollar and rounded to thousands for the statement.

YEAREND ENTRIES 19B

	ACCOUNT BALANCE BEFORE	ENTRY	ACCOUNT BALANCE AFTER
Net loss on sale of bonds (14)	$ 122,676D	$122,676C	$ 0
Amortization of bond losses (16)	0C	40,793D	40,793D
Unamortized losses on bonds (66)	225,000D	81,883D	306,883D
Net gain on sale of shares (15)	238,125C	238,125D	0D
Formula adjustment on shares (17)	0C	28,616C	28,616C
Formula adjustment account (67)	327,000D	209,509C	117,491D
Investment valuation and currency reserve—life (71)	1,252,753C	76,047C	1,328,800C
Additional reserve—life (72)	647,247C	76,047D	571,200C
Investment valuation reserve A&S (71)	27,832C	1,327C	29,159C
Additional reserve A&S (72)	72,168C	1,327D	70,841C
Reserve for miscellaneous assets (69)	487,710C	74,932C	562,642C
Totals	2,051,159C	74,932C	2,126,091C
Balance account	$ 99,465,895C	$ 74,932D	$99,390,963C

FINAL ENTRIES
(ALL INCOME ACCOUNTS CLEARED TO BALANCE ACCOUNT)

Life participating	$ 469,834D
Annuity participating	63,251C
Life nonparticipating	637,805D
Annuity nonparticipating	3,678,997D
Accident and sickness	22,399C
Miscellaneous income life	8,475,431D
Miscellaneous income accident and sickness	143,250D
Net total to balance account	13,319,667C
Balance account previous	99,390,963C
Balance account current	$112,710,630C

The statement of changes in reserves can now be completed from the trial balance, the nonledger accounts and the totals of the reserves required by the Department and additional reserves transferred to the Analysis of Liabilities, Capital and Surplus, which can be completed.

The combined balance sheet is prepared from the total columns of the analyses. Only total amounts for bonds, shares, mortgages and investments in subsidiaries are entered. In the combined liabilities, only the net actuarial reserve is shown.

Example 5.6

NET INVESTMENT INCOME

The exhibit of net investment income can be completed from the calculation of incurred income (Example 5.20) and from the final trial balance (Example 5.14). The reference numbers after the descriptions indicate the sources of the data.

The net rate of investment income is calculated from the net investment income (I) by the formula $2I/(A+B-I)$.

	LIFE	ACCIDENT AND SICKNESS
	($000)	
Invested assets 19A (A) (XI, 3, 7, 10, 11-16, 22 and 23)	$102,352	$1,613
Invested assets 19B (B)	115,975	1,736
Net investment income (I)	8,978	145
A + B - I	209,349	3,204
2I/(A + B - I)	8.577%	9.051%

Example 5.7

ALLOCATION OF INCOME BY FUND

It is necessary to allocate income items, such as net investment income, interest paid on claims, reductions in book values of assets, etc., by fund. The best procedure is to do the allocation by line of business within each fund, so that the data is available both by line of business and by fund.

In this example, we shall allocate the items by mean funds—that is, the funds at the beginning of the year plus half the net increase in funds from directly allocated items. The increase can be taken by using all the items in the analysis of income by line of business (including transfers between lines of business arising from normal transactions) except those to be allocated (in this case items 03 and 16) and then adding back items not affecting funds, such as increases in reserves, etc.

Interest on claims is allocated in the same manner as investment income since it can be assumed that the amounts held pending payment were invested. No charge is made to the shareholders' fund.

The allocated amounts can now be entered where applicable in the analysis of income by line of business and the analysis completed. The fund totals can then be entered in the analysis of income by fund, along with transfers between funds.

When the analysis of income by fund is completed, the combined income statement can be completed by combining the totals for Life and Accident and Sickness. For the combined statement, dividends incurred are entered separately from the increase in the reserve for dividends, and the same procedure is followed for experience rating refunds.

The second part of the combined income statement (income from unusual and extraordinary items and income from subsidiaries and ancillary operations), as well as the reconciliation of unallocated earned surplus, are then completed. The total unallocated surplus so calculated must agree with the corresponding amount in the liabilities, capital and surplus.

ALLOCATION BY LINE OF BUSINESS AND FUND

	PARTICIPATING		NONPARTICIPATING ($000)		SHARE-HOLDERS
	INSURANCE	ANNUITIES	INSURANCE	ANNUITIES	
Direct income	$-4,019	$ -461	$-1,476	$-1,123	$ -250
Plus:					
Increases in reserves					
Actuarial (521)	3,988	343	2,084	4,810	
Amounts on deposit (520)	241	48	49		
Dividend reserve (517)	220	4			
Increase in funds	430	-66	657	3,687	-250
One-half increase	215	-33	329	1,843	-125
Funds 19A*	53,888	6,680	22,400	18,329	2,781
Mean funds	54,103	6,647	22,729	20,172	2,656
Ratio A	.50893	.06253	.21381	.18975	.02498
Ratio B	.52197	.06413	.21928	.19461	
(excluding shareholders)					
Investment income (A)	4,569	561	1,920	1,704	224
Interest on claims (B)	27	3	12	10	
W/D of bonds (A)	38	5	16	14	2
Increase in equity in subsidiary (A)	1	0	1	0	0

*From previous year data.

Example 5.8

RECONCILIATION OF FUNDS

In the reconciliation of funds, the fund totals at the end of the previous year are entered from the previous year statement. The income before unusual or extraordinary items; the adjustment for increases in reserves and any unusual or extraordinary items, and income from subsidiaries and ancillary operations (which must be allocated by fund) are added to the fund totals from the previous year to produce the current year fund totals.

Transfers of surplus between funds are then entered. In this case the only such transfer is a transfer from participating to shareholders. The maximum permitted is one-ninth of the dividends paid to policyholders ($1,784,000) or $198,000, so that the share of the participating policy-holders is 90 percent. The shareholders' fund is charged with the dividends paid to shareholders. The net totals are the fund balances at the end of the year.

Summary of funds and amounts owing
The summary of funds and amounts owing establishes the unappropriated surplus in each fund and checks the total funds, since the sum of the funds, plus amounts owing, must equal the total assets.

The reserves held in the liabilities and appropriated surplus of the insurance funds are entered. The difference between the sums of those items and the fund totals is the unappropriated surplus. The capital and surplus in the shareholders' fund and the totals of all other funds, as well as the total funds are entered. The total amounts owing (from the liabilities) is added. The grand total is compared with the asset total from the balance sheet, with which it must agree.

For comparison, the entries for the insurance and shareholders' funds for the previous year are listed at the bottom of the page.

Funds by line of business
The fund totals by line of business can now be calculated as the starting point for the allocation of income for the next year. The same principles are used as in the reconciliation of funds.

	PARTICIPATING		NONPARTICIPATING	
	INSURANCE	ANNUITIES	INSURANCE	ANNUITIES
		($000)		
Funds 19A	$53,888	$ 6,680	$22,400	$18,329
Income 19B	523	97	432	571
Increases in reserves:				
Actuarial	3,988	343	2,084	4,810
Amounts on deposit	241	48	49	
Dividends	220	4		
W/D of book values	–38	–5	–16	–14
Increase in equity value	1	0	1	0
Transfers to shareholders*	–184	–14		
Funds 19B	$58,639	$ 7,153	$24,950	$23,696

*Transfers to shareholders are one-ninth of dividends paid.

Example 5.9

V: STATEMENT OF CHANGES IN FINANCIAL POSITION

Item 1 of the statement changes, "net income transferred to reconciliation of earned surplus," is shown in total only in item 14 of III: statement of income. In order to obtain figures by branch, we must take the "income before unusual or extraordinary items" from XIII: analysis of income by funds, and adjust the amount for unusual and extraordinary items (split by branch, if necessary) from Statement III.

	LIFE	ACCIDENT AND SICKNESS ($000)	TOTAL
Income before unusual or extra-ordinary items (XIII, 35)	$1,847	$60	$1,907
Nonamortized capital gains and losses (III, 04)	(75)		(75)
Increase in value of sub-sidiaries (III, 12)	2		2
Net income transferred to reconciliation of surplus	$1,774	$60	$1,834

As explained in the text (5.6), the items in the statement of changes of financial position should balance with the changes in assets and liabilities plus items from the reconciliation of earned surplus, and any changes in capital and contributed surplus. In the example of the completed statement, references to increases in the analyses of assets and liabilities during the current year are indicated after the descriptions of most of the items. Numbers in parentheses indicate that the sum of two or three items in this statement should balance with the sum of the indicated items in the assets and liabilities, taking increases in assets as negative and increases in liabilities as positive.

For example, the change in the book values of bonds (Assets, 01) is the sum of three items in the statement of changes:

Item 19 p. 6, Amortization, accrual	-$ 15	$	$
Item 22 p. 6, Reduction in book values	1,931		
Item 08 p. 7, Acquisition of bonds	– 8,455		– 6,539
	19B	19A	NET
Change in book values of bonds	–$56,593	$50,054	–$6,539

A more complicated example arises from items 9 and 20 (Other), because both commissions on due premiums and agents' credit balances are included in other liabilities. The increase in the former is included in item 9 and the increase in the latter in item 20 (which also includes the change in the value of assets of subsidiaries from the statement of assets). The references are L13(2), 10 and L13(2), A17 respectively. The check is made as follows:

Life
Item 9 p. 6 $ 49
Item 20 p. 6   18 $67

	19B	19A	NET
Assets 17	-$21	$ 19	
Liabilities 10	192	- 170	
13	$350	- 303	
	$521	-$454	$67

Example 5.10

XIX: TEST OF COMPLIANCE WITH SECTION 103 ACCIDENT AND SICKNESS

References beside the descriptions indicate the location of additional data for unearned premiums and the analyses of assets and liabilities (accident and sickness) and the statement of changes in reserves for other items. It is assumed that the selected claims ratio is 95 percent or more, so that the 15 percent margin is used for unearned premiums on other than noncancellable policies as well as for the net unpaid claims, other than installment claims.

The margin may be checked as follows:

	($000)	
Unappropriated earned surplus		$ 76
Surplus transferred from life		1,000
Additional reserves		71
		$1,147
Less 15 percent margin (lines 02,04)		17
Excess		$1,130

Example 5.11

Check of Balance Account

The final check is on the balance account, which should equal the net sum of nonledger assets and liabilities plus the unappropriated surplus.

	($000)
Nonledger assets and liabilities	19B
Participating life	$ 52,197L
Participating annuities	6,004L
Nonparticipating life	24,037L
Nonparticipating annuities	21,367L
Accident and sickness	559L
Investment	1,199A
Total	$102,965L
Unappropriated surplus	9,745L
	$112,710L
Balance account	$112,710C

Example 5.12

TRIAL BALANCE YEAR 19A

		PARTICIPATING		NONPARTICIPATING		ACCIDENT AND
		INSURANCE	ANNUITIES	INSURANCE	ANNUITIES	SICKNESS
101	Premiums single	$ 30,000C	$ 30,300C	$ 52,000C	$4,462,000C	$ 79,240C
102	first year	750,000C	163,400C	400,000C		
103	renewal	4,600,000C	770,000C	2,350,000C	4,950C	746,175C
104	Commissions direct single	900D	990D	1,560D	130,300D	
105	first year	525,000D	60,000D	315,872D		33,075D
106	renewal	184,000D	38,500D	97,126D	120D	42,038D
107	Commissions reinsurance first year			35,872C		
108	renewal			11,126C		
109	Death claims	600,000D	18,500D	350,000D	63,550D	
110	Maturity values	300,000D		160,000D		
111	Surrender values	1,250,000D	592,700D	575,000D	306,520D	
112	Disability payments	5,000D		2,400D		631,800D
113	Annuity payments		67,200D		812,350D	
114	Considerations for settlement annuities	82,000C		37,000C		
115	Settlement annuity payments	70,000D		32,500D		
116	Dividends cash	15,745D	3,475D			
117	applied	1,434,255D	101,500D			
118	used to purchase additions	1,020,000C				
119	left on deposit	300,000C	92,700C			
120	withdrawn	250,000D	82,475D			
121	Proceeds left at interest	150,000C		72,000C		
122	Proceeds withdrawn	140,000D		68,000D		
123	Income tax paid	140,000D	8,000D	78,000D	15,000D	15,000D
124	Taxes, licenses, fees	130,500D	1,350D	62,000D	2,650D	17,824D
125	General expenses	1,135,750D	103,500D	578,300D	147,100D	80,807D
126	Increase in provision for agents' debit balances	9,113D	990D	5,500D	1,825D	930D
		$ 741,737C	$ 22,780D	$ 631,740C	$2,987,535C	$ 3,941C

Example 5.13

TRIAL BALANCE YEAR 19B

		PARTICIPATING		NONPARTICIPATING		ACCIDENT AND
		INSURANCE	ANNUITIES	INSURANCE	ANNUITIES	SICKNESS
101	Premiums single	$ 40,000C	$ 43,000C	$ 47,000C	$5,650,000C	$ 82,247C
102	first year	800,000C	137,000C	435,000C		783,508C
103	renewal	4,800,000C	742,000C	2,565,000C		
104	Commissions single	1,200D	1,530D	1,410D	3,850C	
105	direct first year	560,000D	48,200D	347,465D	154,500D	34,362D
106	renewal	192,000D	34,300D	107,773D		44,119D
107	Commissions reinsurance first year			42,965C		
	renewal			14,273C	115D	
109	Death claims	625,000D	19,150D	340,000D	66,700D	
110	Maturity values	330,000D		180,000D		
111	Surrender values	1,375,000D	546,527D	615,000D	497,124D	653,359D
112	Disability payments	8,000D		2,700D		
113	Annuity payments		80,450D		919,000D	
114	Considerations for settlement annuities	94,000C		41,500C		
115	Settlement annuity payments	81,000D		37,600D		
116	Dividends cash	17,530D	4,580D			
117	applied	1,632,470D	121,720D			
118	used to purchase additions	1,100,000C				
119	left on deposit	350,000D	117,350C			
120	withdrawn	315,000D	102,758D			
121	Proceeds left at interest	175,000C		78,000C		
122	Proceeds withdrawn	160,000D		71,000D		
123	Income tax paid	175,000D	48,000D	165,200D	165,000D	40,000D
124	Taxes, licenses, fees	141,500D	1,400D	72,500D	3,970D	19,242D
125	General expenses	1,265,340D	92,894D	639,160D	166,415D	96,042D
126	Increase in provision for agents' debit balances	10,126D	1,092D	6,125D	2,029D	1,030D
		$ 469,834C	$ 63,251D	$ 637,805C	$3,678,997C	$ 22,399D

Example 5.14

Trial Balance—Miscellaneous Income

	Year 19A		Year 19B		
	Life	Accident and Sickness	Life Before Adjusting Entries	Accident and Sickness	Life After Adjusting Entries
01 Interest on bonds	$4,146,881C	$ 113,089C	$4,616,425C	$ 122,850C	$
05 Accrual of discount	15,307C		16,303C		
06 Amortization premium	1,725D		1,635D		
Dividends on shares					
07 preferred	54,125C	993C	59,712C	1,072C	
08 common	117,882C		148,216C		
09 Interest on mortgages	2,985,226C	18,865C	3,384,749C	20,431C	
10 Interest on policy loans	348,000C		378,000C		
11 Interest on bank deposits	17,262C	1,378C	18,872C	1,458C	
Income from real estate					
12 occupied	300,000C		315,000C		
13 other	325,000C		350,000C		
14 Net loss on sale of bonds	22,500D		122,676D	3,124D	0
15 Net gain on sale of shares	9,800C		238,125C	4,875C	0
16 Amortization of loss on bonds					40,793D
17 Formula adjustment on shares					28,616C
18 Interest on borrowed money	73,500D		82,400D		
19 Bonds written down	63,417D		75,474D		
20 Shareholders' dividends	250,000D		250,000D		
21 Interest on claims	47,000D		49,500D		
22 Real estate expenses	45,800D		49,250D		
26 Other investment expenses	121,961D	3,772D	137,826D	4,116D	
27 Investment taxes	8,085D	165D	9,584D	196D	
Depreciation on real estate:					
28 occupied	75,000D		75,000D		
29 other	69,000D		69,000D		
Totals	$7,541,495C	$ 130,388C	$8,603,057C	$ 143,250C	$8,475,431C
	$7,671,883C		$8,746,307C		$8,618,681C

Example 5.15

TRIAL BALANCE—ASSETS AND LIABILITIES

		YEAR 19A		YEAR 19B		
		LIFE	ACCIDENT & SICKNESS	LIFE#	ACCIDENT & SICKNESS#	LIFE##
	Bonds:					
50	nonaffiliated	$ 50,053,470D	$ 1,357,280D	$ 56,593,221D	$ 1,466,105D	$
51	affiliated	250,000D		250,000D		
54	Shares: preferred	772,855D	14,545D	1,035,322D	17,878D	
55	common	2,685,400D		3,376,437D		
56	affiliated	5,000D		5,000D		
57	Mortgages	35,271,596D	189,374D	40,755,249D	203,874D	
	Real estate:					
58	occupied	2,675,000D		2,600,000D		
59	other	2,585,426D		2,516,426D		
60	Policy loans	6,200,000D		7,030,800D		
61	Cash	219,385D	29,639D	176,627D	23,832D	
62	Furniture and equipment less depreciation	237,500D		275,800D		
63	EDP equipment less depreciation	1,250,000D		900,000D		
64	Agents' credit balances	145,075C		164,515C		
65	Agents' debit balances (gross)	425,625D		482,659D		306,883D
66	Unamortized net loss on bonds	225,000D		225,000D		117,491D
67	Adjustment account on shares	327,000D		327,000D		
68	Provision for uncollectable debit balances	175,415C		195,817C		
69	Reserve for miscellaneous assets	487,710C		487,710C		
71	Investment valuation and currency reserve	1,252,753C	27,832C	1,252,753C	27,832C*	562,642C
72	Additional reserve	647,247C	72,168C	647,247D	72,168C*	1,328,800C
73	Capital stock	1,500,000C		1,500,000C		
74	Contributed surplus	1,000,000C		1,000,000C		
75	Surplus transferred	1,000,000D	1,000,000C	1,000,000D	1,000,000C	571,200C
99	Balance account (combined)	$ 98,975,057D	$ 490,838D	$112,301,499D	$ 611,689D	$112,098,941D
		$ 87,451,839C	$ 87,451,839C		$ 99,465,895C	$112,710,630C

*Reserves after adjusting entries 29,159 and 70,841 respectively.
#before adjusting entries.
##after adjusting entries.

Example 5.16

Nonledger Assets and Liabilities Year 19A

	Participating Insurance	Participating Annuities	Nonparticipating Insurance	Nonparticipating Annuities	Accident and Sickness
Premiums					
201 Due and uncollected first year	$ 20,000A	$ 1,190A	$ 11,250A	$	$ 7,969A
202 Renewal	600,000A	27,700A	295,000A		75,046A
203 Deferred first year	202,500A	42,518A	97,550A		
204 renewal	1,431,030A	180,950A	555,241A		
205 Commissions on due first year	16,600L	702L	9,563L		
206 renewal	90,000L	2,216L	38,350L		
207 Loading on deferred first year	172,125L	29,763L	89,746L		
208 renewal	343,447L	27,143L	127,705L		
209 Paid in advance first year	1,000L		450L		
210 renewal	5,000L		2,200L		
211 Outstanding death claims	150,000L	5,560L	75,000L	19,300L	46,498L
212 maturity values	20,000L		10,000L		163,864L
213 disability claims					7,750L
214 Disability payments not yet due					25,574L
215 Unreported outstanding	35,000L		21,000L		
216 Unreported not yet due					
217 Outstanding dividends	35,000L				
218 Due and accrued income tax	33,000L		20,000L		
219 other taxes	27,000L		12,000L		876L
220 general expenses	110,000L		49,800L		2,598L
221 Reserves for settlement annuities	736,506L		330,894L		
222 Other policy reserves	42,236,426L	4,880,415L	19,049,514L	16,545,600L	317,284L
223 Dividends on deposit	2,357,500L	782,580L	840,500L		
224 Proceeds on deposit	1,537,500L				
225 Reserve for dividends	1,700,000L	130,000L			
226 Reserve for unlicensed reinsurance	297,497L		215,428L		
227 Reserve for deficiencies of reserves from cash surrender values			1,714,456L		11,417L*
228 Reserve for deferred acquisition expenses in excess of 30%					1,646L
	$47,650,071L	$ 5,606,021L	$21,647,565L	$16,564,900L	$ 494,492L

*reserve for negative amounts in noncancellable accident and sickness liabilities.

Example 5.17

Nonledger Assets and Liabilities Year 19B

		Participating Insurance	Participating Annuities	Nonparticipating Insurance	Nonparticipating Annuities	Accident and Sickness
	Premiums					
201	Due and uncollected first year	$ 30,000A	$ 550A	$ 14,500A	$	$ 8,496A
202	renewal	680,000A	22,400A	352,000A		80,931A
203	Deferred first year	215,800A	38,415A	106,478A		
204	renewal	1,654,006A	189,715A	633,408A		
205	Commissions on due first year	24,510L	326L	12,687L		
206	renewal	100,640L	1,770L	45,408L		
207	Loading on deferred first year	183,430L	26,891L	97,960L		
208	renewal	396,961L	28,457L	145,864L		
209	Paid in advance first year	1,100L		825L		
210	renewal	6,000L		2,450L		
211	Outstanding death claims	200,000L	3,600L	85,000L	11,700L	
212	maturity values	50,000L		12,000L		
213	disability claims					59,573L
214	Disability payments not yet due					187,329L
215	Unreported outstanding	42,000L		23,000L		8,902L
216	Unreported not yet due					30,496L
217	Outstanding dividends	42,500L				
218	Due and accrued income tax	35,000L		25,000L		
219	other taxes	30,000L		12,000L		1,052L
220	general expenses	120,000L		59,500L		2,942L
221	Reserves for settlement annuities	783,497L		343,837L		
222	Other policy reserves	46,348,834L	5,229,251L	21,181,290L	21,355,200L	343,505L
223	Dividends on deposit	2,511,250L	830,700L			
224	Proceeds on deposit	1,624,625L		889,700L		
225	Reserve for dividends	1,920,000L	134,000L			
226	Reserve for unlicensed reinsurance	356,600L		258,227L		
227	Reserve for deficiencies of reserves from cash surrender values			1,948,679L		12,842L
228	Reserve for deferred acquisition expenses in excess of 30%					2,150L
		$52,197,141L	$ 6,003,915L	$24,037,041L	$21,366,900L	$ 559,364L

Example 5.18

Nonledger Assets and Liabilities
Investment

	Year 19A		Year 19B	
	Life	Accident and Sickness	Life	Accident and Sickness
Interest due				
250 Bonds	$ 4,616A	$ 384A	$ 5,165A	$ 535A
251 Mortgages	25,578A	187A	27,250A	215A
Interest accrued				
252 Bonds	746,744A	20,356A	826,787A	22,113A
253 Mortgages	121,424A	832A	149,133A	901A
256 Policy loans	170,000A		188,435A	
Due and accrued				
258 Investment expenses	11,000L		12,430L	
259 Interest on claims	22,000L		24,742L	
260 Equity in subsidiary*	13,895A		15,762A	
Totals	$ 1,049,257A	$ 21,759A	$ 1,175,360A	$ 23,764A
	$1,071,016A		$1,199,124A	

*These amounts represent the proportion of the excess of the assets of the subsidiary over the liabilities and paid in capital, that the shares owned by the company bear to the total shares outstanding.

Example 5.19

ADDITIONAL DATA: LIFE

ACTUARIAL RESERVES NET OF DEFERRED PREMIUMS AND REINSURANCE CEDED

			PARTICIPATING		NONPARTICIPATING		TOTAL
			INSURANCE	ANNUITIES	INSURANCE	ANNUITIES	
301	Net level premium	19B					$96,267,227
302		19A					84,576,863
303	Minimum reserves	19B	$43,707,636	$ 4,955,340	$20,271,523	$21,034,872	$89,969,371
304		19A	39,884,914	4,619,576	18,241,891	16,297,416	79,043,797
305	Mandatory increase		$ 3,822,722	$ 335,764	$ 2,029,632	$ 4,737,456	$10,925,574

INVESTED ASSETS EXCLUDING SUBSIDIARIES 19B

		CURRENCY	BOOK	CURRENT	PARTICIPATING		NONPARTICIPATING		DEFICIENCY
					BOOK RATES	CURRENT	MARKET BOOK RATES	MARKET CURRENT RATES	(CURRENT)
306	Bonds	Can. $	1.00	1.00	$45,469,221	$45,469,221	$	$44,918,424	$
307		U.S. $	1.15	1.22	11,124,000	11,801,113		10,967,432	
308	Mortgages	Can. $	1.00	1.00	40,755,249	40,755,249		36,272,432	
309									
310	Total debt securities				$97,348,470	$98,025,583		$92,158,288	5,867,295
311	Shares	Can. $	1.00	1.00	4,052,817 (A)	4,052,817	4,522,221 (B)	4,522,221	
312		U.S. $	1.15	1.22	358,942	380,791	387,225	410,795	
313	Total equity securities				$ 4,411,759	$ 4,433,608	$ 4,909,446	$ 4,933,016	$ (499,408)
314	Net market deficiency								$ 5,367,887

(continued)

Example 5.19 (Continued)

ADDITIONAL DATA: LIFE

UNAMORTIZED LOSSES ON SALE OF BONDS

	MATURITY YEAR	CURRENCY	AMOUNT	INCURRED
315	19B+7	Can. $	225,000	Previous years
316	19B+8	U.S. $	36,000	Current year
317	19B+9	Can. $	86,676	Current year
318	Writedown of bonds		Current year $75,474	Previous year $63,417
319	Other U.S. current assets at book rates			$ 474,423
320	U.S. currency liabilities at book rates			10,845,375
321	Profit (loss) on disposition of shares (book)		Can. $242,978	U.S. $(4,853)
322	Adjustment account on shares 19A at book rates		309,148	17,852

INVESTED ASSETS 19B

	BONDS	MORTGAGES	SHARES	POLICY LOANS
323 Book values 19A	$50,053,470	$35,271,596	$ 3,458,255	$6,200,000
324 Accrual of discount	16,303			
325 Amortization of premium	-1,635			
326 Written down	-75,474			
327 Proceeds of sales and repayments	-1,732,518	-3,890,457	-1,783,419	-483,227
328 Gain or loss on sale	-122,676		238,125	
329 New investments	8,455,751	9,374,110	2,498,798	1,314,027
330 Book values 19B	$56,593,221	$40,755,249	$ 4,411,759	$7,030,800

MISCELLANEOUS ASSETS

	COST	19B DEPRECIATION*	BOOK VALUE	COST	19A DEPRECIATION	BOOK VALUE
331 EDP equipment	$2,150,000	$1,250,000	$900,000	$2,150,000	$900,000	$1,250,000
332 Furniture and equipment	590,015	314,215	275,800	517,090	279,590	237,500

*Increase in depreciation included in general and investment expenses.

(continued)

Example 5.19 (Continued)

ADDITIONAL DATA: ACCIDENT AND SICKNESS

		19B	19A
350	Unearned premiums and mid-terminal reserves on noncancellable policies	$295,476	$272,849
351	Unearned premiums less deferred acquisition expense on other policies	48,029	44,435
352	Reserves for claims payable in installments reported	187,329	163,864
353	unreported	30,496	25,574
354		$561,330	$506,722
355	Reserves on noncancellable policies net level premium	322,069	297,678
356	Gross unearned premiums on other policies	71,685	65,830
357	less	48,029	44,435
358	Deferred acquisition expenses	$ 23,656	$ 21,395
359	30% of unearned premiums	21,506	19,749
360	Excess over 30%	$ 2,150	$ 1,646

INVESTED ASSETS 19B

		BOOK	MARKET	DEFICIENCY
361	Short term bonds	$1,002,663	$1,012,690	$(10,027)
362	mortgages	70,823	68,698	2,125
363	Long term bonds	463,442	421,732	41,710
364	mortgages	133,051	123,737	9,314
365	Shares	17,878	16,448	1,430
366	Market deficiency on shares (previous year)			586

(continued)

Example 5.19 (Continued)

ADDITIONAL DATA: ACCIDENT AND SICKNESS

INVESTED ASSETS 19B

		BONDS	MORTGAGES	SHARES
367	Book value 19A	$1,357,280	$ 189,374	$ 14,545
368	Proceeds of sales and repayments	-110,415	-45,826	-14,875
369	Gain (loss) on sale	-3,124		4,875
370	New investments	222,364	60,326	13,333
371	Book values 19B	$1,466,105	$ 203,874	$ 17,878
372	Average two-year market deficiency on shares ½ ($1,430 + $586) = $1,008			

Example 5.20

INCURRED INCOME MISCELLANEOUS LIFE 19B

		LEDGER 19B	NONLEDGER 19B	NONLEDGER 19A	INCURRED
01	Bond interest	$ 4,616,425C	$	$	
250	due		5,165A	4,616A	
252	accrued		826,787A	746,744A	
500	Incurred	$ 4,616,425C	$ 831,952A	$ 751,360A	$ 4,697,017C
05	Accrual of discount	16,303C			
06	Amortization of premium	1,635D			
501	Total	14,668C			14,668C
07	Dividends on shares preferred	59,712C			
08	common	148,216C			
502	Total incurred	207,928C			207,928C
09	Mortgage interest	3,384,749C			
251	due		27,250A	25,578A	
255	accrued		149,133A	121,424A	
503	Incurred	$ 3,384,749C	$ 176,383A	$ 147,002A	$ 3,414,130C
10	Interest on policy loans	378,000C			
256	accrued		188,435A	170,000A	
504	Incurred	$ 378,000C	$ 188,435A	$ 170,000A	$ 396,435C
11	Interest on bank deposits	18,872C			18,872C
12	Income from real estate company occupied	315,000C			
13	other	350,000C			
505	Total	$ 665,000C			665,000C
18	Interest on borrowed money	82,400D			
26	Investment expenses	137,826D		11,000L	
255	unpaid		12,430L		
22	Real estate expenses	49,250D			
27	Investment taxes	9,584D			
28	Real estate depreciation company occupied	75,000D			
29	other	69,000D			
	Charges against investment income	$ 423,060D	$ 12,430L	$ 11,000L	424,490D

(continued)

Example 5.20 (Continued)

INCURRED INCOME MISCELLANEOUS LIFE 19B

		LEDGER 19B	NONLEDGER 19B	NONLEDGER 19A	INCURRED
21	Interest on claims	$ 49,500D	$	$	$
259	accrued		24,742L	22,000L	52,242D
506	Incurred	$ 49,500D	$ 24,742L	$ 22,000L	$ 52,242D
14	Net loss on sale of bonds	122,676D			122,676D
15	Net profit on sale of shares	238,125C			238,125C
19	Bonds written down	75,474D			75,474D
20	Dividends to shareholders	250,000D			250,000D
260	Increase in equity of subsidiary		15,762D	13,895A	1,867C
	Totals (Ex. 5.14, 5.18)	$ 8,603,057C	$ 1,175,360A	$ 1,049,257A	$ 8,729,160C

ACCIDENT AND SICKNESS

		LEDGER 19B	NONLEDGER 19B	NONLEDGER 19A	INCURRED
01	Bond interest	$ 122,850C	$	$	$
250	due		535A	384A	
252	accrued		22,113A	20,356A	
500	Incurred	$ 122,850C	$ 22,648A	$ 20,740A	$ 124,758C
07	Dividends on shares preferred	1,072C			1,072C
09	Mortgage interest	20,431C			
251	due		215A	187A	
253	accrued		901A	832A	
503	Incurred	$ 20,431C	$ 1,116A	$ 1,019A	$ 20,528C
11	Interest on bank deposit	1,458C			1,458C
26	Investment expenses	4,116D			4,116D
27	taxes	196D			196D
14	Net loss on sale of bonds	3,124D			3,124D
15	Net profit on sale of shares	4,875C			4,875C
	Totals (Ex. 5.14, 5.18)	$ 143,250C	$ 23,764A	$ 21,759A	$ 145,255C

Example 5.21

INCURRED INCOME BY LINE OF BUSINESS 19B

		PARTICIPATING		NONPARTICIPATING		ACCIDENT AND SICKNESS
		INSURANCE	ANNUITIES	INSURANCE	ANNUITIES	
Premiums						
101	Single	$ 40,000C	$ 43,000C	$ 47,000C	$ 5,650,000C	$
118	Dividends to purchase additions	1,100,000C				
	Single premiums	$ 1,140,000C	$ 43,000C	$ 47,000C	$ 5,650,000C	$
102	First year	800,000C	137,000C	435,000C		82,247C
201	Due 19B	30,000A	550A	14,500A		8,496A
	19A	(20,000A)	(1,190A)	(11,250A)		(7,969A)
209	Advance 19B	1,100L		825L		
	19A	(1,000L)		(450L)		
	First year premiums	$ 809,900C	$ 136,360C	$ 437,875C		$ 82,774C
103	Renewal	4,800,000C	742,000C	2,565,000C	3,850C	783,508C
202	Due 19B	680,000A	22,400A	352,000A		80,931A
	19A	(600,000A)	(27,700A)	(295,000A)		(75,046A)
210	Advance 19B	6,000L		2,450L		
	19A	(5,000L)		(2,200L)		
	Renewal premiums	$ 4,879,000C	$ 736,700C	$ 2,621,750C	3,850C	$ 789,393C
510	Total premiums	$ 6,828,900C	$ 916,060C	$ 3,106,625C	$ 5,653,850C	$ 872,167C
Commissions						
104	Single	1,200D	1,530D	1,410D	154,500D	
105	First year direct	560,000D	48,200D	347,465D		34,362D
205	Due 19B	24,510L	326L	12,687L		
	19A	(16,600L)	(702L)	(9,563L)		
	First year commissions	$ 567,910D	$ 47,824D	$ 350,589D		$ 34,362D
106	Renewal	192,000D	34,300D	107,773D	115D	44,119D
206	Due 19B	100,640L	1,770L	45,408L		
	19A	(90,000L)	(2,216L)	(38,350L)		
	Renewal commissions	$ 202,640D	$ 33,854D	$ 114,831D	115D	44,119D

(continued)

Example 5.21 (Continued)

INCURRED INCOME BY LINE OF BUSINESS 19B

| | | PARTICIPATING | | NONPARTICIPATING | | ACCIDENT AND SICKNESS |
		Insurance	Annuities	Insurance	Annuities	
511	Total direct commissions	$ 771,750D	$ 83,208D	$ 466,830D	154,615D	$ 78,481D
109	Death claims	625,000D	19,150D	340,000D	66,700D	
211	Outstanding 19B	200,000L	3,600L	85,000L	11,700L	
	19A	(150,000L)	(5,560L)	(75,000L)	(19,300L)	
215	Unreported 19B	42,000L		23,000L		
	19A	(35,000L)		(21,000L)		
512	Death claims	$ 682,000D	$ 17,190D	$ 352,000D	$ 59,100D	
110	Maturities	330,000D		180,000D		
212	Outstanding 19B	50,000L		12,000L		
	19A	(20,000L)		(10,000L)		
513	Matured endowments	$ 360,000D		$ 182,000D		
112	Disability payments	8,000D		2,700D		653,359D
213	Outstanding 19B					59,573L
	19A					(46,498L)
215	Unrep. O/S 19B					8,902L
	19A					(7,750L)
514	Disability claims	$ 8,000D		$ 2,700D		$ 667,586D
111	Surrender values	1,375,000D	546,527D	615,000D	497,124D	
113	Annuity payments		80,450D		919,000D	
116	Dividends cash	17,530D	4,580D			
	applied	1,632,470D	121,720D			
117	Outstanding 19B	42,500L				
217	19A	(35,000L)				
516	Dividends incurred	$ 1,657,500D	$ 126,300D			
225	Reserve for dividends	1,920,000L	134,000L			
	19A	(1,700,000L)	(130,000L)			

Acct.		C1	C2	C3	C4	C5
517	Increase in reserve	$ 220,000D	$ 4,000D			
	Commissions reinsurance					
107	First year			42,965C		
108	Renewal			14,273C		
518	Total commissions reinsurance ceded			$ 57,238C		
119	Dividends deposited	350,000C	117,350C	78,000C		
120	withdrawn	315,000D	102,758D	71,000D		
121	Proceeds deposited	175,000C				
122	withdrawn	160,000D				
223	Liability dividends 19B	2,511,250L	830,700L	889,700L		
	19A	(2,357,500L)	(782,580L)	(840,500L)		
224	Liability proceeds 19B	1,624,625L				
	19A	(1,537,500L)				
519	Interest on amounts on deposit*	$ 190,875D	$ 33,528D	$ 42,200D		
520	Increase in amounts on deposit	240,875	48,120	49,200		
221	Reserve settlement annuity 19B	783,497L		343,837L		343,505L
	19A	(736,506L)		(330,894L)		(317,284L)
222	Policy reserves 19B	46,348,834L	5,229,251L	21,181,290L	21,355,200L	
	19A	(42,236,426L)	(4,880,415L)	(19,049,514L)	(16,545,600L)	
203	Deferred premiums first year 19B	215,800A	38,415A	106,478A		
	19A	(202,500A)	(42,518A)	(97,550A)		
204	Deferred premiums renewal 19B	1,654,006A	189,715A	633,408A		
	19A	(1,431,030A)	(180,950A)	(555,241A)		
207	Loading first year 19B	183,430L	26,891L	97,960L		
	19A	(172,125L)	(29,763L)	(89,746L)		
208	Loading renewal 19B	396,961L	28,457L	145,864L		
	19A	(343,447L)	(27,143L)	(127,705L)		
	Dis. installments					
214	Reported 19B					187,329L
	19A					(163,864L)
216	Unreported 19B					30,496L
	19A					(25,574L)
521	Increase in reserves	$ 3,987,942D	$ 342,616D	$ 2,083,997D	$ 4,809,600D	$ 54,608D
522	Total reserve 19B**	$45,842,916	$ 5,056,469	$21,029,065	$21,355,200	$ 561,330
	19A**	$41,854,974	$ 4,713,853	$18,945,068	$16,545,600	$ 506,722

*should equal the sum of the amounts calculated on credit balances.
**sums of amounts of accounts 221-2, 203-4, 207-8, 214 and 216 for each year.

(continued)

Example 5.21 (Continued)

INCURRED INCOME BY LINE OF BUSINESS 19B

		PARTICIPATING		NONPARTICIPATING		ACCIDENT AND SICKNESS
		INSURANCE	ANNUITIES	INSURANCE	ANNUITIES	
Premiums						
125	General expenses	1,265,340D	92,894D	639,160D	166,415D	96,042D
126	Unpaid 19B	10,126D	1,092D	6,125D	2,029D	1,030D
220		120,000L		59,500L		2,942L
	19A	(110,000L)		(49,800L)		(2,598L)
524	Incurred expenses	$ 1,285,466D	$ 93,986D	$ 654,985D	$ 168,444D	$ 97,416D
124	Taxes, licenses, fees	141,500D	1,400D	72,500D	3,970D	19,242D
219	Unpaid 19B	30,000L		12,000L		1,052L
	19A	(27,000L)		(12,000L)		(876L)
525	Incurred taxes	$ 144,500D	$ 1,400D	$ 72,500D	$ 3,970D	$ 19,418D
123	Income tax	175,000D	48,000D	165,200D	165,000D	40,000D
218	Unpaid 19B	35,000L		25,000L		
	19A	(33,000L)		(20,000L)		
526	Incurred income tax	$ 177,000D	$ 48,000D	$ 170,200D	$ 165,000D	$ 40,000D
114	Considerations for settlement annuities	94,000C		41,500C		
115	Settlement annuity payments	81,000D		37,600D		
226	Reserve for unlicensed reinsurance 19B	356,600L		258,227L		
	19A	(297,497L)		(215,428L)		
		$ 59,103D		$ 42,799D		
227	Reserve for currency valuation deficiencies 19B			1,948,679L		12,842L
	19A			(1,714,456L)		(11,417L)
	Increase			$ 234,223D		$ 1,425D

(continued)

Example 5.21 (Continued)

INCURRED INCOME BY LINE OF BUSINESS 19B

	PARTICIPATING		NONPARTICIPATING		ACCIDENT AND SICKNESS
	INSURANCE	ANNUITIES	INSURANCE	ANNUITIES	
Premiums 228					
Reserve for deferred acquisition expenses 19B					2,150L
19A					(1,646L)
Increase					504D
Total incurred	$ 4,077,236D	$ 461,145D	$ 1,751,671D	$ 1,123,003D	$ 87,271D
Total ledger (Ex. 5.13)	469,834C	63,251D	637,805C	3,678,997C	22,399D
Total nonledger 19B	52,197,141L	6,003,915L	24,037,041L	21,366,900L	559,364L
(Ex. 5.16, 5.17) 19A	(47,650,071L)	(5,606,021L)	(21,647,565L)	(16,564,900L)	(494,492L)
	$ 4,077,236D	$ 461,145D	$ 1,751,671D	$ 1,123,003D	$ 87,271D

Example 5.22

AMORTIZATION OF GAINS AND LOSSES ON BONDS: LIFE (19B)

CURRENCY	YEAR OF MATURITY	UNAMORTIZED PREVIOUS YEAR	INCURRED DURING YEAR	AMOUNT AMORTIZED	UNAMORTIZED (GAIN) LOSS END OF YEAR	CURRENCY ADJUSTMENT
Can. $	YS+7	$225,000	$	$28,125	$196,875	
U.S. $	YS+8		36,000	4,000	32,000	× 7/115 = 1,948
Can. $	YS+9		86,676	8,668	78,008	
		$225,000	$122,676	$40,793	$306,883	+ 1,948 = $308,831

Example 5.23

SCHEDULE B SHARES — PART 3: LIFE (BOOK AND MARKET VALUES YEAR 19B)

	RATES OF EXCHANGE		DEVELOPMENT OF BOOK VALUES		MARKET VALUES	
	BOOK	CURRENT	BOOK RATES (A)	CURRENT RATES	BOOK RATES (B)	CURRENT RATES
Can. $	1.00	1.00	$4,052,817	$4,052,817	$4,522,221	$4,522,221
U.S. $	1.15	1.22	358,942	380,791	387,225	410,795
Total			4,411,759	4,433,608	4,909,446	4,933,016
Formula adjustment (Part 4)			117,491	118,897		
Book values at yearend rates			$4,529,250	$4,552,505		

SCHEDULE B SHARES — PART 4: (FORMULA ADJUSTMENT: LIFE)

(BOOK RATES OF EXCHANGE)

	BALANCE PREVIOUS YEAR	NET CAPITAL (GAIN) LOSS	BALANCE BEFORE ALLOCATION (C)	ALLOCATION TO REVENUE .07 (B-A-C) (D)	FORMULA ADJUSTMENT BOOK RATES (C+D)	CURRENT RATES
Can. $	309,148	(242,978)	66,170	28,226	94,396	94,396
U.S. $	17,852	4,853	22,705	390	23,095	24,501
	$327,000	$(238,125)	$88,875	$28,616	$117,491	$118,897

02

NAME OF COMPANY ▶ EXAMPLE		YEAR OF STATEMENT 19 B

I. ASSETS ($'000)

		CURRENT YEAR 01	PREVIOUS YEAR 02
BONDS	01	58,366	51,636
SHARES	02	4,547	3,800
MORTGAGE LOANS	03	40,959	35,461
REAL ESTATE, LESS ENCUMBRANCES OF $.......	04	5,116	5,260
GROUND RENTS, LESS ENCUMBRANCES OF $.......	05		
POLICY LOANS	06	7,031	6,200
TERM DEPOSITS AND GUARANTEED INVESTMENT CERTIFICATES	07		
CASH, INCLUDING DEMAND DEPOSITS	08	200	249
OTHER INVESTMENTS	09		
INVESTMENTS IN SUBSIDIARIES	10	271	269
INVESTMENT INCOME DUE & ACCRUED	11	1,221	1,090
PREMIUMS OUTSTANDING	12	1,189	1,038
AMOUNTS DUE FROM OTHER INSURERS	13		
MISCELLANEOUS ASSETS	14	1,463	1,738
	15		
	16		
	17		
	18		
ASSETS IN SEGREGATED FUNDS (AT MARKET)	19		
TOTAL ASSETS	▶ 20	120,363	106,741

NOTE: SECTION 48 OF THE CANADIAN AND BRITISH INSURANCE
       COMPANIES ACT REQUIRES THE MAINTENANCE OF SEPARATE
       FUNDS AND ACCOUNTS IN RESPECT OF LIFE AND OTHER THAN
       LIFE BUSINESS. THE REQUIRED DETAILS ARE REPORTED
       ON IN PAGES 05 TO 17 OF THIS STATEMENT.

03

| NAME OF COMPANY ▶   EXAMPLE | | YEAR OF STATEMENT
19 B | |

II. LIABILITIES, CAPITAL AND SURPLUS ($'000)

		CURRENT YEAR 01	PREVIOUS YEAR 02
NET ACTUARIAL RESERVE	01	93,845	82,566
OUTSTANDING CLAIMS AND PROVISION FOR UNREPORTED CLAIMS	02	496	390
AMOUNTS ON DEPOSIT WITH THE COMPANY	03	5,856	5,518
OTHER CONTRACT LIABILITIES	04	78	66
PROVISION FOR DIVIDENDS AND EXPERIENCE RATING REFUNDS TO POLICYHOLDERS	05	2,054	1,830
CURRENT INCOME TAXES, DUE AND ACCRUED	06	60	53
OTHER TAXES, LICENCES AND FEES, DUE AND ACCRUED	07	43	40
GENERAL AND INVESTMENT EXPENSES, DUE AND ACCRUED	08	195	173
AMOUNTS DUE TO OTHER INSURANCE COMPANIES	09		
BANK OVERDRAFT AND BORROWED MONEY INCLUDING INTEREST DUE AND ACCRUED	10		
MISCELLANEOUS LIABILITIES	11	350	303
	12		
	13		
	14		
STAFF PENSION AND INSURANCE FUNDS	15		
SEGREGATED FUND LIABILITIES	16		
TOTAL LIABILITIES (01 TO 16)	▶ 17	102,977	90,939
DEFERRED INCOME TAXES	▶ 18		
CAPITAL, SURPLUS AND RESERVES: RESERVES REQUIRED BY THE DEPARTMENT	19	4,499	4,009
RESERVES REQUIRED BY FOREIGN JURISDICTIONS	20		
ADDITIONAL RESERVES	21	642	719
CAPITAL STOCK ISSUED AND PAID: COMMON STOCK	22	1,500	1,500
: PREFERRED STOCK	23		
CONTRIBUTED SURPLUS	24	1,000	1,000
UNAPPROPRIATED EARNED SURPLUS	25	9,745	8,574
UNAPPROPRIATED SURPLUS (24+25)	▶ 26	10,745	9,574
TOTAL CAPITAL, SURPLUS AND RESERVES (19 TO 25)	▶ 27	17,386	15,802
TOTAL LIABILITIES, CAPITAL AND SURPLUS (17+18+27)	▶ 28	120,363	106,741

04

NAME OF COMPANY ▶ EXAMPLE		YEAR OF STATEMENT 19B

III. INCOME STATEMENT ($'000)

		CURRENT YEAR 01	PREVIOUS YEAR 02
PREMIUMS	01	17,377	
CONSIDERATIONS FOR SETTLEMENT ANNUITIES	02	135	
POLICY DIVIDENDS AND PROCEEDS OF CONTRACTS DEPOSITED IN SEGREGATED FUNDS	03		
NET INVESTMENT INCOME	04	9,123	
NET INVESTMENT GAIN(LOSS) ON SEGREGATED FUND ASSETS	05		
CONTRIBUTION TO STAFF PENSION AND INSURANCE FUNDS	06		
NET GAIN OR (LOSS) ON CURRENCY EXCHANGE TRANSACTIONS	07		
RESERVE ADJUSTMENT ON REINSURANCE CEDED	08		
	09		
	10		
SUBTOTAL (01 TO 10) ▶	11	26,635	
CLAIMS INCURRED	12	6,364	
CLAIMS INCURRED PAID DIRECTLY FROM SEGREGATED FUNDS	13		
PAYMENTS UNDER SETTLEMENT ANNUITIES	14	119	
POLICY DIVIDENDS AND PROCEEDS OF CONTRACTS WITHDRAWN FROM SEGREGATED FUNDS	15		
NORMAL INCREASE IN ACTUARIAL RESERVES - MANDATORY PROVISION	16	10,980	
- ADDITIONAL PROVISION	17	299	
NORMAL INCREASE IN SEGREGATED FUNDS	18		
INCREASE IN STAFF PENSION AND INSURANCE FUNDS	19		
INTEREST INCURRED ON CLAIMS	20	52	
TAXES, LICENCES AND FEES, EXCLUDING INVESTMENT TAXES AND INCOME TAXES	21	242	
COMMISSIONS INCURRED (NET)	22	1,497	
GENERAL EXPENSES (EXCLUDING INVESTMENT EXPENSES)	23	2,300	
PAYMENTS FROM STAFF PENSION AND INSURANCE FUNDS	24		
DIVIDENDS TO POLICYHOLDERS	25	1,784	
INCREASE IN PROVISION FOR DIVIDENDS TO POLICYHOLDERS	26	224	
EXPERIENCE RATING REFUNDS	27		
INCREASE IN PROVISION FOR EXPERIENCE RATING REFUNDS	28		
INTEREST INCURRED ON AMOUNTS ON DEPOSIT	29	267	
	30		
	31		
INCOME TAXES - CURRENT	32	600	
- DEFERRED	33		
SUBTOTAL (12 TO 33) ▶	34	24,728	
INCOME BEFORE UNUSUAL OR EXTRAORDINARY ITEMS (11 MINUS 34) ▶	35	1,907	

05

NAME OF COMPANY ▶ EXAMPLE		YEAR OF STATEMENT 19B

III. INCOME STATEMENT (CONTINUED) ($'000)

		CURRENT YEAR 01	PREVIOUS YEAR 02
INCOME BEFORE UNUSUAL OR EXTRAORDINARY ITEMS (CARRIED FORWARD FROM PAGE 04)	01	1,907	
UNUSUAL CHANGE IN ACTUARIAL RESERVE - LIFE	02		
- ACCIDENT & SICKNESS	03		
NON-AMORTIZABLE GAINS (LOSSES) IN RESPECT OF INVESTED ASSETS - LIFE	04	(75)	
GAIN (LOSS) DUE TO CHANGES IN BOOK RATES OF EXCHANGE	05		
INCOME BEFORE EXTRAORDINARY ITEMS AND INCOME TAXES ON UNUSUAL ITEMS (01 TO 05) ▶	06	1,832	
INCOME TAXES ON UNUSUAL ITEMS: CURRENT	07		
DEFERRED	08		
INCOME BEFORE EXTRAORDINARY ITEMS (06-07-08) ▶	09	1,832	
NET EXTRAORDINARY ITEMS (GIVE DETAILS ON PAGE 08)	10		
NET INCOME FROM INSURANCE OPERATIONS (09+10) ▶	11	1,832	
INCREASE (DECREASE) IN VALUE OF SECTION 64 AND 65 SUBSIDIARIES	12	2	
NET INCOME FROM ANCILLARY OPERATIONS	13		
NET INCOME CARRIED TO RECONCILIATION OF UNAPPROPRIATED EARNED SURPLUS (11+12+13) ▶	14	1,834	

IV. RECONCILIATION OF UNAPPROPRIATED EARNED SURPLUS ($'000)

		LIFE 01	ACCIDENT AND SICKNESS 02	TOTAL 03
UNAPPROPRIATED EARNED SURPLUS, 31 DECEMBER 19 IN SHAREHOLDERS' FUNDS	15	1,281		1,281
IN INSURANCE FUNDS	16	7,275	18	7,293
IN SEGREGATED FUNDS	17		■	
SUB-TOTAL (15 TO 17) ▶	18	8,556	18	8,574
	19			
	20			
NET INCOME FROM INCOME STATEMENT (+ OR -)	21	1,774	60	1,834
DECREASE (INCREASE) IN RESERVES REQUIRED - BY THE DEPARTMENT	22	(487)	(3)	(490)
- BY FOREIGN JURISDICTIONS	23			
DECREASE (INCREASE) IN ADDITIONAL RESERVES	24	76	1	77
DIVIDENDS TO SHAREHOLDERS (-)	25	(250)		(250)
NET INCREASE (DECREASE) IN UNAPPROPRIATED EARNED SURPLUS DURING THE YEAR (SUB-TOTAL 19 TO 25) ▶	26	1,113	58	1,171
UNAPPROPRIATED EARNED SURPLUS, 31 DECEMBER 19 IN SHAREHOLDERS' FUNDS	27	1,451		1,451
IN INSURANCE FUNDS	28	8,218	76	8,294
IN SEGREGATED FUNDS	29		■	
TOTAL UNAPPROPRIATED EARNED SURPLUS, 31 DEC. 19B (27 TO 29) ▶	30	9,669	76	9,745

| NAME OF COMPANY ▶ EXAMPLE | | | YEAR OF STATEMENT 19B | |

V. STATEMENT OF CHANGES IN FINANCIAL POSITION
(EXCLUDING SEGREGATED FUNDS) ($'000)

		LIFE		ACCIDENT & SICKNESS	
		CURRENT YEAR	PREVIOUS YEAR	CURRENT YEAR	PREVIOUS YEAR
A. SOURCES OF CASH:		01	02	03	04
I. OPERATIONS:					
NET INCOME CARRIED TO RECONCILIATION OF EARNED SURPLUS	01	1,774		60	
CHARGES (CREDITS) NOT INVOLVING CASH: NET CHANGES IN:					
NET ACTUARIAL RESERVES LO3	02	11,225		54	
CLAIMS INCLUDING PROVISION FOR UNREPORTED CLAIMS LO4	03	91		15	
PROVISION FOR DIVIDENDS AND E.R.Rs TO POLICYHOLDERS LO7	04	224			
ADJUSTMENT FOR UNAMORTIZED GAIN OR LOSS ON BONDS/MORTGAGES AO2	05	(82)		▓	▓
FORMULA ADJUSTMENT IN RESPECT OF GAINS/LOSSES ON SHARES AO6	06	210		▓	▓
CURRENT TAXES PAYABLE LO8,LO9	07	10			
DEFERRED TAXES	08				
ACCRUED COMMISSIONS, GENERAL AND INVESTMENT EXPENSES L13(2),10	09	49			
OTHER CONTRACTUAL OBLIGATIONS LO6	10	12			
STAFF PENSION AND INSURANCE FUNDS	11				
REINSURANCE PAYABLE/RECEIVABLE TRANSACTIONS	12				
PREMIUMS RECEIVABLE A24	13	(145)		(6)	
INVESTMENT INCOME, DUE AND ACCRUED A23	14	(129)		(2)	
AMOUNTS ON DEPOSIT LO5	15	338			
INTER-BRANCH RECEIVABLES	16				
DEPRECIATION ON REAL ESTATE A11(3)	17	144			
DEPRECIATION/WRITE-DOWN OF MISCELLANEOUS ASSETS A27(2)	18	405			
AMORTIZATION/ACCRUAL ON DEBT SECURITIES A01(3)	19	(15)			
OTHER L13(2),A17	20	18			
SUB-TOTAL: CASH GENERATED BY OPERATIONS (01 TO 20) ▶	21	14,129		121	
II. PRINCIPAL REPAYMENTS ON DISPOSITION OF INVESTED ASSETS:					
REDUCTION IN BOOK VALUES OF:					
BONDS A01(3)	22	1,931		113	
SHARES A04,05(2)	23	1,545		10	
MORTGAGES A08(2)	24	3,891		46	
REAL ESTATE A11(3)	25				
POLICY LOANS A13(2)	26	483		▓	▓
OTHER INVESTED ASSETS	27				
	28				
SUB-TOTAL (22 TO 28) ▶	29	7,850		169	

07

NAME OF COMPANY ▶ EXAMPLE		YEAR OF STATEMENT 19B

V.   STATEMENT OF CHANGES IN FINANCIAL POSITION
(EXCLUDING SEGREGATED FUNDS) - CONTINUED   ($'000)

		LIFE		ACCIDENT & SICKNESS	
		CURRENT YEAR 01	PREVIOUS YEAR 02	CURRENT YEAR 03	PREVIOUS YEAR 04
III. OTHER SOURCES:					
CHANGES IN BORROWED MONEY	01				
CAPITAL AND CONTRIBUTIONS PAID IN DURING THE YEAR	02				
CHANGES IN INTER-FUND TRANSFERS DURING THE YEAR	03				
	04				
	05				
SUB-TOTAL - OTHER SOURCES (01 TO 05) ▶	06				
TOTAL FUNDS GENERATED (06 + PAGE 06, LINES 21+29) ▶	07	21,979		290	
B. APPLICATION OF FUNDS GENERATED:					
I. ACQUISITION OF INCOME PRODUCING ASSETS:					
BONDS A01(3)	08	8,455		222	
SHARES A04,05(2)	09	2,499		13	
MORTGAGE LOANS A08(2)	10	9,374		61	
REAL ESTATE A11(3)	11				
POLICY LOANS A13(2)	12	1,314		■■■■	
OTHER INVESTED ASSETS	13				
	14				
SUB-TOTAL (08 TO 14) ▶	15	21,642		296	
II. OTHER DISPOSITIONS OF CASH:					
DIVIDENDS TO SHAREHOLDERS (R of S)	16	250			
ACQUISITION OF MISCELLANEOUS ASSETS A27(2)	17	130			
OTHER	18				
	19				
SUB-TOTAL OTHER DISPOSITIONS OF CASH (16 TO 19) ▶	20	380			
TOTAL FUNDS APPLIED (15+20) ▶	21	22,022		296	
NET CHANGE IN CASH (07-21) ▶	22	(43)		(6)	
C. RECONCILIATION OF CASH:					
CASH - BEGINNING OF YEAR	23	219		30	
- END OF YEAR (22+23) ▶	24	176		24	

10

NAME OF COMPANY ▶   YEAR OF STATEMENT
        EXAMPLE   19 B

VIII.   CHANGES IN RESERVES ($'000)

		END OF YEAR 01	BEGINNING OF YEAR 02	INCREASE (DECREASE) 03
LIFE				
INVESTMENT VALUATION AND CURRENCY RESERVE (71)	01	1,329	1,253	76
RESERVE FOR CASH VALUE DEFICIENCIES AND AMOUNTS OF NEGATIVE RESERVES (227)	02	1,948	1,714	234
RESERVE FOR REINSURANCE CEDED TO UNREGISTERED REINSURERS (226)	03	615	513	102
VALUATION RESERVE FOR MISCELLANEOUS ASSETS AND OTHER INVESTMENTS (69)	04	563	488	75
	05			
	06			
	07			
SUB-TOTAL - RESERVES REQUIRED BY THE DEPARTMENT (01 TO 07) ▶	08	4,455	3,968	487
RESERVES REQUIRED BY FOREIGN JURISDICTIONS	09			
ADDITIONAL RESERVES (72)	10	571	647	(76)
TOTAL RESERVES APPROPRIATED RE LIFE (08+09+10) ▶	11	5,026	4,615	411
ACCIDENT AND SICKNESS				
INVESTMENT VALUATION AND CURRENCY RESERVE (71)	12	29	28	1
RESERVE FOR NEGATIVE AMOUNTS IN NON-CANCELLABLE ACCIDENT AND SICKNESS LIABILITIES (227)	13	13	11	2
RESERVE FOR REINSURANCE CEDED TO UNREGISTERED REINSURERS	14			
VALUATION RESERVE FOR MISCELLANEOUS ASSETS AND OTHER INVESTMENTS	15			
RESERVE FOR DEFERRED POLICY ACQUISITION EXPENSES IN EXCESS OF 30% OF UNEARNED PREMIUMS (228)	16	2	2	0
	17			
SUB-TOTAL - RESERVES REQUIRED BY THE DEPARTMENT ▶	18	44	41	3
RESERVES REQUIRED BY FOREIGN JURISDICTIONS	19			
ADDITIONAL RESERVES (72)	20	71	72	(1)
TOTAL RESERVES APPROPRIATED RE ACCIDENT AND SICKNESS (18+19+20) ▶	21	115	113	2

IX.   CHANGES IN CAPITAL AND CONTRIBUTED SURPLUS ($'000)

LIFE				
CAPITAL STOCK COMMON: (73)	22	1,500	1,500	0
PREFERRED:	23			
CONTRIBUTED SURPLUS	24	1,000	1,000	0
AGGREGATE TRANSFER OF FUNDS FROM (TO) ACCIDENT AND SICKNESS (70)	25	(1,000)	(1,000)	0
ACCIDENT AND SICKNESS				
CAPITAL STOCK COMMON:	26			
PREFERRED:	27			
CONTRIBUTED SURPLUS	28			
AGGREGATE TRANSFER OF FUNDS FROM (TO) LIFE (70)	29	1,000	1,000	0

12

NAME OF COMPANY	YEAR OF STATEMENT
EXAMPLE	19 B

XI. ANALYSIS OF ASSETS ($'000)

REF. PG. LIFE	A&S			LIFE 01	ACCIDENT & SICKNESS 02	TOTAL 03
54	56 57	BONDS (BEFORE ADJUSTMENT) (50)	01	56,593	1,466	58,059
45	–	ADJUSTMENT FOR UNAMORTIZED (GAIN) LOSS ON DISPOSAL (66)	02	307		307
		BONDS (01+02) ▶	03	56,900	1,466	58,366
58	62	SHARES (BEFORE ADJUSTMENT) – PREFERRED (54)	04	1,035	18	1,053
58	62	– COMMON (55)	05	3,377		3,377
61	–	FORMULA ADJUSTMENT IN RESPECT OF (GAINS) LOSSES (67)	06	117		117
		SHARES (04+05+06) ▶	07	4,529	18	4,547
64	66 67	MORTGAGE LOANS (BEFORE ADJUSTMENT) (57)	08	40,755	204	40,959
46	–	ADJUSTMENT FOR UNAMORTIZED (GAIN) LOSS ON DISPOSAL	09			
		MORTGAGE LOANS (08-09) ▶	10	40,755	204	40,959
68	69	REAL ESTATE, NET OF ENCUMBRANCES (58-9)	11	5,116		5,116
68	69	GROUND RENTS, NET OF ENCUMBRANCES	12			
		POLICY LOANS (60)	13	7,031		7,031
70	71	TERM DEPOSITS AND GUARANTEED INVESTMENT CERTIFICATES	14			
72	73	CASH, INCLUDING DEMAND DEPOSITS (61)	15	176	24	200
74	74	OTHER INVESTMENTS	16			
59		INVESTMENTS IN SUBSIDIARIES: COMMON SHARES (56,260)	17	21		21
59		PREFERRED SHARES	18			
55		BONDS (51)	19	250		250
64		MORTGAGE LOANS ON REAL ESTATE	20			
		OTHER	21			
		SUB-TOTAL INVESTMENTS IN SUBSIDIARIES (17 TO 21) ▶	22	271		271
28	28	INVESTMENT INCOME, DUE AND ACCRUED (500,503,504)	23	1,197	24	1,221
33	33	PREMIUMS OUTSTANDING (201,202)	24	1,100	89	1,189
		AMOUNTS DUE FROM OTHER INSURERS	25			
		INTER-BRANCH RECEIVABLES	26			
74	74	MISCELLANEOUS ASSETS (62,63,65,68)	27	1,463		1,463
			28			
			29			
			30			
		ASSETS IN SEGREGATED FUNDS (AT MARKET)	31			
		TOTAL ASSETS ▶	32	118,538	1,825	120,363

12

| NAME OF COMPANY   EXAMPLE | | | | YEAR OF STATEMENT 19 A |

XI. ANALYSIS OF ASSETS ($'000)

REF. LIFE	PG. A&S			LIFE 01	ACCIDENT & SICKNESS 02	TOTAL 03
54	56 57	BONDS (BEFORE ADJUSTMENT)	01	50,054	1,357	51,411
45	–	ADJUSTMENT FOR UNAMORTIZED (GAIN) LOSS ON DISPOSAL	02	225	▮	225
		BONDS (01+02) ▶	03	50,279	1,357	51,636
58	62	SHARES (BEFORE ADJUSTMENT) – PREFERRED	04	772	15	787
58	62	– COMMON	05	2,686		2,686
61	–	FORMULA ADJUSTMENT IN RESPECT OF (GAINS) LOSSES	06	327	▮	327
		SHARES (04+05+06) ▶	07	3,785	15	3,800
64	66 67	MORTGAGE LOANS (BEFORE ADJUSTMENT)	08	35,272	189	35,461
46	–	ADJUSTMENT FOR UNAMORTIZED (GAIN) LOSS ON DISPOSAL	09		▮	
		MORTGAGE LOANS (08-09) ▶	10	35,272	189	35,461
68	69	REAL ESTATE, NET OF ENCUMBRANCES	11	5,260		5,260
68	69	GROUND RENTS, NET OF ENCUMBRANCES	12			
		POLICY LOANS	13	6,200	▮	6,200
70	71	TERM DEPOSITS AND GUARANTEED INVESTMENT CERTIFICATES	14			
72	73	CASH, INCLUDING DEMAND DEPOSITS	15	219	30	249
74	74	OTHER INVESTMENTS	16			
59		INVESTMENTS IN SUBSIDIARIES: COMMON SHARES	17	19		19
59		PREFERRED SHARES	18			
55		BONDS	19	250		250
64		MORTGAGE LOANS ON REAL ESTATE	20			
		OTHER	21			
		SUB-TOTAL INVESTMENTS IN SUBSIDIARIES (17 TO 21) ▶	22	269		269
28	28	INVESTMENT INCOME, DUE AND ACCRUED	23	1,068	22	1,090
33	33	PREMIUMS OUTSTANDING	24	955	83	1,038
		AMOUNTS DUE FROM OTHER INSURERS	25			
		INTER-BRANCH RECEIVABLES	26			
74	74	MISCELLANEOUS ASSETS	27	1,738		1,738
			28			
			29			
			30			
		ASSETS IN SEGREGATED FUNDS (AT MARKET)	31		▮	
		TOTAL ASSETS ▶	32	105,045	1,696	106,741

13

NAME OF COMPANY ▶ EXAMPLE			YEAR OF STATEMENT 19 B		

XII. ANALYSIS OF LIABILITIES, CAPITAL AND SURPLUS ($'000)

REF PG. LIFE A&S			LIFE 01	ACCIDENT & SICKNESS 02	TOTAL 03
		ACTUARIAL RESERVE BEFORE DEDUCTION OF(301) DEFERRED POLICY ACQUISITION EXPENSES 01	96,267	612	96,879
		DEDUCTION IN RESPECT OF DEFERRED POLICY ACQUISITION EXPENSES 02	2,983	51	3,034
38	38	NET ACTUARIAL RESERVE (01-02) (522) ▶ 03	93,284	561	93,845
23	25	OUTSTANDING CLAIMS AND PROVISION FOR UN-REPORTED CLAIMS (OTHER THAN INSTALMENT CLAIMS) (211-215,life,213,215 A&S) 04 (223,224)	427	69	496
33	33	AMOUNTS ON DEPOSIT WITH THE COMPANY 05	5,856		5,856
40	40	OTHER CONTRACT LIABILITIES (209-10,259) 06	78		78
40	40	PROVISION FOR DIVIDENDS AND EXPERIENCE RATING REFUNDS TO POLICYHOLDERS (225) 07	2,054		2,054
32	32	CURRENT INCOME TAXES, DUE AND ACCRUED (218) 08	60		60
32	32	OTHER TAXES, LICENCES AND FEES, DUE AND ACCRUED (219) 09	42	1	43
31	31	GENERAL AND INVESTMENT EXPENSES, DUE AND ACCRUED (220,258) 10	192	3	195
		AMOUNTS DUE TO OTHER INSURANCE COMPANIES 11			
72	73	BANK OVERDRAFTS AND BORROWED MONEY INCLUDING INTEREST DUE AND ACCRUED 12			
41	41	MISCELLANEOUS LIABILITIES (64,205-6) 13	350		350
		14			
		15			
		16			
41	41	STAFF PENSION AND INSURANCE FUNDS 17			
		SEGREGATED FUND LIABILITIES 18		▓	
		TOTAL LIABILITIES (03 TO 18) ▶ 19	102,343	634	102,977
32	32	DEFERRED INCOME TAXES ▶ 20			
		CAPITAL, SURPLUS AND RESERVES:			
10	10	RESERVES REQUIRED BY THE DEPARTMENT 21	4,455	44	4,499
10	10	RESERVES REQUIRED BY FOREIGN JURISDICTIONS 22			
10	10	ADDITIONAL RESERVES 23	571	71	642
10	10	CAPITAL STOCK ISSUED AND PAID: COMMON STOCK (73) 24	1,500		1,500
10	10	PREFERRED STOCK 25			
10	10	CONTRIBUTED SURPLUS 26	1,000		1,000
10	10	INTER-BRANCH TRANSFER OF FUNDS (70) (FROM)/TO 27	(1,000)	1,000	
05	05	UNAPPROPRIATED EARNED SURPLUS 28	9,669	76	9,745
		UNAPPROPRIATED SURPLUS (26+27+28) ▶ 29	9,669	1,076	10,745
		TOTAL CAPITAL, SURPLUS AND RESERVES (21 TO 28) ▶ 30	16,195	1,191	17,386
		TOTAL LIABILITIES, CAPITAL AND SURPLUS (ITEMS 19+20+30) ▶ 31	118,538	1,825	120,363

ACTUARIAL RESERVE PERTAINING TO LIFE INSURANCE
CALCULATED ACCORDING TO THE METHOD DESCRIBED IN
SUBSECTIONS 82(4) AND 82(7) OR THE MODIFICATION
AS PER PARAGRAPH 82(8)(b) OF THE CANADIAN
AND BRITISH INSURANCE COMPANIES ACT (303)   32   89,969   89,969

13

NAME OF COMPANY ▶ EXAMPLE			YEAR OF STATEMENT 19 A		

XII. ANALYSIS OF LIABILITIES, CAPITAL AND SURPLUS ($'000)

REF PG. LIFE&S				LIFE 01	ACCIDENT & SICKNESS 02	TOTAL 03
		ACTUARIAL RESERVE BEFORE DEDUCTION OF DEFERRED POLICY ACQUISITION EXPENSES	01	84,577	522	85,129
		DEDUCTION IN RESPECT OF DEFERRED POLICY ACQUISITION EXPENSES	02	2,518	45	2,563
38	38	NET ACTUARIAL RESERVE (01-02) ▶	03	82,059	507	82,566
23	25	OUTSTANDING CLAIMS AND PROVISION FOR UN-REPORTED CLAIMS (OTHER THAN INSTALMENT CLAIMS)	04	336	54	390
33	33	AMOUNTS ON DEPOSIT WITH THE COMPANY	05	5,518		5,518
40	40	OTHER CONTRACT LIABILITIES	06	66		66
40	40	PROVISION FOR DIVIDENDS AND EXPERIENCE RATING REFUNDS TO POLICYHOLDERS	07	1,830		1,830
32	32	CURRENT INCOME TAXES, DUE AND ACCRUED	08	53		53
32	32	OTHER TAXES, LICENCES AND FEES, DUE AND ACCRUED	09	39	1	40
31	31	GENERAL AND INVESTMENT EXPENSES, DUE AND ACCRUED	10	170	3	173
		AMOUNTS DUE TO OTHER INSURANCE COMPANIES	11			
72	73	BANK OVERDRAFTS AND BORROWED MONEY INCLUDING INTEREST DUE AND ACCRUED	12			
41	41	MISCELLANEOUS LIABILITIES	13	303		303
			14			
			15			
			16			
41	41	STAFF PENSION AND INSURANCE FUNDS	17			
		SEGREGATED FUND LIABILITIES	18			
		TOTAL LIABILITIES (03 TO 18) ▶	19	90,374	565	90,939
32	32	DEFERRED INCOME TAXES ▶	20			
		CAPITAL, SURPLUS AND RESERVES:				
10	10	RESERVES REQUIRED BY THE DEPARTMENT	21	3,968	41	4,009
10	10	RESERVES REQUIRED BY FOREIGN JURISDICTIONS	22			
10	10	ADDITIONAL RESERVES	23	647	72	719
10	10	CAPITAL STOCK ISSUED AND PAID: COMMON STOCK	24	1,500		1,500
10	10	PREFERRED STOCK	25			
10	10	CONTRIBUTED SURPLUS	26	1,000		1,000
10	10	INTER-BRANCH TRANSFER OF FUNDS (FROM)/TO	27	(1,000)	1,000	
05	05	UNAPPROPRIATED EARNED SURPLUS	28	8,556	18	8,574
		UNAPPROPRIATED SURPLUS (26+27+28) ▶	29	8,556	1,018	9,574
		TOTAL CAPITAL, SURPLUS AND RESERVES (21 TO 28) ▶	30	14,671	1,131	15,802
		TOTAL LIABILITIES, CAPITAL AND SURPLUS (ITEMS 19+20+30) ▶	31	105,045	1,696	106,741

ACTUARIAL RESERVE PERTAINING TO LIFE INSURANCE CALCULATED ACCORDING TO THE METHOD DESCRIBED IN SUBSECTIONS 82(4) AND 82(7) OR THE MODIFICATION AS PER PARAGRAPH 82(8)(b) OF THE CANADIAN AND BRITISH INSURANCE COMPANIES ACT	32	79,044	79,044

19

NAME OF COMPANY ▶ EXAMPLE	YEAR OF STATEMENT 19 B

XIX. TEST OF COMPLIANCE WITH SECTION 103 OF THE CANADIAN AND BRITISH INSURANCE COMPANIES ACT - ACCIDENT AND SICKNESS

REF. PAGE				($'000) 01
	TOTAL ASSETS REQUIRED			
37	NET UNEARNED PREMIUMS OTHER THAN ON NON-CANCELLABLE POLICIES	(351)	01	48
	REQUIRED MARGIN ON LINE 01 AT 15% OR ON SELECTED CLAIMS RATIO IF LESS ('0' IF NEGATIVE)*		02	7
25	NET UNPAID CLAIMS AND ADJUSTMENT EXPENSES OTHER THAN INSTALMENT CLAIMS	(XII-04)	03	69
	REQUIRED MARGIN ON LINE 03 AT 15%		04	10
13	OTHER LIABILITIES	(XII-19 - XIX-01,03)	05	517
10	RESERVE FOR NEGATIVE AMOUNTS IN NON-CANCELLABLE POLICY LIABILITIES	(VIII-13)	06	13
10	REQUIRED COVERAGE FOR REINSURANCE CEDED TO UNREGISTERED COMPANIES		07	
10	RESERVE FOR DEFERRED POLICY ACQUISITION EXPENSES IN EXCESS OF 30% OF UNEARNED PREMIUMS	(VIII-16)	08	2
			09	
			10	
	TOTAL ASSETS REQUIRED (SUB TOTAL 01 TO 10)		▶ 11	666
	TOTAL ASSETS AVAILABLE:			
12	TOTAL ASSETS	(XI-32)	12	1,825
10	INVESTMENT VALUATION AND CURRENCY RESERVE	(VIII-12)	13	(29)
10	VALUATION RESERVE FOR MISCELLANEOUS ASSETS AND OTHER INVESTMENTS		14	
			15	
81	EXCESS (IF ANY) OF MARKET VALUE OVER BOOK VALUE		16	
	TOTAL ASSETS AVAILABLE (12-13-14-15+16)		▶ 17	1,796
	MARGIN OF ASSETS AVAILABLE OVER ASSETS REQUIRED (17-11)		▶ 18	1,130

*MARGIN = .15 OR (SELECTED CLAIMS RATIO - .80; MINIMUM 0, MAXIMUM .15)

NOTE: IF A SELECTED CLAIM RATIO IS USED, PLEASE COMPLETE THE FOLLOWING:
(a) EXPECTED CLAIMS RATIO =   ; (b) SELECTED CLAIMS RATIO =

THE EXPECTED CLAIMS RATIO SHOWN ABOVE IS THE CLAIMS RATIO EXPECTED UNDER ACCIDENT AND SICKNESS POLICIES ISSUED BY THE COMPANY DURING THE UNEXPIRED TERMS OF SUCH POLICIES.

_____
SIGNATURE

_____
TITLE OR POSITION

14 (LS)

NAME OF COMPANY ▶ EXAMPLE		YEAR OF STATEMENT 19 B	

XIII. ANALYSIS OF INCOME BY

		LIFE		
		PAR 01	NON-PAR 02	SHAREHOLD-ERS 03
PREMIUMS	01	7,745	8,760	
CONSIDERATIONS FOR SETTLEMENT ANNUITIES	02	94	41	
POLICY DIVIDENDS AND PROCEEDS OF CONTRACTS DEPOSITED IN SEGREGATED FUNDS	03			
NET INVESTMENT INCOME	04	5,130	3,624	224
NET INVESTMENT GAIN (LOSS) ON SEGREGATED FUND ASSETS	05			
CONTRIBUTIONS TO STAFF PENSION AND INSURANCE FUNDS	06			
NET GAIN (LOSS) ON CURRENCY EXCHANGE TRANSACTIONS	07			
RESERVE ADJUSTMENT ON REINSURANCE CEDED	08			
	09			
	10			
NET TRANSFERS IN RESPECT OF MORTALITY, EXPENSES AND TAXES FROM (TO) SEG. FUNDS	11			
NET TRANSFER OF POLICY LIABILITIES (TO) FROM SEGREGATED FUNDS	12			
INTER FUND TRANSFERS TO MEET LIABILITIES TRANSFERRED	13			
SUBTOTAL (01 TO 13) ▶	14	12,969	12,425	224
CLAIMS INCURRED	15	3,069	2,627	
CLAIMS INCURRED PAID DIRECTLY FROM SEGREGATED FUNDS	16			
PAYMENTS UNDER SETTLEMENT ANNUITIES	17	81	38	
POLICY DIVIDENDS AND PROCEEDS OF CONTRACTS WITHDRAWN FROM SEGREGATED FUNDS	18			
NORMAL INCREASE IN ACTUARIAL RESERVES (TOTAL)	19	4,331	6,894	
NORMAL INCREASE IN SEGREGATED FUNDS	20			
INCREASE IN STAFF PENSION AND INSURANCE FUNDS	21			
INTEREST INCURRED ON CLAIMS	22	30	22	
TAXES, LICENCES AND FEES EXCLUDING INVESTMENT TAXES AND INCOME TAXES	23	146	76	
COMMISSIONS INCURRED (NET)	24	855	564	
GENERAL EXPENSES (EXCLUDING INVESTMENT EXPENSES)	25	1,379	824	
PAYMENTS FROM STAFF PENSION AND INSURANCE FUNDS	26			
DIVIDENDS AND INCREASE IN PROVISION FOR DIVIDENDS TO POLICYHOLDERS	27	2,008		
EXPERIENCE RATING REFUNDS PAID AND INCREASE IN PROVISION .	28			
INTEREST INCURRED ON AMOUNTS ON DEPOSIT	29	225	42	
	30			
	31			
INCOME TAXES - CURRENT	32	225	335	
- DEFERRED	33			
SUBTOTAL (15 TO 33) ▶	34	12,349	11,422	
INCOME BEFORE UNUSUAL OR EXTRAORDINARY ITEMS (14 - 34) ▶	35	620	1,003	224

14 (RS)

NAME OF COMPANY ▶ EXAMPLE

YEAR OF STATEMENT 19 B

FUND ($'000)

	LIFE					ACCIDENT & SICKNESS		
	04	05	06	SEG. FUND 07	TOTAL 08	INS. FUND 09	SHAREHOLD- ERS 10	TOTAL 11
01					16,505	872		872
02					135			
03								
04					8,978	145		145
05								
06								
07								
08								
09								
10								
11								
12								
13								
14					25,618	1,017		1,017
15					5,696	668		668
16								
17					119			
18								
19					11,225	54		54
20								
21								
22					52			
23					222	20		20
24					1,419	78		78
25					2,203	97		97
26								
27					2,008			
28								
29					267			
30								
31								
32					560	40		40
33								
34					23,771	957		957
35					1,847	60		60

15 (LS)

NAME OF COMPANY ▶ EXAMPLE		YEAR OF STATEMENT 19 B	
		XIV.- RECONCILIATION	

		LIFE		
		PAR FUND 01	NON-PAR FUND 02	SHARE-HOLDERS FUND 03
FUNDS, 31 DECEMBER 19	▶ 01	60,568	40,729	2,781
INCOME BEFORE UNUSUAL OR EXTRAORDINARY ITEMS (FROM ANALYSIS OF INCOME)	02	620	1,003	224
NORMAL INCREASE IN ACTUARIAL RESERVE (MANDATORY & ADDITIONAL)	03	4,331	6,894	
NORMAL INCREASE IN SEGREGATED FUNDS	04			
INCREASE IN STAFF PENSION AND INSURANCE FUNDS	05			
NET INCREASE IN AMOUNTS ON DEPOSIT (520)	06	289	49	
INCREASE IN PROVISION FOR DIVIDENDS TO POLICYHOLDERS	07	224		
INCREASE IN PROVISION FOR EXPERIENCE RATING REFUNDS	08			
NET NON-AMORTIZABLE GAINS (LOSSES) IN RESPECT OF INVESTED ASSETS	09	(43)	(30)	(2)
TRANSFERS OF SURPLUS FROM OTHER FUNDS	10			
TRANSFER OF "SEED MONEY" TO (FROM) SEGREGATED FUNDS	11			
	12			
	13			
INCREASE/DECREASE IN VALUE OF SECTION 64 AND 65 SUBSIDIARIES	14	1	1	
NET INCOME FROM ANCILLARY OPERATIONS	15			
EXTRAORDINARY ITEMS	16			
CURRENCY ADJUSTMENT OF FUNDS	17			
	18			
	19			
	20			
	21			
TOTAL (02 TO 21)	▶ 22	5,422	7,917	222
TRANSFERS OF SURPLUS TO SHAREHOLDERS' FUND	23	(198)		198
TRANSFERS OF SURPLUS TO OTHER FUNDS (GIVE DETAILS BELOW)	24			
DIVIDENDS TO SHAREHOLDERS	25			(250)
INCOME TAXES ON UNUSUAL ITEMS: CURRENT	26			
DEFERRED	27			
	28			
	29			
TOTAL (23 TO 29)	▶ 30	(198)		(52)
FUNDS, 31 DECEMBER 19 (1+22-30)	▶ 31	65,792	48,646	2,951

15 (RS)

NAME OF COMPANY ▶ EXAMPLE						YEAR OF STATEMENT 19 B		

OF FUNDS ($'000)

	LIFE					ACCIDENT & SICKNESS		
	04	05	06	SEGREGATED FUND 07	TOTAL 08	INSURANCE FUND 09	SHARE-HOLDERS FUND 10	TOTAL 11
01					104,078	1,638		1,638
02					1,847	60		60
03					11,225	54		54
04								
05								
06					338			
07					224			
08								
09					(75)			
10								
11								
12								
13								
14					2			
15								
16								
17								
18								
19								
20								
21								
22					13,561	114		114
23								
24								
25					(250)			
26								
27								
28								
29								
30					(250)			
31					117,389	1,752		1,752

16 (LS)

NAME OF COMPANY ▶ EXAMPLE	YEAR OF STATEMENT
	19
	XV. SUMMARY OF FUNDS AND

INSURANCE FUNDS; 31 DECEMBER OF CURRENT YEAR

NET ACTUARIAL RESERVE	01
AMOUNTS ON DEPOSIT WITH THE COMPANY	02
PROVISION FOR DIVIDENDS AND EXPERIENCE RATING REFUNDS	03
	04
	05
DEFERRED INCOME TAXES	06
RESERVES REQUIRED - BY THE DEPARTMENT	07
- BY FOREIGN JURISDICTIONS	08
ADDITIONAL RESERVES	09
UNAPPROPRIATED SURPLUS	10
TOTAL INSURANCE FUNDS, 31 DECEMBER OF CURRENT YEAR	▶ 11
SHAREHOLDERS' FUND: CAPITAL	12
: RESERVES ALLOCATED	13
: UNAPPROPRIATED SURPLUS	14
STAFF PENSION AND INSURANCE FUNDS	15
	16
	17
SEGREGATED FUNDS (EXCLUSIVE OF AMOUNTS OWING)	18
TOTAL FUNDS	▶ 19
AMOUNTS OWING BY THE COMPANY ON SEGREGATED FUNDS (PAGE 13, ITEMS 04, 06, 08 TO 16) INCLUDING $_____	20
TOTAL FUNDS AND AMOUNTS OWING	▶ 21
TOTAL ASSETS	▶ 22
INSURANCE FUNDS, 31 DECEMBER OF PREVIOUS YEAR: NET ACTUARIAL RESERVE	23
AMOUNTS ON DEPOSIT WITH THE COMPANY	24
PROVISION FOR DIVIDENDS AND EXPERIENCE RATING REFUNDS	25
	26
	27
DEFERRED INCOME TAXES	28
RESERVES REQUIRED - BY THE DEPARTMENT	29
- BY FOREIGN JURISDICTIONS	30
ADDITIONAL RESERVES	31
UNAPPROPRIATED SURPLUS	32
TOTAL INSURANCE FUNDS, 31 DECEMBER OF PREVIOUS YEAR	▶ 33
SHAREHOLDERS' FUND, 31 DECEMBER OF PREVIOUS YEAR	▶ 34

16 (RS)

	LIFE			ACCIDENT &	GRAND TOTAL
NAME OF COMPANY ▶					**YEAR OF STATEMENT** 19

AMOUNTS OWING BY THE COMPANY ($'000)

	PAR FUND 01	NON-PAR FUND 02	TOTAL FUNDS 03	ACCIDENT & SICKNESS FUND 04	GRAND TOTAL ALL FUNDS 05
01	50,900	42,384	93,284	561	93,845
02	4,966	890	5,856		5,856
03	2,054		2,054		2,054
04					
05					
06					
07	1,457	2,998	4,455	44	4,499
08					
09	328	243	571	71	642
10	6,086	2,131	8,217	1,076	9,293
▶11	65,791	48,646	114,437	1,752	116,189
12					1,500
13					
14					1,452
15					
16					
17					
18					
▶19					119,141
20					1,222
▶21					120,363
▶22					120,363
23	46,569	35,490	82,059	507	82,566
24	4,678	840	5,518		5,518
25	1,830		1,830		1,830
26					
27					
28					
29	1,338	2,630	3,968	41	4,009
30					
31	387	260	647	72	719
32	5,766	1,509	7,275	1,018	8,293
▶33	60,568	40,729	101,297	1,638	102,935
▶34					2,781

17(LS)

NAME OF COMPANY ▶ EXAMPLE				YEAR OF STATEMENT 19 B

XVI.   ANALYSIS OF INCOME

	LIFE - PARTICIPATING				
	INDIVIDUAL		GROUP		
	INSURANCE	ANNUITY	INSURANCE	ANNUITY	TOTAL
	01	02	03	04	05
PREMIUMS (510) 01	6,829	916			7,745
CONSIDERATIONS FOR SETTLEMENT ANNUITIES (114) 02	94				94
NET INVESTMENT INCOME p. 03	4,569	561			5,130
NET GAIN (LOSS) ON CURRENCY EXCHANGE TRANSACTIONS 04					
RESERVE ADJUSTMENT ON REINSURANCE CEDED 05					
06					
07					
08					
NET TRANSFERS IN RESPECT OF MORTALITY, GENERAL EXPENSES AND TAXES FROM (TO) SEGREGATED FUNDS 09					
NET TRANSFER OF POLICY LIABILITIES TO SEGREGATED FUNDS 10					
INTER FUND TRANSFERS TO MEET LIABILITIES TRANSFERRED 11					
SUBTOTAL (ITEMS 01 TO 11) ▶ 12	11,492	1,477			12,969
CLAIMS INCURRED (512-515) 13	2,425	644			3,069
PAYMENTS UNDER SETTLEMENT ANNUITIES (115) 14	81				81
NORMAL INCREASE IN ACTUARIAL RESERVES (TOTAL) (521) 15	3,988	343			4,331
INTEREST INCURRED ON CLAIMS p. 16	27	3			30
TAXES, LICENCES AND FEES (525) 17	145	1			146
COMMISSIONS INCURRED (NET) (511,518) 18	772	83			855
GENERAL EXPENSES (EXCLUDING INVESTMENT EXPENSES) (524) 19	1,285	94			1,379
DIVIDENDS TO POLICYHOLDERS (516) 20	1,658	126			1,784
INCREASE IN PROVISION FOR DIVIDENDS TO POLICYHOLDERS (517) 21	220	4			224
EXPERIENCE RATING REFUNDS PAID 22					
INCREASE IN PROVISION FOR EXPERIENCE RATING REFUNDS 23					
INTEREST CREDITED TO AMOUNTS ON DEPOSIT (519) 24	191	34			225
25					
26					
27					
INCOME TAXES - CURRENT (526) 28	177	48			225
- DEFERRED 29					
SUBTOTAL (ITEMS 13 TO 29) ▶ 30	10,969	1,380			12,349
INCOME BEFORE UNUSUAL OR EXTRAORDINARY ITEMS (ITEM 12 MINUS 30) ▶ 31	523	97			620

17. (RS)

NAME OF COMPANY EXAMPLE								YEAR OF STATEMENT 19 B

BY LINE OF BUSINESS ($'000)

	LIFE - NON-PARTICIPATING					ACCIDENT AND SICKNESS			
	INDIVIDUAL		GROUP						
	INSURANCE	ANNUITY	INSURANCE	ANNUITY	TOTAL	INDI-VIDUAL	GROUP	TOTAL	GRAND TOTAL
	06	07	08	09	10	11	12	13	14
01	3,106	5,654			8,760	872		872	17,377
02	41				41				135
03	1,920	1,704			3,624	145		145	8,899
04									
05									
06									
07									
08									
09									
10									
11									
12	5,067	7,358			12,425	1,017		1,017	26,411
13	1,152	1,475			2,627	668		668	6,364
14	38				38				119
15	2,084	4,810			6,894	54		54	11,279
16	12	10			22				52
17	72	4			76	20		20	242
18	410	154			564	78		78	1,497
19	655	169			824	97		97	2,300
20									1,784
21									224
22									
23									
24	42				42				267
25									
26									
27									
28	170	165			335	40		40	600
29									
30	4,635	6,787			11,422	957		957	24,728
31	432	571			1,003	60		60	1,683

28

NAME OF COMPANY ▶ EXAMPLE	YEAR OF STATEMENT 19B

EXHIBIT 6 - INVESTMENT INCOME
(EXCLUDING SEGREGATED FUNDS) ($'000)

	LIFE		ACCIDENT & SICKNESS	
	EARNED	DUE AND ACCRUED	EARNED	DUE AND ACCRUED
	01	02	03	04
BONDS: INTEREST **(500)** 01	4,697	832	125	23
AMORTIZATION OF PREMIUM AND ACCRUAL OF DISCOUNT **(501)** 02	15			
AMORTIZATION OF NET REALIZED GAINS AND LOSSES IN LIFE BRANCH **(16)** 03	(41)			
SHARES: DIVIDENDS **(502)** 04	208		1	
AMORTIZATION OF REALIZED AND UNREAL-IZED GAINS AND LOSSES IN LIFE BRANCH 17 05	28			
MORTGAGE LOANS: INTEREST **(503)** 06	3,414	176	20	1
AMORTIZATION OF PREMIUM AND ACCRUAL OF DISCOUNT 07				
AMORTIZATION OF NET REALIZED GAINS AND LOSSES IN LIFE BRANCH 08				
INCOME FROM REAL ESTATE INCLUDING $ 315 **(505)** FOR COMPANY'S OCCUPANCY OF ITS OWN BUILDINGS 09	665			
INCOME FROM GROUND RENTS 10				
INTEREST ON POLICY LOANS **(504)** 11	397	189		
INTEREST ON TERM DEPOSITS AND GUARANTEED INVESTMENT CERTIFICATES 12				
INTEREST ON BANK DEPOSITS **(11)** 13	19		1	
INTEREST ON OVERDUE PREMIUMS 14				
INCOME FROM OTHER INVESTMENTS 15				
CAPITAL GAINS & LOSSES ON INVESTED ASSETS - ACCIDENT & SICKNESS **(14,15)** 16			2	
TOTALS: GROSS INVESTMENT INCOME ▶ 17	9,402	1,197	149	24
INVESTMENT AND REAL ESTATE EXPENSES INCLUDING INTEREST INCURRED ON BORROWED MONEY (18,20,259,22) 18	271		4	
INVESTMENT TAXES **(27)** (28,29) 19	9		0	
REGULAR ANNUAL DEPRECIATION OF REAL ESTATE 20	144			
TOTAL: INVESTMENT EXPENSES, INVESTMENT TAXES ▶ & DEPRECIATION (ITEMS 18 TO 20) 21	424		4	
NET INVESTMENT INCOME (ITEMS 17-21) ▶ 22	8,978		145	

EXHIBIT 7 - AVERAGE NET RATE OF INVESTMENT INCOME EARNED DURING THE YEAR

	(01) LIFE	(02) A&S
NET INVESTMENT INCOME: ITEM 22 COLS. 01/03 = I 23	8,978	145
INCOME-PRODUCING ASSETS (LESS BANK INDEBTEDNESS) AT BEGINNING OF YEAR = A 24	102,352	1,613
AT END OF YEAR = B 25	115,975	1,736
NET RATE OF INVESTMENT INCOME EARNED = $\frac{2I}{A + B - I}$ = ▶ 26	8,577	9,051

Review Questions

1. What were the reasons for the 1978 and 1981 revisions of the Canadian statement?
(**Answer:** See section 5.1.)

2. How are statutory requirements reconciled with GAAP?
(**Answer:** See section 5.1.)

3. Why are assets and liabilities in the life and accident and sickness branches shown separately?
(**Answer:** See section 5.1.)

4. What are the reasons for the analysis of income by fund?
(**Answer:** See section 5.1.)

5. Describe the treatment of capital gains and losses on debt securities in the Canadian statement.
(**Answer:** See section 5.2.)

6. How are gains and losses on shares brought into the Canadian statement?
(**Answer:** See section 5.2.)

7. Where do capital gains and losses on real estate appear in the Canadian statement?
(**Answer:** See section 5.4.)

8. What asset values may be shown for furniture and equipment and agents' debit balances in the Canadian statement? How do these values affect the unappropriated surplus?
(**Answer:** See section 5.2.)

9. Describe the 1978 Canadian reserve method.
(**Answer:** See section 5.3.)

10. Outline the requirements for the report of the valuation actuary which must be attached to the Canadian annual statement.
(**Answer:** See section 5.3.)

11. Describe the various actuarial reserves for life insurance and annuities which must be shown in the Canadian annual statement.
(**Answer:** See section 5.3.)

12. How are deferred policy acquisition expenses shown in the Canadian annual statement?
(**Answer:** See section 5.3.)

Chapter 6: Management Reports and Other Required Statements

Reports for management / general description and principles / insurance data / investment data / use of gain and loss exhibit for validation of statement data / NAIC early warning system / interim statements / NAIC quarterly statements / segregated funds / NAIC separate account statements / Canadian segregated fund statement / NAIC credit insurance exhibits / statement of changes in investments and loans (Canada) / provincial exhibits (Canada) / group life insurance / group annuities / statements of nonresident companies / internal GAAP reports / formulas for analysis of increases in reserves / example of analysis of increases in reserves

6.1 Management reports

The results of the operations of any company depend partly on external factors and partly on internal factors which, in some measure, are subject to control. For instance, the net investment income of a life insurance company depends on the level of interest rates in the investment market and on the demand for policy loans, both external factors not controllable by the company. It also depends on the types of investments made; how quickly cash receipts can be placed in appropriate investments, and expenses incurred in investment operations. All these factors can be controlled to some extent by the company.

Annual corporate financial statements display the results of operations during the year. Unfortunately, they are usually too late and contain insufficient detail to enable management to detect and eliminate the causes of unfavorable results.

All companies want to improve the results of their operations, in comparison with those of other companies, with those of the previous year, or to reach planned objectives. In order to monitor the results of operations in time to exert control over them, reports are needed more frequently than annually and in sufficient detail so that variances may be explained and, if possible, controlled. For example, a decrease in net investment income may be due to a fall in market yield on new investments below that expected, or to increases in investment expenses due to a reduction in the efficiency of investment operations. In the former case, if a change in investment policy is not practical, expectations for the year will have to be revised; in the latter, efforts can be made to improve efficiency and reduce costs in the future.

It is obvious that sufficient detail must be available so that the causes of variances may be diagnosed. In the above example, if the increase in expenses was due, say, to the cost of mortgage collections, it would be counterproductive to attempt to reduce all types of investment expenses in order to remedy the situation.

Therefore, although all financial reports may be considered to be management reports, in a narrower sense the term is usually restricted to those reports which provide information that enables managers to monitor the results of operations for which they are responsible and to improve the results of those operations.

For instance, the manager of a claims department is responsible for processing claims promptly and economically. For him or her, a management report should concentrate on the cost of processing claims and the time required to process them, which may be measured by the average time between receipt of notice and the final disposition of the claim. For such a report, the number of claims, rather than their amounts, will be important, except in the few cases where the amount of individual claims may affect the time or the cost of processing them.

The manager may be responsible for keeping the cost per claim and the average time of processing below those for previous years or below planned standards. The report should indicate the target figures and any variances from target. If the variances are unfavorable, further information may be required to establish the cause and enable the manager to institute remedial measures.

Management reports required by insurance companies depend on the organizational structure of the company and vary considerably from one to another. However, a few general principles may be established.

First, because lower level managers are responsible for the processing of transactions but not for their number or amount, managerial reports at that level are principally comparisons of expenses with budgeted figures. For example, the manager of a policy issue department is responsible for the efficiency of his or her department. The number of applications received, and hence of policies issued, is beyond his or her control. At a higher level, however, a manager will be responsible for the volume of transactions as well as the costs. The officer responsible for the marketing of individual insurance, for example, must be concerned with the number and amount of new policies issued as well as the cost of obtaining the new business.

Reports, therefore, should focus on the significant controllable items upon which a manager can act. The distribution of reports should be limited to those who can act on the information. In making comparisons between periods, care must be taken to ensure that the data are comparable (e.g., number of pay periods per quarter) and that ratios are used if applicable, e.g., cost of agent recruiting to number of agents recruited or production of new agents.

Thus, the scope of management reports increases in direct proportion to the manager's area of responsibility. At the same time, the detail of reports must decrease as the scope increases, if the reports are to be useful. The total of claims expenses listed in the report to the claims manager may be a single item in a department budget report. In the report of operations of a line of business, on the other hand, it may be combined with other items in total general expenses.

However, since managers at each level are responsible for the operations of managers who report to them, variations from target in items included in summary totals should be specifically noted when they exceed some minimum percentage or amount. Explanations of the deviations and proposed corrective actions should also be included. This enables the reader of the report to concentrate on significant items and any suggestions proposed to remedy unfavorable deviations.

It is important to classify revenues and costs so that they can be matched for each area of responsibility. This requires the establishment of cost centers and the allocation of revenues and costs by cost center, taking into account the operational responsibilities of each center for which revenues and costs will be accumulated; cost centers from which work is received; those benefiting from work performed, and plans or major types of insurance served by each center.

The design of the system should provide for the most efficient preparation of the reports, to keep the cost of producing them reasonable and make them available before they are outdated. The structure of accounting and other data should be designed so that the information for management reports may be a byproduct of the normal collection of data, with a minimum of special requirements.

For example, in the accounting for expenses, cost centers should match management reporting requirements, so that, as far as possible, required data can be obtained directly from the ledger. Advantage should be taken of the fact that, especially with computerized accounting systems, it is easier to allocate transactions to appropriate subaccounts at the time of entry, and to combine the subaccounts into larger groups as required, than it is to break down account totals by analyzing individual entries.

The principles of management reporting may be summarized in the following manner:

1. Purpose: to improve company performance in controllable areas of the business relating to revenues and costs.

2. Data: significant items of cost and revenue on which managers can act, with emphasis on variances from target.

3. Scope: corresponding to responsibilities of recipient.

4. Distribution: only to those who can be expected to act on the information.

5. Requirement: an accounting system in which revenues and costs are allocated to the areas responsible for them.

In addition to revenues and costs, a number of other important items affect operating results of life insurance companies. Reports related to these items can have definite value for management.

Insurance data

a) Numbers of policies and average amounts of insurance issued and in force, and summaries by plan of insurance, marketing division or agency. These will serve to check actual results against sales forecasts and point out deviations of individual performances from the average.

b) Termination rates by plan, mode of premium payment and agency. This information is required for estimating the recovery of deferred policy acquisition costs and the profitability of different types of insurance. Comparisons may also be made with industry rates and trends, such as those published by the Life Insurance Marketing and Research Association.

c) Ratios of actual to expected mortality can be developed by major plan of insurance (e.g., life, endowment, term), by type of underwriting (e.g., medical, paramedical, nonmedical), and by risk category (e.g., smoker, nonsmoker, standard, substandard) in order to indicate mortality trends and assist in developing bases for premium rates and valuation. Again, comparisons may be made with industry trends, such as those shown in the reports of the mortality committees of the Society of Actuaries and the Canadian Institute of Actuaries.

d) Expense ratios by category, such as first year and renewal, individual and group. Again, these may be compared with the expense investigations of the Life Office Management Association and the Canadian Institute of Actuaries.

e) Reports on the activities of the marketing area, such as the number of agents recruited and terminated during the period and the number under contract at the beginning and end of the period. The quality of the agency force may also be measured by the ratio of the number of agents currently under contract compared with the number recruited (by duration of contract). The average current production for agents recruited during the period is another measure of the quality of the agency force.

Investment data

a) **Cash flow reports.** Life insurance companies receive cash from a number of sources, such as premium income, investment income and repayments of principal on investments (either regularly on amortized mortgages or periodically on the sale or maturity of investments). They disburse this cash in claims; commissions and other expenses, and the purchase of investments.

While cash balances are needed to pay claims and expenses, it is important to maintain them at minimum levels, since excess cash balances reduce investment income. For this reason, many companies estimate net cash receipts for the near future so that the investment department can plan its investments. Cash flow statements are necessary to provide data for estimating future cash flows, check the accuracy of previous estimates and monitor both the efficiency with which the net cash received from operations has been invested and the distribution of those investments.

Cash flow statements are similar to the statements of changes in financial position required in both the NAIC and Canadian annual statements (Chapter 3, section 3.9 and Chapter 5, section 5.6). However, the statement form should be changed to suit the purpose for which it is needed. For instance, in the statutory statements, policy loan advances, which are contractual obligations and not discretionary investments, are included with new investments made. Most companies would prefer to show them elsewhere so that new investments will indicate the disposition of moneys available for investment.

If the ledger is on a cash basis, the data for the cash flow statement can be taken directly from the ledger. The normal net income from operations is the difference between income and disbursements for the period. This figure must be adjusted for accounts not affecting cash (such as accrual of discount and amortization of premium on investments and depreciation and writedowns of assets) plus the increase in ledger liabilities. To this must be added the principal repayments on investments, including sales and maturities. The amount remaining after deduction of the increase in policy loans is available for investment. It must balance with the sum of the new investments made and the increase or decrease in cash balances.

If the ledger is on an accrual basis, income and disbursement items must be adjusted for the increase in the relevant outstanding accounts. For instance, the increase in outstanding premiums must be deducted from the total premiums and the increase in premiums paid in advance of the due date added, and the increase in outstanding claims deducted from claims figures.

In preparing forecasts, most of the items can be determined from trend analyses of data for previous years. Other items, e.g., bond and mortgage maturities, may be estimated from an analysis of the investment portfolio. Information regarding substantial disbursements likely in the near future, such as income tax payments and proposed purchases of real estate or computer equipment, should be obtained from the departments responsible.

b) **Investment yields.** Reports of average investment income by type of investment (bonds, mortgages, real estate, common and preferred shares, etc.) will enable management to monitor the performance of the investment department, and provide data for use in rate and dividend calculations and future planning. In the case of some investments, such as shares and real estate, some estimate of unrealized capital gains may be used to make current yields more comparable with those of other investments.

c) **Structure of investment portfolio.** Analysis of investments by maturity date will make cash flow forecasts more accurate and will provide data for checking the match between future income from premiums and investments and future insurance and annuity disbursements.

d) **Average yield on new funds.** The average yield on new investments, both by investment category and in total, helps management, especially in times of significant fluctuations in investment yields, to forecast future yields on current investments (for instance, determining valuation interest rates), and to calculate rates on new policies with a large investment element.

If, during a period of high interest rates, some contracts are issued with interest assumptions or guarantees at current rates, it is important to check the yield on the investment of funds from such contracts against assumed or guaranteed interest rates. For companies issuing participating contracts and using average portfolio rates rather than yields based on the investment year method for allocating excess interest, it is also important to be able to deduct the funds and income on "new money" contracts from total funds and income to determine the rate to be used for policies other than "new money" contracts.

6.2 Gain and loss exhibit

The gain and loss exhibit (see section 6.13), formerly included in the NAIC statement, can be misleading as an indication of sources of increases in surplus, but it is nevertheless of value in validating data in the annual statement. By far the largest liability item of a life insurance company is the policy reserve, the liability for future benefits under insurance and annuity contracts. The increase in this liability is a substantial element in the income statement. For example, the total policy reserves of a number of life insurance companies in 1979 was $24.2 billion, the increase in the reserve for the year was $2.9 billion, and the net income $555 million. An error of one-half of one percent in the 1979 reserve would have been $121 million—4.2 percent of the increase in reserve and 22 percent of the net income.

Because the policy reserve is determined by a large number of calculations, it is subject to error, and its accuracy is difficult to check by inspection. The gain and loss technique can indicate at least whether the increase in the reserve is reasonable by breaking it down into smaller elements, such as the cost of insurance, interest required, net premiums, etc.; each of those elements can be compared with related accounting data, such as actual mortality costs, net investment income and gross premiums less commissions and expenses. If these comparisons are made in reasonable groupings (e.g., line of business, participating and non-participating, and, for premiums, first year and renewal), the result will be a number of smaller items (e.g., interest required on reserves and tabular gains and losses from mortality, loadings, etc.) in relatively homogeneous groups. Because the size of these groupings will normally change by small percentages from year to year, any unusually large variation will be a signal to examine all the data involved to determine whether the variation is due to unusual circumstances or actuarial or accounting error. (The net sum of the individual items, plus net investment income, should, of course, equal the normal income before income tax and dividends. Example 6.1 illustrates this.)

In addition to the formulas used for the NAIC analysis of increases in reserves (section 6.13), simpler formulas may be used for segments of the life insurance business where the amounts involved are relatively small. For instance, the gain or loss on dividend additions may be calculated by a simple formula such as the following:

  (a) reserve at end of previous year
+(b) amount used to purchase dividend additions during the year
−(c) dividend addition surrender values paid
−(d) dividend addition death claims incurred
−(e) dividend addition maturity values incurred
+(f) interest at valuation rate on [(a) +.5(b − c − d − e)]
−(g) reserve at the end of the current year
=   net gain or loss on dividend additions

The year-to-year variation in net gain should be relatively small. If it is too large to be explained by a variation in death claims, an error should be suspected and further checking done.

Similar formulas can be used for disability benefits (separately for active and disabled lives), additional accidental death benefits, etc., using reasonable percentages of gross premiums as net premiums. (In order for the net total to balance with the net income, net premiums for the benefits must be deducted from the gross premiums in the calculation of the gain from loadings.)

If systems are designed so that most of the data are byproducts of the valuation and accounting systems, such a report can be produced with little extra work in time to confirm the accuracy of the valuation and accounting data before the statement is completed.

Gains and losses indicated on a U.S. statutory reserve basis will not usually be a true indication of the sources of gains and losses, especially if multiple valuation bases are used. Nevertheless the data from such a gain and loss exhibit, properly interpreted, can provide some insight into relevant trends.

For companies which prepare statements on the GAAP basis, a gain and loss exhibit using data from the GAAP valuation can give auditors some assurance that the reserve is consistent with that of the previous year and also indicate trends in GAAP income.

In this analysis, as can be seen, all items of the income statement are entered. Items from the analysis of increases in reserves are entered twice, once with a positive sign and once with a negative sign, so that they balance out, leaving the net income as the balance. (The interest required could be deducted from net investment income to give the excess interest earnings, but for this analysis it is better to compare interest required with the figure for previous years, since comparisons of excess interest may be distorted by variations in net investment income.)

Example 6.1

GAIN AND LOSS ANALYSIS

Let us take a simple case with the following data:

Income Statement

Premiums	$ 8,167,444
Net investment income	3,753,043
	$11,920,487
Death claims	3,752,012
Maturities	368,382
Surrender values	1,786,688
Increase in reserves	1,832,570
Commissions	1,016,208
General expenses	2,168,460
Taxes, licenses and fees	208,463
	$11,132,783
Net income before dividends and tax	787,704

Analysis of Increase in Reserves

Net premiums	$ 6,560,964
Interest required	1,745,733
Cost of insurance	−2,962,953
Reserves released: by death	−867,441
by other terminations	−2,643,733
Increase in reserves	$ 1,832,570

The analysis of gains and losses can be set up as follows:

Analysis of gains and losses

	INCOME STATEMENT	INCREASE IN RESERVES	GAIN/LOSS
Gross premiums	$8,167,444		$
Net premiums		−6,560,964	
Commissions	−1,016,208		
General expenses	−2,168,460		
Taxes, licenses, fees	−208,463		
Loss on loadings	$4,774,313	−$6,560,964	−1,786,651
Cost of insurance		2,962,953	
Death claims	−3,752,012		
Reserves released		867,441	
Gain from mortality	−$3,752,012	$3,830,394	78,382
Reserves released by terminations		2,643,733	
Maturity payments	−368,382		
Surrender values paid	−1,786,688		
Gain from surrenders	−$2,155,070	$2,643,733	488,663
Interest required		−1,745,733	−1,745,733

(continued)

	INCOME STATEMENT	INCREASE IN RESERVES	GAIN/LOSS
Increase in reserves	−1,832,570		
Net premiums		6,560,964	
Cost of insurance		−2,962,953	
Reserves released: by death		−867,441	
by other terminations		−2,643,733	
Interest required		1,745,733	
	−$1,832,570	$1,832,570	0
			−$2,965,339
Net investment income	3,753,043		3,753,043
Totals	$ 787,704	$ 0	$ 787,704

6.3 NAIC early warning system

To identify companies whose operations require special attention by insurance departments, the NAIC has set up an early warning system under which statement data is analyzed and various ratios determined. The results are reported to state insurance departments, and individual companies are provided with their own ratios along with percentile rankings for all participating companies. Certain tolerances are established for each ratio, and attention is paid to those companies with ratios outside the tolerances. The tests are divided into two groups: 1) financial and 2) stability.

Financial tests

1. Rate of change of the surplus at the end of the current year to that at the end of the previous year.

2. Ratio of net gain from operations to gross income. A zero or negative ratio is a warning signal, as may be a downward trend.

3. Ratio of commissions and expenses to total premiums. Any ratio over 60 percent is regarded as an exception, although the composition of the business must be taken into account. For instance, if the percentage of term insurance is growing, the ratios may be expected to increase.

4. Ratio of net investment income to the average of current and previous cash and invested assets. If the ratio is less than four percent the return on investments is likely too low. If it is over 9.9 percent, the security of investments may be doubtful.

5. Ratio of nonadmitted assets to admitted assets. Any ratio over ten percent is regarded as an exception.

6. Ratio of real estate to capital and surplus. The ratio should be less than 100 percent.

7. Ratio of investments in affiliates to capital and surplus, which should also be less than 100 percent.

8. Ratio of commissions and expense allowances on reinsurance ceded to capital and surplus, which should be below 20 percent.

Stability tests

1. Percentage change in premiums received to those of the previous year. The change should be between –10 percent and 50 percent.

2. The changes in the percentages of premiums for the various lines of business to total premiums from the previous year to the current year. The average of the absolute values of the percentage changes should be less than three percent.

3. The two-year average change in the percentage of each component of cash and invested assets to the total, which should be less than five percent.

4. The change in the ratio of the increase of individual life insurance reserves to the total of individual life insurance renewal and single premiums. It should be between –20 percent and +10 percent.

Most insurance companies are required to submit their statements for this test, and many make the tests themselves. Since the data are taken from the annual statement, special procedures are not required for their generation. It is important for insurance companies to monitor the ratios at least quarterly. Although ratios outside the tolerances are not necessarily danger signs, for example, if there is a substantial change in the distribution of new policies between permanent insurance and term, or if there is an increase in policy surrenders due to economic conditions, it is important to ascertain the reasons for the changes in the ratios so that explanations may be made and, if necessary, corrective action taken to reverse any unfavorable trend.

6.4 Interim statements

Interim statements (prepared during the year at quarterly or monthly intervals) are becoming more common among life insurance companies. Management uses these statements to keep track of current progress and forecast yearend results. They are also required by some supervisory authorities (see below).

Data from ledger accounts present few problems, because these accounts are normally kept up to date. Nonledger data are another matter. Policy reserves, accrued interest, due and deferred premiums etc., generally require the analysis of large volumes of data and, even if EDP equipment permits accurate calculations, the long runs involved may make reasonable approximations more economical. However, since the amount entered in the income statement is the difference between the nonledger asset or liability at the end of the period and that at the beginning, any approximate calculation should be based on assumptions which will reproduce the amount at the previous yearend.

Moreover, the reproduction of the yearend figure is a necessary but not sufficient condition. For example, the accrued interest on bonds depends on the dates on which interest is due. If these are not uniformly distributed over the year, the ratio of accrued interest to total value of bonds will vary significantly from month to month. In this case, before deciding on an approximation, a random sample of bonds may be analyzed to determine the variation of accrued interest according to the date on which it is calculated. If the variation is significant, factors based on the sample may be used.

For policy reserves, the reserves on new issues and terminations are often calculated accurately, because the volume is relatively small and the calculations have to be made for the yearend in any event. For the business in force at the end of the previous year, a calculation of reserves at the end of the current year will enable the net premiums, interest required and cost of insurance to be determined. Interim reserves may be calculated by adding the proportionate amount of net premiums and interest to the previous reserve and deducting the proportionate cost of insurance.

Again, a determination of the variance from uniform distribution over the year will provide data for adjusting the proportions to give more accurate values.

Minor items of reserves (active life disability and additional accidental death benefits, etc.), can usually be estimated from the growth of the reserve from year to year, because any errors will be small relative to the total increase in reserve.

If it is possible to make accurate calculations, this should be done from time to time to check the accuracy of the approximations. Some companies calculate accurate figures for September, which will provide a check on the approximations and avoid inconsistencies between the yearend and September statements.

NAIC quarterly statements

Certain states, including New York, Ohio and California, require quarterly statements from all domiciled companies. Others require them under special circumstances. For example, one state requires quarterly statements if:

1. the company has been consolidated with another within three years, or
2. the company has been under total new management for three years or less, or
3. the company has been under a management contract for three years or less, or
4. the company has been incorporated for five years or less, or
5. the company has failed to file data with the data base, or
6. the company has not met surplus requirements, or
7. if there are special problems (at the discretion of the commissioner).

The quarterly statement is basically a modified form of the NAIC life and accident and health statement with the following statements and schedules. (The balance sheet is as of the end of the quarter and the other statements are for the year to date.)

Statements

1. Assets
2. Liabilities, capital and surplus
3. Summary of operations
4. Capital and surplus account
5. Reconciliation of ledger assets

Schedules

   I. Bonds and stocks acquired during the quarter
  II. Cash deposits at the end of each month in the quarter
 III. Investments in mortgages, real estate and other invested assets during the quarter
 IV. Investments in collateral loans during the quarter
  V. Changes in collateral loans during the quarter
 VI. Sales or redemptions of securities during the quarter:
     a) bonds
     b) stocks

       c) collateral loans
       d) real estate
       e) foreclosures of real estate
       f) mortgages
       g) other invested assets
   VII. Premiums and annuity considerations for the year to date allocated by states and territories

6.5 Segregated funds (separate accounts)

For a long time, shares of stock were not considered appropriate investments for life insurance companies, because the lack of a fixed maturity date and fluctuations in market values make it difficult to match their yields to life insurance fixed dollar obligations. Most jurisdictions in the United States and Canada limited such investments to a small percentage of assets, and the majority of companies were content to hold less than the permitted amount.

However, postwar inflation, which reduced the purchasing power of traditional fixed dollar investments, and the long period of increases in market values of shares after 1940 renewed interest in equity investments. An analysis of past trends in consumer prices and market values of shares showed some historical correlation between them (Duncan, T.S.A. IV). This led to the concept of issuing variable annuities, under which the amount of the annuity payments would vary with the market value of an equity fund in which the premiums had been invested. The objective of the variable annuity was to maintain the purchasing power of pensions. At the same time, the popularity of mutual funds, in which deposits were invested in equities, and the return on the investment was based on the performance of the securities in the fund, created serious competition for life insurance companies.

Eventually, life insurance companies in both the United States and Canada were permitted to accept deposits to be invested in securities (including bonds and mortgages as well as shares of stock). These deposits are segregated from the general funds of the company, and the liability is determined by the market value of the fund. Essentially, the investment risk is borne by the policyholder, and the insurer's guarantee is limited to mortality and expense charges. Such contracts are known as separate account contracts in the United States and segregated fund contracts in Canada.

In such contracts, accounting for the interests of policyholders is based on fund units. When the fund is set up, usually by a transfer of surplus from the general funds of the company, an arbitrary value is set for a unit, and the initial deposits are used to purchase units at that value. Thereafter, the value of a unit is the market value of the fund divided by the number of units outstanding. All deposits and withdrawals are converted into units on the basis of unit values at the time of the transaction.

The number of units payable annually on a variable annuity is determined by dividing the number of units purchased with the premium by an annuity factor based on estimates of future mortality; interest or dividend earnings on the fund, and expenses. The amount paid each year is the current value of the number of units payable.

Under variable life insurance contracts all or a portion of the reserve may be invested in the segregated fund and the benefits adjusted in accordance with unit values. Most jurisdictions require a guarantee that death and survivor benefits will not fall below some minimum amount. The guarantee is provided by the general fund, and the segregated fund is charged with a premium.

In Canada, for income tax purposes, income and capital gains and losses on segregated funds are assumed to flow through to the possession of the policyholders, who must include them in their taxable income. Policyholders whose contracts are registered retirement savings plans (treated as employee pension plans for tax purposes) pay no tax on such amounts, but other policyholders must pay income tax on their shares of income and net capital gains. The company is taxed only on the earnings of any surplus contributed to the funds.

The total amounts of assets, liabilities and surplus in segregated funds must be included in the balance sheet of statutory life insurance company statements. Other statements respecting such funds also must be furnished. In the United States, companies must file the NAIC separate account statement (for contracts not involving life insurance) and the NAIC variable life insurance separate account statement. In Canada companies must file the segregated fund statement.

Generally, deposits intended for segregated funds are included in the premium income of the general fund and transferred to the segregated fund less commission, premium tax (if applicable) and collection expenses. In the case of variable insurance, a portion of the reserve may be so transferred. Administrative expenses and taxes incurred in the segregated fund are usually transferred to the general funds of the company and paid out of those funds. Payments to policyholders may be treated similarly.

NAIC separate account statement

The NAIC separate account statement contains a balance sheet of the separate accounts; a summary of operations; an analysis of operations by line of business (individual annuities, individual supplementary contracts and group annuities), and an analysis of increases in reserves.

Assets include:
1) bonds, separated into long-term (maturing more than one year from the date of the statement) and short-term (all other),
2) preferred stocks,
3) common stocks,
4) mortgage loans
5) real estate, separated into properties acquired in satisfaction of debt and investment real estate,
6) cash on deposit and
7) other invested assets, with
8) a total of cash and invested assets.

The remaining items are due and accrued investment income; receivables for investments sold and net adjustment in assets and liabilities due to foreign exchange rates (see Chapter 3, 3.2,20).

Liabilities include:
1) aggregate reserves for contracts with life contingencies,
2) liabilities for supplementary contracts without life contingencies,
3) liabilities for annuity and other deposit funds,
4) charges (owing to the general fund) for investment management, administration and contract guarantees, due or accrued,
5) investment expenses due or accrued,
6) investment taxes, licenses and fees due or accrued,
7) federal income tax due or accrued (excluding deferred taxes),
8) reserve for future income taxes,
9) unearned investment income,
10) other transfers to general account due or accrued,
11) remittances and items not allocated,
12) amounts payable for investments purchased, and
13) net adjustment in assets and liabilities due to foreign exchange rates.

Because assets are included at market value and liabilities vary according to the market value of assets, the mandatory securities valuation reserve is not required. The total liabilities are shown, with the net due or accrued transfers to or from the general account noted. The surplus, split into special surplus funds and unassigned surplus, is then shown, followed by the total surplus and the final total to balance with the assets.

The summary of operations includes, in income:
a) transfers to separate accounts due to
  1) annuity considerations (net),
  2) annuity and other fund deposits, (e.g., on deposit administration contracts) and
  3) considerations for supplementary contracts with and without life contingencies, and
b) the sum of net investment income and net capital gains or losses.

Deductions include:
a) transfers to the general funds for
  1) contract benefits,
  2) policy or contract reserves and
  3) other transfers for charges made by the general fund and taxes incurred.
b) increases in reserves on life contracts,
c) increases in reserves for supplementary contracts,
d) investment income and net capital gains credited to annuity and other fund deposits and
e) increase in reserve for future federal income taxes.

These items are added to produce total deductions, with a final item for the net gain or loss from operations.

The surplus account combines the total surplus at the end of the previous year, plus the net gain from operations; adjustments for surplus contributed or withdrawn during the year; changes in reserves due to changes in valuation bases, and increases or decreases in special reserves. The result is the total surplus at the end of the current year.

The analysis of operations by line of business splits the summary of operations into individual annuities, supplementary contracts and group annuities.

The analysis of increases in reserves, taking into consideration the nature of separate account business, replaces the item "tabular interest" with "increase or decrease from investment results after provision for federal income tax." There is also a deduction for charges for investment management, administration and contract guarantees.

Exhibits include:

1) Net investment income and capital gains and losses.

2) Gross investment income (by category of investment) similar to that in the Life and Accident and Health statement.

3) Capital gains and losses by category, showing net unrealized gains at the beginning and end of the year and the difference; the realized gains, and the net gain or loss (the net sum of the preceding two items).

4) Investment expenses paid directly from the separate account.

5) Investment taxes, licenses and fees (excluding federal income tax).

6) Aggregate reserves for contracts with life contingencies (ordinary and group).

6A) Changes in reserves due to changes in valuation bases.

7) Present value of amounts not due on supplementary contracts without life contingencies.

8) Reconciliation of cash and invested assets.

The asset schedules are similar to those in the life and accident and health statement except that bonds are separated into long-term and short-term, and statement values are market values.

NAIC variable life insurance separate account statement

The variable life insurance separate account statement is similar in many respects to the previous statement, with a few differences due to the nature of the business. In the assets, there is provision for policy loans but not for mortgages or real estate, while the liabilities include reserves for life policies and contracts and for dividend accumulations. There is no provision for investment expenses or taxes paid directly from the account. Therefore, the summary of operations includes gross investment income and net capital gains and losses separately, and charges for investment management are deducted. Lines of business are divided into ordinary and group insurance.

Exhibit 1 is an exhibit of gross investment income, similar to that in the life and accident and health statement.

Exhibit 2 is an exhibit of net capital gains and losses, similar to that in the previous statement.

Exhibit 3 shows the aggregate reserve for life policies and contracts by valuation basis by line of business.

Exhibit 4 is a reconciliation of cash and invested assets.

Exhibit 5, Part 1 shows the investment results by account. It lists the monthly average of assets in each account and the amounts and percentages of the monthly average of assets of:

1) charges for investment management,
2) charges for mortality and interest guarantees,
3) charges for federal income taxes,
4) other charges,
5) total charges,
6) gross investment income,
7) net capital gains or losses,
8) gross investment return (6)+(7),
9) net investment return (8)–(5) and
10) charges incurred in the acquisition or disposal of assets.

Exhibit 5, Part 2 is a calculation of the turnover rate of portfolio securities (excluding short-term and U.S. government securities), showing the ratio of disposals of portfolio securities to the monthly average of such securities.

Exhibit 6 shows ordinary and group life insurance, including the number and amount of policies in force at the beginning of the year, movements during the year and the number and amount of policies in force at the end of the year.

Schedules of assets are similar to those in the previous statement.

Canadian segregated fund statement

The Canadian segregated fund statement includes all funds and all types of business (variable life insurance and annuity). Details must be provided for each fund.

Assets and liabilities must be shown for each fund and in total. Assets are shown by type of asset (bonds, common and preferred shares, mortgages, real estate, etc.) at market values. The date of valuation also must be shown. Liabilities are split into amounts owing (amounts due to other funds, taxes and expenses due or accrued, etc.) and funds held for the benefit of policyholders (actuarial reserves, amounts on deposit and amounts transferred from other funds).

A reconciliation of the funds at the end of the year with those at the beginning is required, along the following lines:

Funds at the beginning of the year
+ net balance of investment operations (income and net realized and unrealized capital gains less investment expenses)*
+ net transfers re policyholders' benefits (premiums, reserve transfers, payments to policyholders, etc.)*
+ net contributions from surplus of other funds during the year*
+ miscellaneous items (currency adjustments, suspense items, etc.)
= funds at end of year.

---

*Details of these amounts are shown in **Exhibits 1, 2** and **3**.

Exhibit 4. Reconciliation of accumulation and annuity units in force.
Units in force at the end of the year are reconciled with those in force at
the beginning by adjusting the latter for the units credited and debited to
each fund for receipts from and payments to policyholders and for
transfers to and from other funds of the company. The units credited and
debited will be the amounts shown in the exhibits of contributions and
payments to policyholders converted into units at the transaction dates.
The results of investment operations are not included in this reconciliation because they affect unit values, not the number of units.

Exhibit 5. Valuation and statistical exhibit. The contents of this exhibit
are best described by quoting the instructions:

"For each fund, describe the bases of valuation where applicable.
Where there is a guarantee of the annuity rates which will be applied
over a period, show the basis of the guarantee and the amount of
funds to which it applies. Where there is a mortality guarantee, the
basis of valuation of actuarial reserves should be given as well as the
amount of reserves to which each basis pertains. Give the number of
persons covered and the amount of annuities payable for immediate
annuities.

"Reserves and other liabilities should be reported separately for
the various types of units to which they appertain."

A certificate attesting to the adequacy of reserves held and signed by the
valuation actuary must be included.

Exhibit 6. Exhibit of unit values. This exhibit shows, for each fund, the
net assets and unit values on monthly valuation dates throughout the
year.

Exhibit 7. Exhibit of movement of policies (other than group). This
exhibit must include brief descriptions of the types of individual contracts
in force in each fund. For each fund, the amount in force at the end of the
previous year, movements (new issues, increases, terminations by type
and duration) and the amount in force at the end of the year must be
shown by number of contracts and amount. The amount may be the initial
sum insured, estimated annuity per annum or some other measure of size
of policy (e.g., single or annual premium).

The remaining data are schedules of investments, similar in format to
those in the statement of the general funds of the company, although only
par and market values are shown for securities.

6.6 NAIC credit insurance exhibits

Companies writing credit insurance in the United States must file, by
April 1, a statistical report on direct credit life insurance for the preceding
calendar year, split by group, individual with level amounts and
individual with decreasing amounts.

The required data are:
1. Gross premiums collected
2. Return premiums on cancelled policies

   3. Gross premiums less return premiums (1 – 2)
   4. Unearned gross premiums at beginning of year
   5. Unearned gross premiums at end of year
   6. Earned premiums (3 + 4 – 5)
   7. Losses paid during year
   8. Unpaid losses at end of year
   9. Unpaid losses at beginning of year
 10. Losses incurred (7 + 8 – 9)

A second statement, the credit life and accident and health exhibit, must be filed by May 1. Data must be shown for direct, reinsurance assumed and reinsurance ceded, separately for group and individual, with individual life split into level amounts and decreasing amounts.

The required data for life insurance are:
   1. Gross premiums
   2. Return premiums on cancelled policies
   3. Gross premiums less return premiums (1 – 2)
   4. Increase in reserve liability
   5. Earned premiums (3 – 4)
   6. Losses: a) death benefits
             b) other benefits
   7. Loss expense
   8. Commissions
   9. General insurance expense
 10. Taxes, licenses and fees
 11. Other disbursements
 12. Total (sum of lines 6 to 11)
 13. Net gain before dividends and experience refunds
 14. Dividends and experience refunds
 15. Net gain after dividends and experience refunds
 16. Amount of insurance in force December 31, previous year
 17. Amount of insurance in force December 31, current year

The data called for in the first 15 lines of the life insurance exhibit are also required for accident and health insurance. The only differences are that there is, of course, no provision for death claims among the losses, and line 11 is called "other reserve increases."

6.7 Changes in investments and loans (Canada)

The NAIC statements include schedules of investments acquired and disposed of during the year by category. In Canada, this information must be submitted semiannually for the six-month periods ending June 30 and December 31 in a special statement, "Changes in Investments and Loans." Separate schedules are required for the life insurance fund and for the segregated funds.

The categories which must be covered are:
1) bonds,
2) shares,
3) real estate,

4) term deposits and guaranteed investment certificates,
5) collateral loans and
6) other investments.

For each type, a listing is required of investments acquired, investments disposed of, and (for the first three) investments held at the end of the period under the "basket clause," followed by a reconciliation of the investments held at the end of the period with those held at the beginning. Reconciliation schedules must also be included for mortgages, policy loans and investments under the "basket clause." This reconciliation is of book values for life insurance market values for segregated funds. (The "basket clause" refers to investments held under permission granted by the Canadian and British Insurance Companies Act for companies to hold investments not authorized by the Act up to a maximum of seven percent of the total book value of assets.)

In the schedules for secregated funds, the investments of each segregated fund must be listed separately in all schedules with a consolidated reconciliation of bonds and shares for all funds.

6.8 Provincial exhibits (Canada)

Companies doing business in Canada must file with the insurance department of each province and territory in which they are licensed a special statement containing provincial exhibits in addition to copies of the life and accident and sickness and segregated fund statements.

The provincial exhibits provide data on transactions with policyholders by residence. The data are shown for each province or territory of residence, with a miscellaneous category for insurance originally written on Canadian residents who now reside elsewhere; the total for Canadian policies, and data for out-of-Canada business (policies written on non-residents), followed by a grand total which must balance with the appropriate total in the combined statement.

Premiums and dividends (direct, reinsurance acquired, reinsurance ceded, and net written) are shown for:
• life insurance, individual
• life insurance, group
• life insurance, total
• annuities, individual
• annuities, group
• annuities, total

Movements of life insurance and annuities (direct) are shown separately for individual, group and total. Claims and dividends incurred (direct) for life insurance and annuities are also shown for individual, group and total.

For accident and sickness business, a separate schedule shows premiums (direct, reinsurance acquired, reinsurance ceded and net); dividends (direct and net); premiums less dividends (direct and net), and claims (direct and net).

6.9 Group life insurance

Group insurance may be broadly defined as insurance written on groups of people associated in some way apart from the insurance, such as employees of a common employer or group of employers; members of trade or professional associations, or debtors of a common creditor (group credit insurance). The contract is generally made with the employer, association or creditor, who is responsible for the payment of premiums and through whom claims are paid.

The most common group life insurance plan is one-year renewable term insurance with premiums based on the age, sex and amount of insurance on each life (although, after an initial calculation, average premiums per thousand may be used for convenience). Credit insurance premiums may be based on the total indebtedness or on single premiums charged as each debt is incurred. A small proportion of groups provide some form of permanent insurance with level premiums, and permanent insurance on retired lives may be provided by single premiums paid at retirement.

Group insurance may be either participating or nonparticipating. Experience refunds are common on policies classed as nonparticipating. Very often, group life insurance is part of a package which includes medical, disability and accidental death benefits.

Government statements require the separation of group accounts from individual to monitor the progress of the business and to ensure that group business is self-supporting and not likely to endanger the security or interests of individual policyholders, whose contracts tend to be for much longer terms.

In the United States, the NAIC statement requires the reporting of credit insurance, both individual and group, as one line of business, and all other group life insurance as another. In Canada, participating and nonparticipating group life insurance are separate lines of business.

The items in the income statement (statement of operations) are the same as those for other lines of business, but some explanations are required in view of the differences between group and individual life insurance contracts.

Premiums. In the United States, experience refunds on nonparticipating group policies are treated as deductions from premium income rather than as dividends or other payments to policyholders. In Canada they are shown as disbursements.

Investment income. Investment income must be allocated according to some reasonable formula, as with other lines of business.

Conversion charges. Group policies provide that, when an insured leaves the group, he or she may purchase an individual policy for an equivalent amount of insurance at standard rates without evidence of insurability. Since the mortality experience on such converted policies is usually higher than on policies written with normal evidence of insurability, an amount to cover the expected additional mortality costs (less some allowance for commissions and underwriting costs not incurred) is usually charged to the group account and credited to the appropriate individual account when a converted policy is issued. (In the individual account, a reserve may be set up for the credit, reducing to zero over the period during which the extra mortality is expected to persist.)

In the NAIC statement, such charges are included in "all other charges." In the Canadian statement they are listed as "inter-fund transfers to meet liabilities transferred." For transfers within the company, the net amount will, of course, be zero. However, this may not be the case for plans in which a number of companies participate, such as the federal employees group life insurance plan and the servicemen's group life insurance plan in the United States. The mortality experience of policies converted to individual insurance under each of these plans is pooled, and any profit arising from the excess of the conversion charges over the mortality experienced is passed on to the participating insurers. The net credit is the cash payment received less amounts disbursed, plus the increase in the company's share of the assets in the pool. A net credit would be shown in the income statement of the NAIC statement under "other income."

Other charges. In package plans, it may happen that the experience of one line, say life insurance, is better than that anticipated in the premiums, while the experience of others, such as accident and health, is worse. The experience rating refund, in this case, would therefore be the excess, if any, of the credit from the life account over the debit from the accident and health account. The amount withheld would be charged to the life account and credited to accident and health.

Increase in reserves. The reserves include unearned premium reserves on one-year term insurance (the portion of the net premiums received applicable to the period following the valuation date); single premium reserves for credit insurance if required; paid-up life reserves; reserves for waiver of premium and extended death benefits, and, if considered necessary, preconversion reserves for group conversions (the buildup of reserves to provide conversion charges on future conversions) and incurred but unreported claims under the waiver of premium benefit.

Dividends and experience rating refunds. In the NAIC statement, the increase in the reserve for dividends payable in the following year is added to the incurred dividends for the year, and the increase in the reserve for experience rating refunds is deducted from incurred premiums. In the Canadian statement, the reserve increases are shown as separate items in the income statement.

While the reserve for dividends on individual policies normally includes the full dividend payable in the following year (and may be included in actuarial reserves in the Canadian statement if explicit provision for dividends is made), for group insurance the reserves for dividends and experience rating refunds include only the amounts earned from the policy anniversary to December 31.

6.10 Group annuities

Group annuities are contracts made with employers to provide pensions for their employees at retirement. They may provide for the accumulation of premiums paid on behalf of the employees and the payment of withdrawal benefits and pensions to employees, or merely for the investment and accumulation of deposits and the disbursement of funds as instructed by the employer (deposit administration contracts). Under the former type of contract, the insurance company determines the premiums to be paid to provide the benefits and is responsible for paying the benefits as they fall due. Under deposit administration contracts, the insurance company acts as trustee for the funds deposited, paying them out or providing annuities at guaranteed rates as required. In the latter case, actuarial advice is secured from either an independent consultant or the actuarial staff of the insurer for an additional fee.

In the case of group annuities proper, the amount of the retirement annuity is determined in one of two ways. Under the unit benefit plan, the amount of the benefit is based on some formula (e.g., two percent of salary for each year of service) and the total contributions of employer and employees are determined by the benefits to be provided. Under the money purchase plan, the contributions for each employee are fixed, and the benefits are the amounts that can be purchased at retirement by the accumulation of the contributions at interest.

Generally, the benefits for each year of service are purchased annually on the policy anniversary, with the contributions for the year used to purchase single premium deferred annuities. The interest and mortality rates used are generally guaranteed for limited periods, and changed, if necessary, at the end of each period in accordance with current conditions.

In deposit administration contracts, deposits are usually made into the general funds of the company, with guarantees for limited periods of the interest rates at which funds will be accumulated and interest and mortality rates for the purchase of annuities as members retire.

Under some contracts, part of the funds may be deposited in separate (segregated) equity or fixed interest funds in which the accumulation is dependent on the performance of the investments in the funds. However, mortality and expense rate guarantees may be provided, and a premium charged for the guarantee. As employees retire, amounts may be withdrawn from the separate funds and fixed dollar annuities purchased from the general funds, or the amounts may be left in the separate funds and variable annuities purchased, with guarantees only as to the mortality and expense rates.

Group annuities, like group insurance, may be either participating or nonparticipating, and experience refunds are common on the latter contracts. In the NAIC life and accident and health statement, group annuities are a single line of business, while in the Canadian statement, they are split into participating and nonparticipating.

Most of the income entries are straightforward, although, if guarantees are provided for amounts deposited in separate funds, the premiums for the guarantees will be charged to the separate funds and credited to the general funds.

Investment income must be allocated to the group annuity line of business in accordance with a reasonable formula, as with other lines of business. Because interest guarantees on group annuities tend to be based on current investment yields, many companies with substantial volumes of such business use a method such as the investment year method, in which the investment income is distributed by a formula which takes into account the yields current at the time moneys were invested. When such a method is used, a description must be included in the NAIC life and accident and sickness statement. (See Chapter 1, section 1.6.)

The reserve on group annuities is the reserve for the annuities purchased to date. If the amount of annuity used is the amount purchased as of the previous policy anniversary, the deposits made since the anniversary plus accrued interest to the end of the year must be added to the reserve.

In deposit administration contracts, the reserve will be the amount of the fund (less any surrender charge applicable if the case is surrendered). However, if the guaranteed interest rate exceeds the maximum valuation rate, a reserve should be held to provide for increases in the fund due to the excess of the guaranteed rate over the valuation rate. At least one state (New York) requires that such a reserve be held.

Two accounts are usually maintained for deposit administration contracts: one based on the guarantees in the contract, and one on actual experience. The guarantee account determines the guaranteed accumulation, and therefore the reserve which must be maintained, and the experience account the actual amounts to the credit of the policyholder, on which dividends or experience refunds may be based.

Tables 6.1 and **6.2** are examples of the two accounts. **Table 6.3** illustrates the relevant entries in the annual statement income account (summary of operations), and **Table 6.4** shows the reconciliation between the net income from the statutory account and the increase in the experience account. The reconciliation is similar to the reconciliation of funds in that the increase in reserves and items not affecting the income account, such as capital gains and losses, are added to the net income.

Table 6.1

GUARANTEED ACCOUNT
Active lives

1. Amount December 31, 19A	$465,327
2. Deposits	135,814
3. Transfers to separate accounts	(45,271)
4. Annuity purchases	(33,415)
5. Tax on annuity purchases*	(334)
6. Surrender values paid	(738)
7. Expense charges (premium formula)	(4,782)
8. Total before interest and dividends	$516,601
9. Interest at guaranteed rate	34,472
10. Dividends accrued	9,135
11. Amount December 31, 19B	$560,208

*If applicable; many states and all Canadian provinces exempt annuity premiums from premium tax.

Retired lives

20.	Account December 31, 19A	$ 52,375
21.	Net premiums [95% of gross (4)]	31,744
22.	Tabular interest	2,095
23.	Tabular less actual reserves released	730
24.	Annuity payments	(5,200)
25.	Account December 31, 19B	$ 81,744

Table 6.2

EXPERIENCE ACCOUNT

30.	Balance December 31, 19A	$560,000
31.	Deposits (2)	135,814
32.	Transfers to separate accounts (3)	(45,271)
33.	Annuity payments (24)	(5,200)
34.	Surrender values paid (6)	(738)
35.	Expenses (actual)	(5,435)
36.	Premium tax (5)	(334)
37.	Investment income credited	50,965
38.	Capital gains (less tax)	850
39.	Balance December 31, 19B	$690,651

Table 6.3

INCOME STATEMENT
(SUMMARY OF OPERATIONS)

50.	Premiums (annuity purchases) (4)		$ 33,415
51.	Deposits (2)	$135,814	
52.	accrued dividends (10)	9,135	
53.	less annuity purchases (4)	(33,415)	111,534
54.	Transfers from separate account (premiums for guarantees)		650
55.	Net investment income (37)		50,965
56.	Total income		$196,564
	Less: Annuity benefits		
57.	Payments (24)	$ 5,200	
58.	Surrender values (6)	738	$ 5,938
59.	Transfers to separate accounts (3)		45,271
	Increases in reserves:		
60.	Active lives* (11)	560,208	
	(1)	(465,327)	94,881
61.	Retired lives (25)	$ 81,744	
	(20)	(52,375)	29,369
62.	General expenses (35)		5,435
63.	Premium tax (5)		334
64.	Accrued dividends (10)		9,135
65.	Total disbursements		$190,363
66.	Net income (gain from operations)		$ 6,201

*The active life reserves may be reduced by the amount of any surrender charges applicable on termination of the contract.

Table 6.4

RECONCILIATION OF NET INCOME AND INCREASE IN
EXPERIENCE ACCOUNT

70. Experience account: December 31, 19A (30)	$560,000
71. December 31, 19B (39)	690,651
72. Increase	$130,651
73. Net income (gain from operations) (66)	$ 6,201
74. Increase in reserves: active lives (60)	94,881
75. retired lives (61)	29,369
76. Transfer from separate accounts* (54)	(650)
77. Capital gains (less tax) (38)	850
78. Net increase	$130,651

*This item is a charge against the funds in the separate account, not against the experience account.

6.11 Statements on nonresident companies

Traditionally, insurance companies have carried on business in jurisdictions other than the one in which they are chartered by setting up branches rather than by establishing subsidiaries. This enables them to pool risks and investments and provide all policyholders with the security of the total surplus. (In recent years, however, many companies have set up resident subsidiaries in foreign countries.) Because no country has jurisdiction over assets in another country, branches of insurers chartered in other countries are required to hold sufficient assets in the country in which the branch is located to protect policyholders who reside in that country.

In branch operations, although assets must be physically present in the country in which the branch is situated, income from such assets and other sources is part of the general funds of the company and need not be retained by the branch as long as adequate assets are held. A subsidiary, on the other hand, is a separate entity initiated by a legal transfer of assets from the parent company. Thereafter, it operates in a financially independent manner, and any future transactions with the parent are in compensation for assets or liabilities transferred; dividends paid on the shares held by the parent, and investments, such as the purchase of additional shares or contributions to surplus.

In general, such companies (alien insurers in the United States, British and foreign insurance companies in Canada) must maintain assets deposited or held in trust (that is, not under the sole control of the company) at least equal to the liabilities to residents minus loans secured by policies held by residents. In the United States, a minimum deposit with the appropriate government authority must be held in addition to the amount of assets specified above. In Canada, the minimum deposit may be included to make up the total of assets required. In Canada, the amounts held in trust for accident and sickness policyholders must at least equal the greater of the minimum deposit required for accident and sickness business and the amount required by Section 103 of the Canadian and British Insurance Companies Act (see Chapter 5, section 5.12).

In the United States, while most deposits and trusteed assets are for the benefit of all U.S. policyholders, some states require special deposits for the benefit of residents of that state only. Other states normally accept such deposits only as offsets to the liabilities to policyholders of the states requiring the special deposit.

The statement requirements for assets of nonresident companies are generally the same as for residents. In Canada, however, realized gains and losses on all investments are brought into income so that book values of debt securities are not adjusted for unamortized gains and losses and there is no formula adjustment of book values of equities.

Valuation requirements for liabilities are also similar to those for resident companies, except that, in the United States, the mandatory securities valuation reserve is not required (since its main purpose is to cushion the impact of capital gains and losses). In Canada, the investment valuation reserve is more stringent.

The investment valuation reserve for the life branch of nonresident companies in Canada is:

    a) the net market deficiency of redeemable securities, perpetual bonds, equity assets and real estate, plus

    b) if the book value of mortgages is greater than 40 percent of the total book value of assets in Canada, a fraction of the market deficiency of mortgages.

    The fraction is the ratio of:

    a) the excess of

        1) the book value of mortgages over

        2) 40 percent of the sum of

            i) the total book value of assets less assets in segregated funds, plus

            ii) the total of loans secured by policies in Canada

to

    b) the book value of mortgages.

For example, if the total book value of assets in Canada is $12,000,000, of which $2,000,000 are in segregated funds, total mortgages amount to $5,000,000, and loans on Canadian policies to $1,000,000, the fraction would be:

$$[5,000,000 - .4(12,000,000 - 2,000,000 + 1,000,000)]/5,000,000$$
$$= (5,000,000 - 4,400,000)/5,000,000$$
$$= 600,000/5,000,000 = .12$$

This fraction would be applied to the total market deficiency of mortgages.

The investment valuation reserve for the accident and sickness branch of nonresident companies in Canada is the lesser of:

    a) the net market deficiency of debt securities, equity assets and real estate combined, and

    b)

1) the net market deficiency of long-term (over five years to maturity) redeemable securities, long-term mortgage loans, perpetual bonds, equity assets and real estate, plus

2) if the total book value of mortgages exceeds 20 percent of the total book value of assets, the amount of the market deficiency of short-term mortgages minus any market excess of short-term bonds.

However, British and foreign companies in Canada may obtain permission from the Minister of Finance to file the annual statement required of Canadian companies. In that case, the requirements for the valuation of assets and for the investment valuation reserve will be the same as for resident companies. One requirement for such permission is that the branch be operated in the same manner as a subsidiary.

In both countries, the statements required of nonresident companies are designed to demonstrate compliance with special requirements. These requirements are intended to ensure that assets and liabilities consist only of assets held in the country and liabilities to policyholders resident in the country. A statement which compares required assets with those actually held, must also be filed, because assets and liabilities normally do not balance. Instead of an income statement, there is merely a synopsis of operations of the branch. The excess of income over disbursements is not shown since it is not important to the security of policyholders, who are protected by the maintenance of sufficient assets in the country.

The exhibits of transactions in the country and schedules are similar to those required of resident companies.

Statements of alien insurers in the United States

The statement of admissible assets includes assets held in the United States by an approved trustee or on deposit with an official of a state or territory for the benefit and protection of United States policyholders and items representing admissible assets relating to the Company's United States business.

The statement of liabilities includes liabilities to United States policyholders and the statutory deposit.

The synopsis of operations shows the operations in the United States in total and by line of business, excluding capital gains and losses on investments. Income and disbursement items are totalled, but no net income is shown, because it has no meaning for branch operations.

A special statement is the development of net admissible assets, which shows the excess of U.S. assets over liabilities related to U.S. policies, plus the statutory deposit. Admissible trusteed assets are shown, and loans on U.S. policies; due and accrued investment income on trusteed assets, and due and deferred premiums on U.S. business are deducted from U.S. liabilities.

The exhibits and schedules of U.S. business and assets are similar to those required in the NAIC life and accident and sickness statement with the addition of a home office expense exhibit, in which total home office expenses are shown by category, along with the percentage and amount charged to the U.S. branch.

There is also a special deposits schedule which shows:
1) All deposits or investments in the United States not held for the protection of all U.S. policyholders and
2) All deposits made with governments, firms or individuals for the benefit of all U.S. policyholders.

Canadian British and foreign insurance company statement (Form INS-55)

Assets in Canada are shown in two sections: (A) those under the control of the Minister of Finance (including assets held by trustees), and (B) those under the control of the Chief Agent. Liabilities and reserves in Canada include those reserves required by the Department of Insurance which are treated as appropriations of surplus by resident companies.

Instead of a conventional income statement, the statement consists of a statement of income in Canada (including investment income and net capital gains and losses on investments), and a statement of expenditures in Canada.

There are separate tests of adequacy of assets in Canada for life and accident and sickness business.

In calculating the assets required in Canada for the life branch, the following items may be deducted from liabilities and reserves in Canada:
a) net liability to segregated fund policyholders,
b) the investment valuation reserve and
c) policy loans secured by policies in Canada.
The amount of assets required is the net amount calculated above or the minimum deposit, if greater.

For the assets available, book and market values of invested assets under the control of the Minister are shown. The amount used is the greater of the total market value and the total book value less the investment valuation reserve. Cash and income due or accrued on investments under the control of the Minister are added, and assets in segregated funds and nonadmitted assets under the control of the minister deducted to give the assets available. (Outstanding premiums on policies in Canada may not be included in the assets available, although net deferred premiums are effectively included, since they are deducted from the actuarial liability.)

The excess or deficit must be shown, as well as the monthly prorata increase in assets required (the difference between assets required at the end of the current and previous years divided by 12).

For accident and sickness business, the development of the assets required is similar to the Section 103 test in the resident statement (see Chapter 5, section 5.12).

Exhibits of transactions in Canada are similar to those required of Canadian companies except for the changes required by the elimination of amortization of realized gains and losses on debt securities and of realized and unrealized gains and losses on equities. The exhibit of capital gains and losses on investments includes only those on investments under the control of the Minister.

In addition, there are separate summaries of bonds and shares under the control of the Minister for life and accident and sickness business.

6.12 Internal GAAP reports

Comparisons of gross premiums received with the sum of benefits and expenses can be misleading, even when they are prepared according to GAAP. The reason is that a substantial portion of benefits to policy-holders (e.g., interest included in the increase in reserves) is properly not a charge to premiums but to investment income. On the other hand, if interest is charged to unamortized deferred policy acquisition expenses (DPAC), the amount charged to expenses will be understated by the amount of such interest.

For example, if interest credited to the deferred policy acquisition cost in Example 4 was $200,000, then the table in Example 4.1 (2a) would read as follows:

1.	Unamortized acquisition costs, 19A	$3,768,935
2.	Commissions deferred 19B	775,795
3.	General expenses deferred 19B	134,000
4.		$4,678,730
5a.	Interest credited	200,000
		$4,878,730
5b.	Less amount charged to expense 19B	691,024
6.	Unamortized acquisition costs, 19B	$4,187,706

Edward S. Silins, FSA, in an article in *Best's Review* (March 1983), has pointed out that this can result in inadequate and misleading internal GAAP statements, since investment income and benefit costs are overstated, while expenses are understated.

For example, adjusting the data in the Example 4.5 to exclude supplementary contracts and accident and health business, we get this income statement:

		($000)
Premiums		$16,574
Net investment income		8,424
		$24,998
Policy benefits:		
Death claims	$ 1,034	
Annuity payments	2,119	
Endowments and surrender values	2,532	
Increase in reserves	10,917	
Dividends to policyholders	1,783	18,385
Amortization of deferred policy acquisition cost		491
Commissions, expenses, taxes		2,715
		$21,591
Income before income tax		$ 3,407

(Interest on policy or contract funds has been deducted from investment income, and, for simplicity, the investment income and expenses allocated to supplementary contracts and accident and health business are taken from the statutory statement.)

In this case, as Silins points out, it appears that gross premiums are deficient, since the net income is much less than the investment income. However, if we take into account interest on reserves of, say, $6,000,000, the benefits paid will be decreased by that amount to $12,385,000, expenses will be increased by the interest on the deferred policy acquisition cost to $3,406,000, and investment income will be reduced by the difference to $2,624,000.

The revised income statement will be:

	($000)
Premiums	$16,574
Net investment income	2,624
	$19,198
Policy benefits	12,385
Amortization of deferred policy acquisition cost	691
Commissions, expenses, taxes	2,715
	$15,791
Income before income tax	$ 3,407

Note that benefits and expenses amount to 95 percent of gross premiums.

Silins' method consists of four steps:

1) establish expected GAAP results by line of business as percentages to gross premiums of:

   a) policy benefits (excluding interest on reserves),
   b) commissions,
   c) acquisition expenses,
   d) policy maintenance expenses,
   e) overhead expenses and
   f) margin for taxes and profit.

2) Adjust investment income, policy benefits and increases in deferred policy acquisition cost (separated into those arising from commissions and those arising from other acquisition expenses) for interest on reserves and deferred policy acquisition cost.

3) Allocate actual expenses to acquisition costs, maintenance expenses, and overhead.

4) Adjust the expenses for increases and decreases in deferred policy acquisition cost, calculate the ratios of the adjusted figures to gross premiums, and compare with expected GAAP results.

(A more detailed explanation will be found in Silins' article cited above.)

6.13 Formulas for the analysis of increases in reserves

The analysis of increases in reserves (for which formulas are included in the NAIC statement instructions) is based on the relation between successive terminal reserves. If V_0, V_1, and V_2 are successive terminal reserves, P the constant net premium, and i and q_0, q_1 the interest and mortality rates applicable to the first and second policy years respectively, then, assuming premiums are payable annually and death claims paid at the end of the policy year,

$V_1 = (V_0 + P)(1 + i) - q_0(1 - V_1)$ (Jordan, p. 107)

$V_2 = (V_1 + P)(1 + i) - q_1(1 - V_2)$

$V_1 + V_2 = (V_0 + V_1 + P)(1 + i) + P(1 + i) - q_0(1 - V_1) - q_1(1 - V_2)$

Adding P to both sides and dividing by 2,

$.5(V_1 + V_2 + P) = .5(V_0 + V_1 + P)(1 + i) + P(1 + .5i) - .5[q_0(1 - V_1) + q_1(1 - V_2)]$

If we assume that policy issue dates are uniformly distributed over the calendar year, then we can set M_0, the medial reserve at the end of the previous calendar year, $= .5(V_0 + V_1 + P)$, and, if M_1 is the next medial reserve, C = the average cost of insurance, and I = the required interest, then

$M_1 = M_0 + iM_0 + P + .5iP - C$

$C - I = M_0 + P - M_1$ F.1

$I = .5i(2M_0 + P) = .5i(M_0 + M_0 + P)$
$= .5i[M_0 + M_1 + (C - I)]$ F.2

To simplify calculations we have assumed that deaths are uniformly distributed over policy years, and that other terminations occur on the policy anniversary before payment of the annual premium.

For terminations other than death, using the above assumptions,

Dividing the basic formula by 2, we get

$.5V_1 = .5(V_0 + P) + .5i(V_0 + P) - .5q_0(1 - V_1)$

and, adding $.5V_1$ to both sides,

$V_1 = .5(V_0 + V_1 + P) + .5i(V_0 + P) - .5q_0(1 - V_1)$

$V_1 = M_0 + .5i(V_0 + P) - .5q_0(1 - V_1)$ (1)

$V_1 = M_0 - (C - I)$

$C - I = M_0 - V_1$ T.1

$I = .5i(V_0 + P) = .5i(2M_0 - V_1)$

$= .5i(M_0 + C - I)$ T.2

For new policies,

$$M_1 = P(1 + .5i) - .5q_0(1-V_1)$$
$$= P + I - C$$
$$C - I = P - M_1 \qquad\qquad\qquad\qquad\qquad\qquad\qquad\qquad\qquad\qquad\qquad\qquad\text{N.1}$$
$$I = .5i(P) = .5i(M_1 + C - I) \qquad\qquad\qquad\qquad\qquad\qquad\qquad\qquad\text{N.2}$$

Deaths must be divided into those occurring before the anniversary, D^B, and those occurring after the anniversary, D^A. For D^B the same formulas apply as for other terminations. For D^A we use the relationship,

$$V_2 = V_1 + P + i(V_1+P) - q_1(1-V_2)$$
$$= M_0 + .5i(V_0+P) - .5q_0(1-V_1) + P + i(V_1+P) - q_1(1-V_2) \qquad\qquad \text{from (1)}$$
$$= M_0 + P + .5i(V_0 + 3P + 2V_1) - [.5q_0(1-V_1) + q_1(1-V_2)]$$

so that

$$C-I = M_0 + P - V_2 \qquad\qquad\qquad\qquad\qquad\qquad\qquad\qquad\qquad\qquad\text{D.1}$$
$$M_0 + P = C-I + V_2 \qquad\qquad\qquad\qquad\qquad\qquad\qquad\qquad\qquad\qquad\text{(2)}$$
$$I = .5i(V_0 + P + V_1 + 2P + V_1) = .5i(2M_0 + 2P + V_1)$$
$$= .5i[M_0 + (M_0+P) + P + V_1]$$
$$= .5i(M_0 + C-I + V_2 + P + V_1) \qquad\qquad\qquad\qquad\qquad\qquad \text{from (2)}$$
$$= .5i(M_0 + C-I + V_1{}^B + V_2) \qquad\qquad\qquad\qquad\qquad\qquad\qquad\text{D.2}$$

if we ignore $.5iP$ (i.e., one-half of a year's interest on premiums received on policies terminated by death after the anniversary) and put $V_1{}^A = V_1{}^B$, using the assumption of uniform distribution of deaths.

Adding these formulas together we get, for $C-I$,

EQUATION

In force	F.1	M_0	$+P$	$-M_1$
Deaths before anniversary	T.1	M_0		$-V_1$
Deaths after anniversary	D.1	M_0	$+P$	$-V_2$
Other terminations	T.1	M_0		$-V_1$
New issues	N.1		P	$-M_1$

The first column includes the total mean reserves at the end of the previous year; the second, the total net premiums (no premiums are assumed to be collected on deaths before the policy anniversary or on other terminations); the third, the total mean reserve at the end of the current year, and the fourth, the reserve released by terminations. This agrees with the formula prescribed for $C-I$ in the NAIC statement instructions:

Mean reserve December 31 of previous year
Tabular premiums
Other increases
    Total

Deduct:
Mean reserve December 31 of current year
Terminal reserves released by death
Net reserves released by other terminations

For I, the factor to be multiplied by .5i is:

In force	F.2	M_0	$+M_1$	$+(C-I)$
Deaths before anniversary	T.2	M_0		$+(C-I)$
Deaths after anniversary	D.2	M_0		$+(C-I)$ $+V_2+V_1$
Other terminations	T.2	M_0		$+(C-I)$
New issues	N.2		M_1	$+(C-I)$

Corresponding to the formula for I in the instructions:

One half year's interest on: mean reserve December 31 of previous year
mean reserve December 31 of current year
$(C-I)$
terminal reserves released by death

Adding I to $C-I$ gives C, the tabular cost.
(See **Table 6.5**)

(For an example of the above calculation see **Example 6.2**.)

For annuities, since $a_x = 1 + vp_x a_{x+1}$,

$$(a_x - 1)(1+i) = p_x a_{x+1}$$
$$a_x + i(a_x - 1) - 1 = p_x a_{x+1}$$

and, if R_0 and R_1 are the reserves at the end of the previous and current years, respectively, and P is the total annuity payments during the year, we see that, if actual reserves released equal tabular reserves released, and there are no new considerations,

$$R_0 + I - P = R_1.$$

If C is the amount of new considerations received, and actual reserves released (A) are greater than tabular reserves released (T), then

$$R_0 + I + C - P = R_1 + A - T$$
$$C - P = R_1 - R_0 - (T - A + I)$$
$$T - A + I = R_1 + P - R_0 - C$$
$$R_0 + C - P = R_1 - (T - A - I)$$

And on the assumption of uniform distribution of payments and considerations over the calendar year,

$$I = iR_0 + .5iC - .5iP$$
$$= .5i(R_0 + R_0 + C - P)$$
$$= .5i[R_0 + R_1 - (T - A + I)]$$

This agrees with the formula:

Tabular less actual reserve released plus tabular interest
    Mean reserve December 31 of current year
    Annuity payments incurred during year
    Less:
    Mean reserve December 31 of previous year
    Tabular considerations for annuities and supplementary contracts
    Other increases (net)
Tabular interest
    One half year's interest on:
    Mean reserve December 31 of previous year
    Mean reserve December 31 of current year
    Less:
    Tabular less actual reserve released plus tabular interest.

For interest only reserves, it is obvious that

$$R_1 = R_0(1+i) + (C-P)(1+.5i)$$
$$I = iR_0 + .5i(C - P)$$
$$= R_1 + P - R_0 - C$$

The formula for required interest is
    Mean reserve December 31 of current year
    Payments during year
    Less:
    Mean reserve December 31 of previous year
    Other increases

Example 6.2

ANALYSIS OF INCREASE IN RESERVES: LIFE INSURANCE

To illustrate the formulas for required interest and cost of insurance on life insurance, let us take a simplified example of $100,000,000 of insurance at the end of a year, consisting entirely of whole life insurance issued at age 35 ten years previously. Of this, $150,000 terminates by death before the policy anniversary in the following year, $150,000 terminates by death after the anniversary and $10,000,000 terminates for other reasons. There are also $15,000,000 in new issues, all whole life at age 35.

Using net level premium reserves on 1958 C.S.O. 2½ percent,

$P = P_{35} = 17.67$ per M

$V_0 = {}_{10}V_{35} = 167.90$ $M_0 = 185.71$ $q_0 = q_{45} = .00535$

$V_1 = {}_{11}V_{35} = 185.85$ $M_1 = 203.74$ $q_1 = q_{46} = .00583$

$V_2 = {}_{12}V_{35} = 203.97$

For new issues, $V_1 = {}_1V_{35} = 15.64$, $q_N = q_{35} = .00251$, $M_1 = 16.65$

$½I_0 = ½i(V_0 + P) = .0125(185.57) = 2.32$
$½I_1 = ½i(V_1 + P) = .0125(203.52) = \underline{2.54}$

     I_F 4.86

$½C_0 = ½q_0(1000 - V_1) = .002675(814.15) = 2.18$
$½C_1 = ½q_1(1000 - V_2) = .002915(796.03) = \underline{2.32}$

     C_F 4.50

In force: $M_1 = M_0 + P + I_F - C_F$
          $= 185.71 + 17.67 + 4.86 - 4.50 = 203.74$

Deaths before anniversary:
Other terminations:

$V_1 = M_0 + ½I_0 - ½C_0 = 185.71 + 2.32 - 2.18 = 185.85$
$I_T = I_{DB} = 2.32$ $C_T = C_{DB} = 2.18$

Deaths after anniversary:

$V_2 = M_0 + ½I_0 - ½C_0 + P + I_1 - C$
      $= 185.71 + 2.32 - 2.18 + 17.67 + 5.09 - 4.64 = 203.97$
         $I_{DA} = 7.41$ $C_{DA} = 6.82$

New issues:

$M_1 = P + ½iP - ½q_N(1000 - V_1^N)$
     $= 17.67 + .0125(17.67) - .001255(984.36)$
     $= 17.67 + .22 - 1.24 = 16.65$
         $I_N = .22$ $C_N = 1.24$

Table 6.5
CALCULATION OF C–I FROM FACTORS

	F	D^B	D^A	T	N	IN-FORCE END OF YEAR
'000	$ 89,700	$ 150	$ 150	$ 10,000	$ 15,000	$104,700 *Totals*
I/M	4.86	2.32	7.41	2.32	.22	
C/M	4.50	2.18	6.82	2.18	1.24	
I	435,942	348	1,111	23,200	3,300	463,901
C	403,650	327	1,023	21,800	18,600	445,400
C – I						−$18,501

CALCULATION OF C–I FROM FORMULA

	F	D^B	D^A	T	N	TOTAL
(a) M$_0$	$ 16,658,187	$ 27,857	$ 27,856	$ 1,857,100	0	$ 18,571,000
(b) P	1,584,999		2,651		265,050	1,852,700
(c) −M$_1$	−18,275,478				−249,750	−18,525,228
(d) −V^D		−27,878	−30,595			−58,473
(e) −V^T				−1,858,500		−1,858,500
(f) C–I	$ −32,292	$ −21	$ −88	$ −1,400	$ 15,300	$ −18,501

	F	D^B	D^A	T	N	TOTAL
a)	$ 16,658,187	$ 27,857	27,856	$ 1,857,100		$ 18,571,000
c)	18,275,478				$ 249,750	18,525,228
d)			27,878* 30,595			58,473
f)	−32,292	−21	−88	−1,400	15,300	−18,501
Sum	$ 34,901,373	$ 27,836	$ 86,241	$ 1,855,700	$ 265,050	$ 37,136,200

I = .0125 × sum,
C = C − I + I.

*Assuming V$_1^A$ = V$_1^B$

	F	D^B	D^A	T	N	TOTAL
I	$ 436,267	$ 348	$ 1,078	$ 23,196	$ 3,313	$ 464,202
C	403,975	327	990	21,796	18,613	445,701
Error in I	−325	0	+33	+4	−13	−301
per M	−.0037	0	+.2200	+.0004	−.0009	−.0029

Interest required and cost per thousand may have errors of up to .005, so that it is evident that the differences between the two methods are well within that limit, except for D^A, for which the error is caused by the neglect of $\frac{1}{2}iP = .0125 \times 2651 = 33$. In this case, of course, the use of V_1^B for V_1^A does not introduce an error. If the deaths were not evenly distributed between deaths before and after the anniversary, but, for example, $D^B = 100,000$ and $D^A = 200,000$, $V_1^B = 18,525$ and $V_1^A = 37,170$ so that the error, $\frac{1}{2}i(V_1^A - V_1^B) = .0125 \times 18,525 = 232$, which is still not significant in the total interest required of \$460,000.

Review questions

1. Why are special reports required for management?
(**Answer:** See section 6.1.)

2. What restrictions should be placed on the circulation of management reports?
(**Answer:** See section 6.1.)

3. How are the data in management reports related to the scope of the report?
(**Answer:** See section 6.1.)

4. What are the requirements for an accounting system if management reports are to be produced economically?
(**Answer:** See section 6.1.)

5. Can the average portfolio rate be used for the excess interest element in dividends on participating policies if the company issues a substantial volume of "new money" contracts?
(**Answer:** No, the average portfolio rate includes the higher earnings on new money contracts which are required for those contracts. See section 6.1.)

6. What condition must an approximation meet in order to be suitable for use in calculating nonledger items for interim statements?
(**Answer:** See section 6.4.)

7. In the Canadian segregated fund statement why is investment income excluded from the reconciliation of accumulation and annuity units in force?
(**Answer:** See section 6.5.)

8. What are the fund units used for segregated funds and how are they calculated?
(**Answer:** See section 6.5.)

9. Why is it reasonable to charge the group account and credit the individual account when a group certificate is converted to an individual policy?
(**Answer:** See section 6.9.)

10. Why are two accounts usually maintained for deposit administration contracts?
(**Answer:** See section 6.10.)

11. Why have insurance companies operated in other countries through branches rather than subsidiaries?
(**Answer:** See section 6.11.)

12. How does a branch differ from a subsidiary?
(**Answer:** See section 6.11.)

13. Why are branches of nonresident companies required to maintain assets in trust in excess of domestic liabilities?
(**Answer:** See section 6.11.)

Conclusion

As background for the description of the financial statements required of life insurance companies in the United States and Canada, I have attempted to describe the effects of recent changes in the business of life insurance and the environment on financial reporting principles of life insurance companies, reflected in the development of GAAP accounting for stock companies in the United States and recent changes in both statutory and published financial statements of all companies in Canada.

While the effect of these changes has been an improvement in the information provided to policyholders, shareholders and the public, and some of the distortions of statements due to solvency requirements of life insurance have been eliminated, a number of problems remain. In 1981 an attempt was made by the NAIC to change the format of the NAIC Life and Accident and Sickness Statement to simplify the financial exhibits by showing data only on the accrued basis and to streamline the asset, liability and income statements. However, this was defeated by failure to secure unanimous approval.

The NAIC has now proposed a number of substantive changes, such as a new form of statement of changes in financial position and the disclosure of dividend practices of mutual companies, including an actuarial certificate that the dividends have been determined in accordance with the actuarial principles and practices of the American Academy of Actuaries.

The development of new plans of insurance, such as universal life*, and the increase in single premium deferred annuity (SPDA) sales using current high interest rate assumptions, has prompted discussions of changes in NAIC and GAAP rules to deal with these matters. The AICPA has proposed that, on SPDA, no profit should emerge with premium receipt, while, for universal life, a "composite" approach has been adopted. This permits profit to emerge as a percentage of premiums, but emphasizes provisions for margins that go beyond margins for adverse deviations. In addition, a limitation on lump sum payments and limited premium plans was adopted. The maximum premium that could be utilized in profit recognition would be that which would provide the benefits of the plan in 20 level annual premiums. These conclusions have been referred to the FASB for consideration, and a discussion paper is expected in 1985.

---

*Universal life policies are combinations of term insurance and an investment fund with guarantees of interest and mortality rates and expense charges, under which the amount and frequency of premium payments are at the option of the owner. The amount of insurance is specified in the policy and may either include the investment fund or be added to it. The amount of insurance may be increased at any time subject to evidence of insurability or be decreased subject to certain minimums.

In Canada, the joint task force of the CIA and CICA has recommended financial reporting and disclosure principles which would become generally accepted actuarial principles and GAAP for both solvency reporting and income reporting in the single Canadian statement which is used for both statutory reporting and published statements. These recommendations have been discussed by the CIA committee on financial reporting and there was general agreement on many of the recommendations.

In addition to those which have been implemented as amendments to the Regulations under the Insurance Acts in 1984, referred to in chapters 2 and 5, these recommendations were made:

1. The accrual method with discounting for interest and an assumption as to future tax rates should be employed in the calculation of deferred taxes.

2. The option to use a cash value floor (see Section 5.3) in the valuation of liabilities rather than explicitly valuing the withdrawal risk should be discontinued.

3. All recoverable acquisition expenses should be deferrable, rather than be limited to 150% of the net level premium.

The CIA committee has reported disagreement with some of the recommendations dealing with actuarial liabilities:

1. Although it agrees that actuarial liabilities should include a provision for adverse deviations which appropriately tests solvency, the CIA suggests that the additional margin required for solvency be an appropriation of surplus rather than a deduction from income.

2. The CIA agrees that the effect of changes in valuation assumptions be reflected in income, but maintains that the extra charge should be accounted for in the current year instead of being spread over future years as the Task Force recommended.

Another joint CIA-CICA task force has addressed the roles of the auditor and the actuary with respect to financial statements. The auditors felt that requiring the auditor to indicate in the opinion statement that the actuarial liability was determined by the valuation actuary amounted to a qualification of his opinion. The Task Force report recognizes the reporting responsibilities of both the auditor and the valuation actuary and sets out the criteria which would allow one professional to use the work of the other. The report also requires the disclosure of the respective roles of the auditor and the actuary in the financial statement as part of management's report in the statement or in a note to the financial statements. The Task Force report has been accepted in principle by both professional bodies, and subgroups are working out the details.

Glossary

Accrual accounting. Same as **revenue accounting.**

Actuarial reserves. The excess of the present value of future benefits provided under life insurance and annuity contracts over the present value of the benefit premiums to be received.

Agents' credit balances. Amounts due to agents arising from the excess of amounts earned over amounts paid.

Agents' debit balances. The excess of payments made to agents over commissions and other amounts earned. The conditions under which these amounts are repayable depend on the terms of the agent's contract.

Amortization (of expenses, gains or losses). The spreading of an amount incurred in one year over future years to match that amount against income.

Amortized value (of investments). The value, at any date after purchase, so determined that if the security were purchased on that date and at that value, the yield would be the same as the yield at the date of purchase.

Amounts withheld as agent or trustee. Amounts deducted from payments to policyholders, employees or creditors to be remitted to a third party, such as income tax or group insurance premiums deducted from salaries.

Association values. Values of assets established by the National Association of Insurance Commissioners for use in statutory annual statements of insurance companies in the United States.

Automatic premium loan. A policy loan made automatically under the terms of the policy contract to pay all or part of an unpaid premium, as long as the net cash surrender value is sufficient to cover the loan and interest to the next policy anniversary.

Balance account. In a modified double entry accounting system, in which some assets and liabilities may not be included in the ledger, an account which contains the net sum of the nonledger items, so that the ledger accounts will balance.

Beneficiary. The person entitled to the amount payable in the event of the death of the life insured.

Book values of assets. Values at which assets are recorded in the ledger.

Cash accounting. The entry of transactions in the ledger only when amounts are received or paid. (See **revenue accounting.**)

Coinsurance. Reinsurance under which the reinsurer accepts a share of the original policy, receiving a proportionate amount of the gross premiums less an allowance for commissions and expenses.

Collateral loans. Loans made to individuals or corporations on the security of assets deposited with the lender.

Cost center. A unit of the company set up to facilitate control of expenses and their allocation to departments and functions.

Coupons (on insurance policies). Guaranteed refunds provided on some nonparticipating policies payable in the same manner as dividends on participating contracts.

Debt securities. Securities representing loans to borrowers, such as bonds and mortgages.

Deferred maternity benefits. An estimate of maternity benefits payable after the date of the statement to those entitled to such benefits who may be pregnant at the date of the statement.

Deferred policy acquisition expenses (DPAE). Expenses incurred in the acquisition of new policies which are deferred and charged against subsequent premiums collected on the policies.

Deferred premiums. Premium payments on a policy falling due after the date of the statement and prior to the next policy anniversary.

Dividends (to policyholders). Refunds allotted to holders of participating policies out of profits earned on such policies.

Dividend accumulations. Dividends credited to policyholders which are left with the company to accumulate interest.

Dividend additions. Additional amounts of insurance purchased by dividends credited to policyholders.

DPAE. (See **deferred policy acquisition expenses.**)

Earned surplus. The amount of surplus arising from profits, in contrast to surplus contributed by shareholders.

Equity securities. Securities representing an equity in an enterprise, such as shares of stock in a corporation.

Extended term insurance. Paid-up term insurance purchased by the net cash value as a nonforfeiture benefit. The amount is equal to the face amount of the policy less any indebtedness, and the term of the insurance depends on age and net cash value.

Extraordinary income. Gains, losses and provision for losses which result from occurrences which are not typical of the normal business activities of the enterprise, are not expected to occur regularly over a period of years, and are not considered as recurring factors in any evaluation of the enterprise.

FRRI. Financial Reporting Recommendations and Interpretations of the Academy of Actuaries.

Funds. Shares of assets of an insurance company arising from transactions with different classes of clients, such as participating policyholders, non-participating policyholders, segregated fund policyholders, and shareholders, or dedicated to specific purposes, such as staff pensions or investment reserves.

GAAP. Generally accepted accounting principles, usually established by recognized accounting institutes, which must be followed in the preparation of financial statements if an independent auditor is to give an unqualified report on them.

Incontestable provision. A clause in life insurance policies, required by law in the United States and Canada, providing that, in the absence of fraud, statements of the insured in his or her application for insurance will be deemed true and incontestable after a certain period (commonly two years) if the insured is alive at the end of the period.

Incurred accounting. Same as **revenue accounting.**

Modified coinsurance. Reinsurance on a coinsurance basis in which the reserve on the reinsurance accepted is loaned by the reinsurer to the ceding company.

Mutual life insurance company. A life insurance company without stockholders, owned by the policyholders.

NAIC. National Association of Insurance Commissioners (United States). An association of insurance commissioners of all the states which co-ordinates their regulatory activities.

Net cash value. The cash surrender value of a policy plus the value of any dividend accumulations or additions, minus any indebtedness secured by the policy such as policy or premium loans.

Nonadmitted assets. Assets of an insurance company not permitted by supervisory authorities to be included in the company's balance sheet.

Nonforfeiture benefits. Benefits (such as cash payments, paid-up insurance for a reduced amount, extended term insurance, etc.) available to a policyholder on premature termination of premium payments.

Premium note. A promissory note given by a policyholder in partial payment of a life insurance premium. Since life insurance premiums are not legal debts, such notes are not regarded as valid assets by supervisory authorities unless the cash value is sufficient security for the amount owing.

Policy loans. Loans advanced to policyholders on the security of the cash surrender values of their policies.

RAIA. Record of the American Institute of Actuaries, Chicago.

Reduced paid-up insurance. Paid-up insurance purchased as a nonforfeiture benefit on the same plan of insurance but for a reduced amount.

Revenue accounting. The entry in the ledger of income transactions as income is earned and of disbursement transactions as the amount due is incurred (e.g., premiums and taxes when due). (Amounts received or paid prior to the due date are treated as liabilities or assets and amounts unpaid at the date of the statement are treated as assets or liabilities respectively.)

SAP. Statutory accounting practices. Accounting practices of insurance companies required by regulatory authorities.

Segregated fund contracts (Canada). Contracts whose benefits vary in accordance with the market value of a special fund in which the premiums or deposits are invested. Such funds are segregated from other assets of the company and cannot be used for the satisfaction of liabilities to other policyholders.

Separate account contracts (United States). See **segregated fund contracts** (above).

Settlement annuities (Canada). See **supplementary contracts.**

Shares. Shares of stock in corporations (Canadian usage).

Stock life insurance companies. Life insurance companies owned by stockholders.

Stocks. Shares of stock in corporations (U.S. usage).

Supplementary contracts. When a policy terminates by death, maturity or surrender, the beneficiary or insured may have the right to purchase an annuity with all or part of the proceeds at rates guaranteed in the original contract. Such annuity contracts are called supplementary contracts and are treated differently in the annual statement from other annuities since they arise from claims and not from annuity considerations received.

Surplus. The excess of assets over liabilities and capital. It may be divided into:
(a) contributed surplus (amounts paid in by shareholders in addition to capital).
(b) appropriated surplus (amounts set up to provide for special contingencies) and
(c) unappropriated or unallocated surplus (the balance).

Tax allocation basis. A method of charging income tax on specific transactions in the period in which the transactions are recognized for accounting purposes.

Tax payable basis. Income tax charged in the annual report using the amount estimated to be payable for the year of account.

TSA. Transactions of the Society of Actuaries, Chicago.

Unrealized gains and losses (on investments). The excess or defect of the statement value of investments at the end of one period compared with that at the end of a previous period. (See Chapter 2, 2.3.)

Unusual income. Gains, losses and provision for losses resulting from normal business activities which are both abnormal in size and caused by rare and unusual circumstances.

Bibliography

American Academy of Actuaries. *Financial Reporting Recommendations and Interpretations.* Society of Actuaries, Chicago, IL, 1981.

American Academy of Actuaries. *Guides to Professional Conduct.* Society of Actuaries, Chicago, IL, 1981.

American Institute of Certified Public Accountants. *Audit Guide for Stock Companies, 1979.* New York, 1979.

Attwood, James A., and Ohman, Carl R. "Segmentation of Life Insurance Company General Accounts", *TSA,* XXXV, 1984, Chicago, IL, p. 585.

Broad, Samuel J., "The Applicability of Generally Accepted Accounting Principles", the *Journal of Accountancy,* September, 1957.

Canadian and British Insurance Companies Act and Regulations.

Canadian Institute of Actuaries. *Rules for Professional Conduct.* Ottawa, Canada, 1984.

Canadian Institute of Actuaries. *Recommendations for Insurance Company Financial Reporting.* Ottawa, Canada, 1979.

Canadian Institute of Actuaries. *Report of the CIA Committee on Financial Reporting.* Ottawa, Canada, 1973.

Canadian Institute of Chartered Accountants. *CICA Handbook,* Toronto, ON, 1972.

Canadian Institute of Chartered Accountants. *Financial Reporting for Life Insurance Companies (a research study),* Toronto, ON, 1973.

Canadian Life Insurance Association. *Report of the CLIA Committee of Financial Reporting,* Toronto, ON, 1973.

Corbett, Gary. "Accounting for Purchase of a Life Insurance Company", *TSA,* XXVII, 1975, Chicago, IL, p. 313.

Davidson, Sidney and Weil, Roman L. *Handbook of Modern Accounting.* McGraw Hill, New York, NY, 1977.

Department of Insurance, Ottawa, Canada. *Instructions for the Completion of Canadian Statement (Form 54) 1983.*

Department of Insurance, Ottawa, Canada. *Report of the Superintendent of Insurance—Insurance, 1972, Vol. 1,* 1973.

Duncan, Robert M. "A Retirement System Granting Unit Annuities and Investing in Equities", *TSA,* IV, 1952, Chicago, IL, p. 317.

Eckley, Douglas A., "Purchase Accounting, A Fresh Look", *TSA,* XXXIV, 1983, Chicago, IL, p. 449.

Financial Accounting Standards Board. Financial Reporting Recommendations and Interpretations of the FASB. Stamford, CT, 1982.

NAIC Statement Instructions (included with statement).

Noback, Joseph C., *Life Insurance Accounting,* Homewood, IL: Richard D. Irwin, Inc., 1969.

Robertson, Richard S. "GAAP Accounting for Reinsurance Accepted," *TSA,* XXVII, 1976, Chicago, IL, p. 375.

Robertson, Richard S. "GAAP Accounting for Reinsurance Ceded," *TSA,* XXVII, 1976, Chicago, IL, p. 397.

Shepherd, C. O., "The 'Convention' Statement of Life Insurance Companies," *RAIA,* XXVI, 1975, Chicago, IL, p. 317.

Silins, Edward S., F.S.A., "Internal GAAP Reports", *Best's Review,* March, 1983.

Strain, R. W. (ed.) *Life Insurance Accounting.* Santa Monica, CA, 1977, Insurance Accounting and Statistical Association and The Merritt Company.

Index